W9-BCV-434

Client/Server Computing
for Technical Professionals

Client/Server Computing for Technical Professionals

Concepts and Solutions

Johnson M. Hart
Barry Rosenberg

▲
▼▼
ADDISON-WESLEY PUBLISHING COMPANY

Reading, Massachusetts Menlo Park, California New York
Don Mills, Ontario Wokingham, England Amsterdam Bonn
Sydney Singapore Tokyo Madrid San Juan
Paris Seoul Milan Mexico City Taipei

Many of the designations used by manufacturers and sellers to distinguish their products are claimed as trademarks. Where those designations appear in this book and Addison-Wesley was aware of a trademark claim, the designations have been printed with initial capital letters.

The authors and publishers have taken care in preparation of this book, but make no expressed or implied warranty of any kind and assume no responsibility for errors or omissions. No liability is assumed for incidental or consequential damages in connection with or arising out of the use of the information or programs contained herein.

The publisher offers discounts on this book when ordered in quantity for special sales. For more information please contact:

Corporate & Professional Publishing Group
Addison-Wesley Publishing Company, Inc.
One Jacob Way
Reading, Massachusetts 01867

Library of Congress Cataloging-in-Publication Data

Hart, Johnson M., 1944—
        Client/server computing for technical professionals: concepts and solutions/Johnson M. Hart, Barry Rosenberg.
        p.   cm.
        Includes bibliographical references and index.
        ISBN 0-201-63388-4 (alk. paper)
        1. Client/server computing. I. Rosenberg, Barry, 1958—   .
II. Title.
QA76.9.C55H37   1995
004' .36--dc20   95-32282
                                                                        CIP

Copyright © 1995 by Addison-Wesley Publishing Company, Inc.

All rights reserved. No part of this publication may be reproduced, stored in a retrieval system, or transmitted, in any form, or by any means, electronic, mechanical, photocopying, recording, or otherwise, without the prior consent of the publisher. Printed in the United States of America. Published simultaneously in Canada.

ISBN 0-201-63388-4
Text printed on recycled and acid-free paper.
1 2 3 4 5 6 7 8 9 CRW 98979695
First Printing, September 1995

To Linda, Bob, and Elizabeth

—J. M. H.

To Marilyn, Danny, Rachel,

Papa Mel, Honey,

Papa Louis, and Grandma Evelyn

—B. J. T. R.

Table of Contents

CHAPTER 5   Client/Server Security   53

CHAPTER 6   Distributed File System Concepts   75

CHAPTER 13   Binding Clients to Servers   191

CHAPTER 14   Distributed Object-Oriented Computing   209

CHAPTER 17   Two Client/Server Frameworks   263

List of Figures

List of Tables

Preface

"Client/server" is one of the most ubiquitous phrases of the '90s. The trade press, advertisements, and news media are filled with stories of client/server products and solutions. The client/server concept and the closely related development of distributed computing solutions reflect a sweeping change in how computer systems are designed and deployed.

Anyone who deals with modern computing technology, whether as a user, purchaser, administrator, or vendor must understand what client/server means and does not mean, and what its benefits and risks are. We wrote this book to describe distributed client/server computing to a broad class of computer professionals, users, and decision makers.

In the simplest possible terms, client/server computing means that two parts of a single program are run by two (or more) computers. The two parts of the program are called, naturally enough, the client and the server. The server provides services to the client. This simple idea quickly leads to powerful capabilities, extended requirements, interesting technical issues, and sophisticated solutions, which we explore and explain.

Client/server computing embraces numerous products, strategies, and standards. We portray client/server computing as a natural, inevitable, and beneficial step in the evolution of computing technology. In the process we make some generalizations and cite many examples. We even make a few provocative statements, and venture risky predictions about future developments. We stand by these opinions, which we have tried out in designs, product development, installations, seminars, and conversations. In this book, we share our observations and predictions with you.

Audience

We have aimed this book at you, the computer professional. We feel that there is value in this book for a wide audience. You are in the audience if:

- You program computers for a living and your livelihood depends on knowing client/server programming and systems.

- You are a computer architect designing a client/server application or planning how your organization can move to client/server computing.

- You are a technical professional designing a distributed application for your organization and need to understand the variety of design approaches, products, and frameworks that are available.

- You are studying computer science and want to learn more about distributed computing issues and solutions.

- You are involved with hardware and software acquisition for your organization and want to know what your choices are in the client/server arena. You want to know how to look under the hood of a client/server system, kick its tires, and be able to choose from the many alternatives.

- You manage people doing any of these activities and need to learn more about the choices, the technologies, and how they work.

- You are simply curious about client/server computing.

Portions of Part 3 assume that you know something about programming. The rest of the book requires no programming experience, but computing experience and knowledge always help. We have written examples for Part 2 in the C programming language, but familiarity with nearly any other programming language should be sufficient to follow the general concepts.

Organization

The book covers all the major aspects of client/server computing.

The first two chapters position client/server computing as the natural and most efficient architecture to integrate networked hardware and software. We develop a vocabulary and show the major forms of client/server computing. We introduce the major benefits, problems, and risks.

In Part 1, we introduce the basic distributed computing services, security, and naming and location. Client/server computing is both interesting and difficult largely because the computing systems are distributed, communicating over local and wide area networks. Key issues are that communication is not secure and it is necessary to identify and locate computing resources. By discussing these topics early, we give a taste of the problems caused by distribution and lay the groundwork for what follows.

In Part 2, we discuss distributed information systems, including today's popular implementations (such as NFS and Novell NetWare) and candidates for future popularity (such as DFS). implementations that are may become popular in the next few years (such as DFS). We also describe how distributed databases work and explain database replication. In addition, Part 2 describes wide area, distributed information systems such as the World Wide Web.

In Part 3, we explain models for distributed program logic, especially remote procedure calls (RPCs) and distributed objects. We use a small client/server program to show basic principles. We discuss DCE and ONC implementations of RPCs and we compare RPCs to other programming models using messaging or distributed objects. Client/server programming has a unique set of problems, such as how to ensure security and reliability. We discuss these problems and show how to solve them in an RPC environment. We emphasize RPCs because they most directly embody the client/server concept. Part 3 concludes with a discussion of distributed object-oriented computing, using CORBA and OLE/COM as examples.

In Part 4, we describe what we call the distributed user interface, followed by discussions of systems management and client/server frameworks. We show how a client and server can cooperate to render graphics on a screen. We summarize the X Window System, the primary implementation for distributed presentation. Next, Part 4 discusses the problems of managing distributed computing resources. Finally, we pull all this information together to show how complete client/server computing environments can be built. We use the Distributed Computing Environment (DCE) and the Common Object Request Broker Architecture (CORBA) as examples, and discuss current and possible future developments.

Standards, Products, and Reference Systems

We want to say a word or two about the standards, operating systems, and commercial products that we mention in varying detail from time to time. Not everyone will agree with all of our choices, but we believe that they illustrate the points well and make good "reference systems" against which to compare similar systems.

Some products and standards, such as UNIX, the Microsoft Windows family (Windows 3.1, NT, and 95), TCP/IP, DCE, NFS, and CORBA are discussed because of their clear importance. Other products are mentioned only in passing or as being representative of a class of product. The field is so broad and diverse that some of our choices are arbitrary; we apologize for those systems that we have doubtlessly overlooked. This book is not a product catalog, a buyer's guide, or a product endorsement. We do, however, provide sufficient information so that products can be understood, properly positioned in the client/server world, and evaluated.

In particular, we discuss the Distributed Computing Environment (DCE) extensively to illustrate the components of a client/server system and how they work together. Why DCE? DCE is not perfect, it is not the most widely used system, and its future is unclear. Nonetheless, DCE is our client/server reference point for several reasons:

- DCE is open, interoperable, scalable, and integrated. DCE is available on a wide class of host systems, from PCs to mainframes.

- DCE is more complete than any other widely available system, and it addresses the major requirements. Therefore, DCE is a good reference model for evaluating other systems.

- DCE was designed for client/server computing. An understanding of the DCE components, their operation, their methods for addressing requirements, and their integration can help you understand other solutions.

- More advanced systems such as those based on distributed object-oriented computing, are not yet as firmly established.

Acknowledgments

Many people have generously contributed their time to review all or parts of this book. They have made numerous helpful and insightful comments, and this book would not have been possible without them. Numerous friends and colleagues have helped out as well with advice, information, and valuable encouragement. So, we would like to express our gratitude alphabetically to: Jeff Allen, Robert Attwood, Matthias Autrata, Doug Blewett, Sumner Blount, David Chappell, Ellis Cohen, Joe Comuzzi, Daniel Dardailler, Frank D'Arrigo, Kathryn DeNito, Holgar Denk, Gail Driscoll, Eric Eldred, Art Gaylord, Rosa Gonzalez, Janet Gunn, Paul Hagstrom, Arthur Lewbel, Robert Mathews, Scott Meeks, Andy Nemec, Rich Salz, Douglas Schmidt, and Paul Shalek. Sample home pages are courtesy of The MathWorks, Inc. and of Barry Bakalor. The image of two jugglers passing computers and clubs is courtesy of Greg Cohen. Responding to all the suggestions was time-consuming but definitely worthwhile. Remaining errors are ours, despite the best efforts of all those named above.

Our long-suffering literary editor, Judy Tarutz, spread a healing balm of red ink over our disease-ridden prose. Sarah Tuttle took on a goodly percentage of the dreaded production edit.

Our editor, Carol Long, deserves a special vote of thanks for just the right mix of carrots and sticks, encouragement and cajoling. Carol kept us on track and almost on schedule.

Finally, we wish to thank our friends and colleagues from long ago at Apollo Computer who showed us what it could be even before it was called "client/server."

My wife Linda has been a steadfast supporter throughout this effort with her invaluable love and understanding.

John Hart
jmhart@world.std.com

I want to thank my wonderful wife Marilyn for her wisdom, patience, and suggestions. I'd also like to thank my father for suggesting that my books would read
better if only there was more sex in them. (Look dad: Page 1, Line 1!)

Barry Rosenberg
juggler@world.std.com

CHAPTER 1

What Is Client/Server?

Tabloid newspaper editors try to put three words (*win*, *free*, and *sex*) on the front page of every edition. Those three words sell a lot of newspapers. Similarly, computer marketers like to place the term *client/server* on every product they sell. So the term has expanded to mean, well, almost nothing.

A client requests services from a server.

To us, all client/server systems contain a client part and a server part. The *client* makes requests for some service and the *server* responds by providing that service. You might see other terms used in place of client and server. For instance, the client might be referred to as a *master* and the server referred to as a *slave*. Network management uses the terms *managers* and *agents* instead of *clients* and *servers*.

Client and server are usually on different nodes.

Most client/server systems are *distributed*; that is, the client part runs on one computer and the server part runs on another computer. However, some client/server systems are not distributed. In these systems, the client and server are merely separate processes running on the same computer.

1

Client/server is everywhere.

Client/server computing is everywhere. It is used in business, universities, government, homes, and in all fields of activity, including science, banking , engineering, medicine, and even leisure.

Anyone who is involved with purchasing, planning, using, managing, or just talking about computing must be able to understand:

- How client/server computing can solve real problems.
- How client/server systems are constructed and how they work.
- The impact of client/server technology on existing systems.
- The conflicting claims of different client/server vendors.
- The limitations of client/server technologies and products.

This chapter introduces client/server computing at a high level. In the process, we explain the factors that make client/server computing both possible and necessary.

A Typical Client/Server Environment

Most sites contain a mixed bag of systems.

Figure 1 illustrates the computing equipment that you might find installed at nearly any medium or large enterprise. This figure shows the following:

- PCs (IBM compatibles) and Apple Macintosh computers.
- UNIX workstations.
- Graphical X terminals connected to powerful multi-user systems.
- Dumb terminals.
- Mainframes and multi-user systems managing large databases.
- File servers maintaining documents, spreadsheet files, program source code, and other data.
- Specialized server systems for communications, printing, and number crunching.

This diverse collection of computers, networks, operating systems, and applications is the result of an ongoing evolution. Some systems were acquired to meet the needs of individual users, and others were purchased to serve the needs of small departments or even the entire enterprise. Most large enterprises have numerous operating systems, networking protocols, and user interfaces. In all likelihood, more variety is on the way.

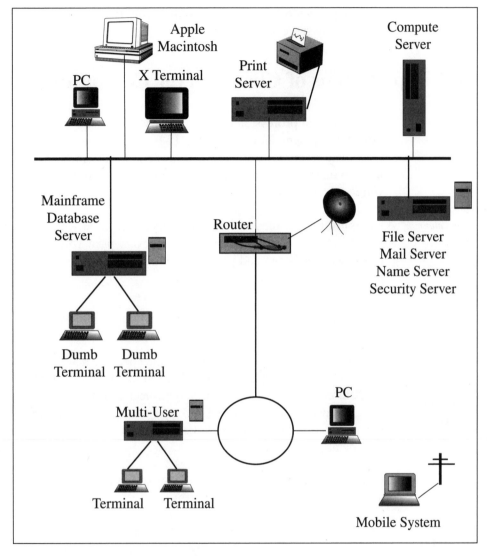

Figure 1   A Typical Client/Server Environment

All these systems are connected by a high-speed local area network (***LAN***). The local area network is, in turn, connected to wide area networks (***WAN***). Mobile users connect through laptops. Whether connected through terminals, laptops, or desktop PCs, people in an organization use resources within the local area network as well as resources networks in the wide area network.

Client/server computing lets desktop and laptop PCs, and even UNIX workstations act as clients in accessing and sharing the extensive and diverse resources provided by servers.

Our Expectations of Client/Server Computing

Single-system view turns network into a virtual system.

As a technical professional or manager, what do you want to do with the collection of equipment shown in Figure 1? Basically, you want to access any system's power and resources from any other system. Furthermore, you want all of the systems to interoperate seamlessly, as if they were a single system. We call this the **single-system view**.

You cannot have everything.

Computing resources are needed everywhere in an enterprise, but you cannot spend an unlimited amount of money on every user. You want to spend as little as possible on each user and yet give each user access to as many shared resources as possible.

Integrating the Parts

Clients should be able to access distributed resources.

You want to integrate the best aspects and special capabilities of each system. For instance, you want to extract a table from the manufacturing database; you want the data pricing to go into a PC spreadsheet and the part numbers to go into the design drawing. Going another step, you want the servers themselves to appear integrated so that there appears to be a single large database instead of several distinct database servers.

Of course, you want to integrate all the parts without worrying about which parts are being done on which systems.

Security

Restrict access to authorized clients only.

You need comprehensive **security**. That is, you expect servers to provide services to authorized clients only. For example, you do not want unauthorized engineers to have access to the payroll database.

Reliability

Failure must have minimal impact.

You need **reliability**. Network and individual system failures should affect only a limited number of users. You also expect your system to recover gracefully from failures.

Scalability

Solutions should work on networks of all sizes.

You need **scalability**. The solutions that "work" in a small department with ten PCs must also work in organizations of a hundred, a thousand, or tens of thousands of computers of all types. By "work" we mean that all of the functionality, security, performance, and other features of the small network are available in the large network without any significant degradation in performance or increase in cost-per-user.

When Can You Have Your Needs Met?

Some features are available now; others are years away.

The good news is that client/server systems already achieve many of your requirements. In fact, PC networks with file and print servers are a widely used form of client/server computing. These networks satisfy many needs even though they may not scale or may lack some security features. The popular Internet provides a limited, but very useful form of wide-area client/server computing. Yet, more advanced concepts, such as distributed object-oriented computing, are just starting to be used.

Size is a
relative term
and a fast-
moving target.

Scale and Size

We frequently talk about large file systems, databases, and networks. We also talk of smaller systems, such as PCs and workstations. Terms such as *large*, *small*, *fast*, and *slow* are relative, Their meaning depends on the environment, the applications, and many other factors. Furthermore, the expectations change continually. Size and speed definitions are moving targets.

A few examples and anecdotes illustrate the possibilities and the rate of change.

Databases at large corporations (such as life insurance companies) routinely contain terabytes (a trillion, or 10^{12}, bytes). A small company, however, may have a *large* central database containing a mere gigabyte of data (a gigabyte is a billion, or 10^9, bytes). Both databases can be considered large and appropriate for database servers, even though their sizes differ by a factor of 1,000.

A department or small company may have 40 or 50 desktop systems (PCs) networked to a file server with, perhaps, a few gigabytes of storage. A multinational corporation, by contrast, may have tens (or hundreds) of thousands of systems of all sizes, all requiring access to corporate databases and other services. Both networks are *large,* and both require client/server solutions. The two authors, as long ago as the mid-1980s, worked at a company (Apollo Computer, Inc.) where 4,000 workstations and PCs were seamlessly integrated in what would now be called a medium-sized client/server network.

In early 1995, we are preparing this book on a $1,500 laptop PC with a 33 MHz Intel 80486 CPU, 8MB RAM, 170MB disk, and a monochrome monitor. This is definitely a *small* and nearly obsolete system; it is barely an acceptable client. Not so many years ago, it would have made a departmental server worth fighting for.

Client/Server Computing: The Driving Factors

What makes it worthwhile and possible? Client/server computing is worth the effort only if it offers more features and better overall price/performance than alternative systems. We now take a quick look at the technical and economic reasons leading to client/server computing.

Technical Enabler: Hardware

Hardware improves in many ways. Dramatic increases in performance, capability, reliability, and cost-effectiveness for computers and networking equipment are the most significant factors in making the client/server vision achievable. It is impossible to overstate the extent of these improvements in the 1980s and early 1990s, and these improvements continue.

Desktop systems (PCs, workstations, and even laptops and notebooks) now have sufficient computing power, memory, disk space, and display capabilities to run client software.

File, database, and computing servers are available in all price and performance ranges. Meanwhile, mainframe, fault-tolerant, and other traditionally expensive systems are decreasing in price; such machines can be reconfigured to perform their traditional duties in client/server environments.

Applications that once required a large, expensive mainframe computer that required its own air-conditioning system can now run on small servers that draw no more power than a television set. We can now ***downsize*** or ***rightsize*** our applications onto cheaper computers.

Technical Enabler: Software

Software exploits hardware advances. Software has evolved to exploit the improved hardware and to enable distributed client/server computing.

Operating systems such as UNIX, Mac/OS, and Microsoft Windows provide sophisticated graphical user interfaces, which make them excellent systems to run clients.

Many operating systems such as UNIX and Microsoft Windows NT now provide the necessary features to run servers. These features include multiprocessing and thread support.

Middleware integrates clients and servers.

Client/server **middleware**, a distributed client/server operating environment, extends the basic system software. A good middleware package makes it much easier to create robust clients and servers. Middleware also smooths out the rough edges on systems where clients run on one kind of machine and servers on another kind. The Open Software Foundation's Distributed Computing Environment (**DCE**) is an example of middleware that we will explore in more detail.

Application software for both clients and servers continues to advance and to become integrated. Client software can access, modify, and present server information. Many new applications do more than solve old problems in better ways; they create solutions that were not feasible without distributed client/server computing.

Open systems provide an additional stimulus.

Software at all levels is increasingly open, conforming to relevant standards. This openness allows systems of all sorts to interoperate. Furthermore, standards simplify the porting of software to a wide variety of host computers. Where standards compete or popular implementations are not standardized, it is usually possible to obtain software to bridge systems.

Technical Enabler: Networking

Many advances have contributed to making network access nearly universally available at reasonable costs.

Reliable, high-performance networking is essential and fields growth.

LANs can be installed using inexpensive twisted pair wiring. High-speed, wide-area digital communication is also available. Smart switches and hubs enable fast and reliable data communication. Routers extend the local networks throughout large buildings and campuses and connect to WANs, including the Internet. Systems software is continually improving to exploit networking technology.

The very near future will bring even faster and cheaper long-distance data communication.

Economic Enabler: Cost

Client/server systems can be faster, better, and cheaper.

The effective integration of computing equipment can provide solutions more efficiently than traditional centralized computing. Client/server computing allows for:

- Balanced, cost-effective, and shared use of resources.
- The proper blend of centralization and decentralization.
- Modular, incremental, and evolutionary growth.

Users need open, distributed computing for several compelling economic reasons. Standards-based systems drive prices down and prevent any single vendor from gaining control. Client/server computing gives users on small machines the opportunity to run applications once reserved for big machines.

In turn, vendors are meeting the demand by supplying client/server products and developing new product niches. In short, the demand is there and is being met vigorously.

Client/Server Computing: Issues and Barriers

There are many client/ server successes.

Distributed client/server computing is possible, cost-effective, and necessary. Numerous organizations have already implemented client/server systems of some form. What, then, remains to be done? Are there any remaining problems to solve? What are the factors delaying the deployment of systems that achieve the vision?

Still, much remains to be done.

Many current systems only partially implement the client/server concept. For instance, a network of PCs and workstations with shared files may have neither uniform database access nor integrated applications. Furthermore, these networks are likely to have severe security limitations. Also, a PC-only network may not scale well; a network may work well with a hundred PCs, but not with a thousand.

Changes can be far-reaching.

Distributed client/server systems force organizational changes. Existing ways of doing business must change as operations are decentralized, workflow patterns are changed, and processes are reengineered to match the new computing capabilities. These changes can be painful, expensive, and time-consuming.

Legacy Systems

Large, nonmodular, old-fashioned (yet still useful) programs are often called *legacy* programs. In an industry where last year's hardware is already obsolete, it is hard to believe how many enterprises still rely on software written in the 1960s.

Many enterprises want to update their legacy programs to the client/server model. However, doing the necessary updates is not for the squeamish. Not only is the code nonmodular and sometimes undocumented, but some of the code was written in languages that became obsolete 20 or 30 years ago. In addition, users worry about losing data in existing databases. Nevertheless, distributed object-oriented programming techniques can go a long way toward migrating legacy programs to the client/server era.

Many standards issues are unresolved. Many client/server solutions are proprietary in some significant way. Any barrier to openness will hinder and delay user commitment. Many of the old "UNIX wars" are still being fought on new battlefields over new objectives such as distributed objects. Vendors and customers have investments in proprietary, and often excellent, technology that they are reluctant to give up for the benefits of unproved standards. That standards, products, and concepts often conflict or overlap only serves to make customers wary.

Can client/server be managed? Manageability is often cited as the single largest barrier to client/server computing. All the diverse hardware, software, servers, files, and security services must be manageable in a coherent way. Client/server management software is not unified; users must acquire and operate several distinct management applications.

Summary

Distributing client/server computing is a natural and desirable consequence of rapid advances in hardware, software, and networking. The next chapter explains what elements of a program can be distributed.

CHAPTER 2

Partitioning Programs into Clients and Servers

This chapter explains how to partition programs.

A ***distributed client/server program*** is any program that divides computational tasks among two or more distinct computer systems. This chapter explains the various ways in which a program's code and data can be ***partitioned*** between clients and servers.

Most programs, whether distributed or nondistributed, are partitioned into discrete modules, variously called procedures, functions, subroutines, objects, or processes. These modules traditionally run on a single machine.

Networking now allows programmers to put these modules on different systems. Before getting to networked systems, let's look at partitioning old-fashioned programs that run on a single machine.

Partitioning a Nondistributed Program

Figure 2 shows a simple nondistributed program and its data running on a single computer.

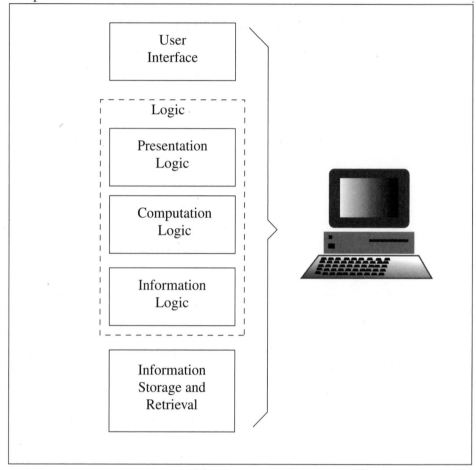

Figure 2   Nondistributed, Single-System Computing

This program contains five modules. We have lumped three of the modules into the Logic category. The resulting three modules (User Interface, Logic, and Information Storage and Retrieval) compose what is often called the ***three-tiered client/server model.***

The Information Storage and Retrieval Module

Storage and Retrieval includes file systems and database management.

The ***Information Storage and Retrieval module*** reads data from and writes data to long-term ("persistent") storage (disks, tapes, CD-ROMs, and many other media). It also has a convenient interface for the logic modules. Later, you will see that the information interface can be divided into submodules, including file systems, database systems, and block storage devices.

The Three Logic Modules

Logic modules perform the computation.

The three logic modules perform all of the CPU-based processing that you normally think of as computation. The logic modules store and retrieve data, process that data, prepare it for presentation, and interact with the user through the User Interface module. They run on a single CPU in one or more processes for each user (or display).

The ***Presentation Logic*** module displays graphical output and processes user input. A sophisticated Presentation Logic module performs the calculations for tables and graphs. A simple Presentation Logic module might only be smart enough to handle character terminals.

The ***Computation Logic*** module interfaces with the other two submodules. This is where computationally intensive tasks take place, such as computing economic forecasts, simulating mechanical designs, or performing statistical analysis.

The ***Information Logic*** module accesses the information storage system, determining how to access it, what data to store, and what data to retrieve. This module, for instance, would determine a query to send to a database.

The User Interface Module

The ***User Interface*** module controls all user interaction through displays, keyboards, mice, and so on. The display may be graphical or character based. For example, a PC running Microsoft Windows is graphical based, and a VT100 dumb terminal is character based.

Distributing the Modules

Any of the modules can be distributed as clients and servers.

You can partition the modules of Figure 2 at the following three junctures:

- You can detach the Information & Storage Retrieval module from the Logic modules.
- You can detach one Logic module from the other two Logic modules.
- You can detach the User Interface module from the Logic modules.

We now take a closer look at each of these partitions.

The Logic-Information Partition

You can place the Information Storage and Retrieval module on a different node from the rest of the modules. If you do, the Logic modules and the User Interface module form the client, and the Information Storage & Retrieval module is the server. The client requests access to the data, and the server provides that access.

The five categories of interfaces between the Logic modules and the Information Storage and Retrieval module are as follows:

- Distributed file system
- File transfer
- Distributed DBMS
- Distributed data objects
- Distributed block-level interface

Distributed file systems are quite popular.

A *distributed file system* serves files to a requesting client. A distributed file system can perform the same file operations as a nondistributed file system, including the following:

- Basic create, open, close, read, write, seek, and delete operations
- Extended file operations such as record locking
- Extended features such as structured, keyed files

Popular distributed file systems include Novell NetWare and the Network File System (NFS).

File transfer is also popular, but rather limited.

File transfer, such as **ftp**, provides a limited and nontransparent interface between the Logic modules and the Information Storage and Retrieval module. A file transfer server allows a client to copy files to and from a server. In addition, some file transfer servers allow the client to request limited directory manipulation. In many practical situations, file transfer is adequate or even optimal. For instance, anonymous **ftp** sites provide a powerful way to distribute documents and programs.

A DBMS allows clients to access and integrate shared data.

Distributed database management systems (DBMS) are also widely used as information interfaces. The server manages a database (usually relational). The client sends queries to the server, which returns a response, often in the form of a "relation" or table. The client computational logic can do nearly anything with the results. For instance, a PC can place the response in a spreadsheet, perform analysis on the data, and, perhaps, return the result to the database.

Figure 3 shows a distributed DBMS server running in the Information Storage and Retrieval module. This distributed DBMS server maintains and updates the database. The Information Logic module generates database queries.

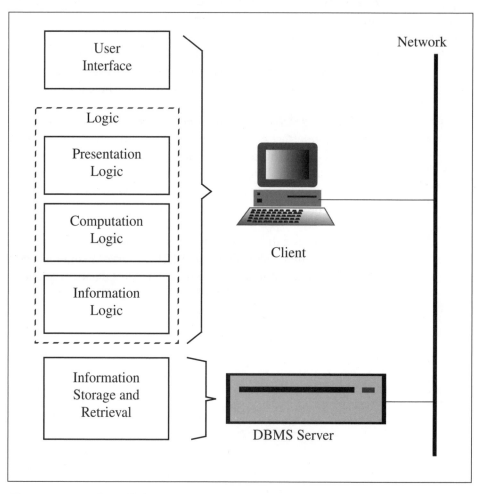

Figure 3   A DBMS Server Implementing the Logic-Information Partition

Distributed data objects extend the object-oriented computing model and allow clients to integrate distributed data modeled as compound documents directly into client applications. For example, distributed object-oriented technology provide an efficient way for a spreadsheet to automatically gather its data from a remote database server. Distributed object technology is one of the most active and promising areas in client/server technology.

Block-level interfaces are rarely distributed.

In a ***distributed block-level interface*** , the partition is at the access level of the disk device. In this design, a file system would be a client to a server that actually manipulates the disk media. The disk device, in turn, uses the most cost-effective technologies for performance and reliability. This partition would allow for networks of distributed mass storage devices. However, this partition is not widely used.

The Logic-Information partition is the subject of Part 2 of this book.

Logic-Logic Partitions

You can also divide up the Logic modules. In other words, you can put different Logic modules on different nodes. Distributing Logic modules allows us to use specialized or expensive systems more efficiently.

The logic modules can be distributed to different systems.

For instance, suppose a company owns one high-speed computer optimized for numerical computation. It makes sense to put the computationally intensive Logic modules on this fast machine. It generally does not make sense to put all Logic modules on the expensive high-speed computer. The high-speed computer does not need to be bogged down working on mundane chores that a PC or Macintosh could handle just as easily. Computationally intensive chores include economic forecasting, business modeling, and mechanical design simulation.

Figure 4 shows a Computation Logic module split off from the rest of the program. In this figure, the Computation Logic module runs on a high-speed compute server, while the rest of the program runs on a PC. The Computation Logic module is a server and the Logic module that calls the Computation Logic module is the client.

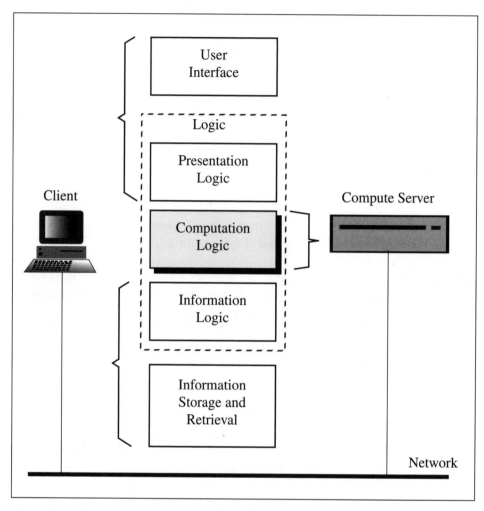

Figure 4   *A Compute Server Implementing the Computation Logic
             Module*

*There are three
different
distributed
programming
models, all
backed by
standards.*

The client Logic modules could use **remote procedure calls** (**RPCs**), **interprocess
communication** (**IPC**), or **distributed objects** to communicate with the server
Logic modules. We describe these different communication models in later chapters, but here's a a quick preview. Remote procedure calls behave very much like
familiar local procedure calls, yet also insulate the application programmer from
the details of the underlying network. A remote procedure call is usually no harder
to code than a local procedure call. RPC programming is the core of such systems

as the Distributed Computing Environment (DCE) from the Open Software Foundation (OSF) and Open Network Computing (ONC) from SunSoft. Likewise, distributed object-oriented programming is the core of systems based on the Common Object Request Broker Architecture (CORBA) and the Common Object Model (COM).

The Logic-Logic partition is the subject of Part 3 of this book.

The User Interface-Logic Partition

You can split off the User Interface module from the Logic modules, as shown in Figure 5. That is, you can place the actual user interface devices (the display, keyboard, and mouse) away from the CPU running the Logic Modules. Communication is over the connecting network.

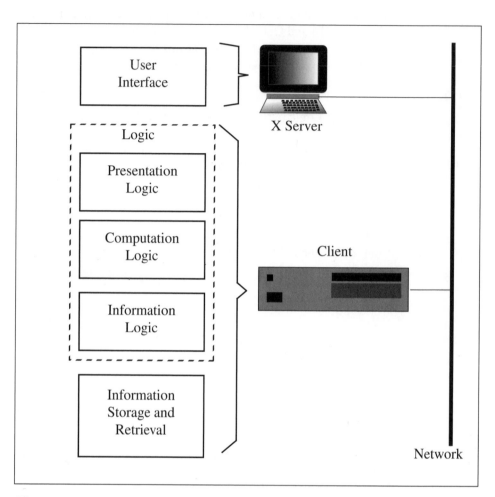

Figure 5   *Using the X Windows System to Implement the User Interface-Logic Split*

X Windows provides a way to partition the User Interface module from the Logic modules.

A true User Interface-Logic partition has the following characteristics:

- The user interface includes an intelligent graphical display, or Graphical User Interface (GUI).

- The communication between the Logic modules and the User Interface module uses the full network transport protocol.

- The communication between the Logic modules and the User Interface module consists of high-level graphics commands, for example, to draw circles, lines, characters, and so on.

- The user interface can maintain concurrent connections with different programs (different logic modules on different machines).

The X Windows System is the most important technology for implementing the User Interface-Logic partition.

Legacy applications are often converted to a distributed user interface, where a character-based user interface is presented in a window with various mouse-activated controls, colors, and other enhancements. Facelifting and screen-scraping are two methods we will examine.

The User Interface-Logic partition is one of the subjects in Part 4 of this book.

Partitioning Everything

Why not distribute an entire application, partitioning as shown in Figure 6? This figure shows a client/server application in which one client requests services from four different servers. Each server provides one service. Each server could run on a different machine (as shown in the figure) or be different processes on the same machine.

Clients usually run on PCs because PCs are relatively cheap.

Database servers tend to run on more expensive hardware that incorporates all the latest technology for high-speed storage devices, fault-tolerant computing, transaction auditing, security, and fast recovery. Distributed client/server computing allows the high costs of these systems to be amortized over the large user base without compromising convenience and usability.

Computation and logic servers often run on expensive massively parallel computers. Such computers can support computationally intensive work by engineers, scientists, business analysts, and others requiring fast numerical computation.

X servers typically run on UNIX workstations or X terminals. However, software is now available that allows most popular terminals (including PC terminals) to act as an X server.

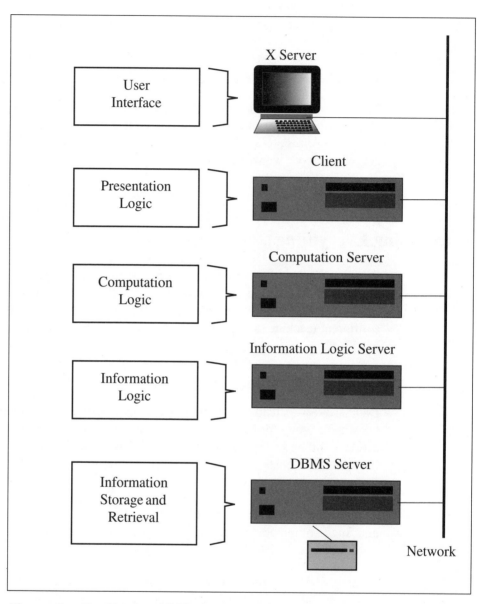

Figure 6   Partitioning All Modules

Other forms of servers are possible. Specialized and physically distributed machines perform other tasks, such as communications, printing, or control. A factory floor controller or an employee badge reader would fall into this category.

Any of the servers can serve multiple clients concurrently.[1]

"Client" and "server" are relative terms. For example, suppose a client calls Server A but Server A needs some help from Server B. Thus, although Server A is obviously a server to the original client, Server A is also a client to Server B.

Using Frameworks to Implement Partitions

DCE, ONC, and CORBA are frameworks.

You use one or more client/server *frameworks*[2] to implement partitioning. Frameworks provide the necessary *application programming interface (API)* and services to make partitioning a reality. Some common implementations of frameworks include DCE, ONC, and CORBA. Before we compare and contrast the different framework implementations, we will examine what a good framework must supply.

What a Framework Must Supply

Frameworks provide programming support.

First and foremost, a distributed client/server computing framework must simplify the coding of client/server applications. The different frameworks provide different ways for clients and servers to communicate. Some frameworks support remote procedure calls, others support distributed objects, and still others support only distributed interprocess communication.

Distributing a program causes many problems.

Partitioning a program into client and server modules running on separate nodes creates issues not present when writing an application that runs on a single node. For instance, you have to consider the following:

- Performance
- Scalability
- Single-system view
- Heterogeneity
- Reliability

[1.] With client/server computing, you really can serve two masters.

[2.] The term "framework" is widely used with a variety of meanings and shades of meaning. Our use of the term is consistent with much common practice.

- Security
- Naming and location
- Replication
- Time synchronization
- Transparency

A distributed program should run nearly as fast as a nondistributed program.

Performance is often the first objective. How can it be possible for a remote procedure to execute as quickly as a local procedure, considering the unavoidable network communication and overhead? The answer lies in the fact that the specialized server may excel at its task and make up for the overhead. Furthermore, dramatic increases in computing speed and good framework implementations can make up for the overhead computation; the gains realized from distributed client/server computing compensate for any performance losses. Finally, there really may be no alternative, as the resource must be shared among many users, regardless of location. Balancing these factors is a problem for the application designer.

How do client/server programs run in very large enterprises?

Scalability is another frequent concern. Will the distributed application work as well in an environment with 10,000 computers as in a network of ten systems? Alternatively, can the system at least limit the degradation as the environment grows? The answer will vary with loads on the server, the network design, and other factors. Nonetheless, maintaining applications on a single system is not a scalable solution either.

The client/server partition should be transparent to the user.

The framework should create a **single-system view** insofar as possible. Users and administrators want to regard the system as a unified entity that is easy to manage and in which the resources (such as the file system) behave as if they are on a single large computer. The single-system view also means that a user, ideally, can log in at any workstation, PC, or terminal and have his or her "home" environment (directories, applications, window environment, and so on).

Client/server programs must handle diversity.

Heterogeneity requires that the different system architectures (hardware and software) be hidden from programs and users. A PC client should not be concerned with whether its database server runs on an HP-UX (UNIX) departmental server or on an IBM MVS mainframe. Heterogeneity requires that systems of all types interoperate freely and are, to some extent, "plug compatible" with one another in the client/server environment.

Reliability is a far bigger concern in distributed computing than in single-system computing. Networks can fail or perform erratically. What happens to the client application when its file server crashes or the network link fails? What happens if a client locks a file for editing and then crashes without releasing the lock so that no one else can use the file? A distributed environment has numerous points of potential failure. Good frameworks must address reliability concerns. Application designers recognize that total reliability is impossible and must prepare applications to recover from failures. Reliability encompasses both the issue of correct, error-free operation and of availability, the assurance that the client/server system can always function.

Security is vital in client/server programs.

Security becomes a much bigger issue in distributed computing than on a single system. Conventional single computers typically require user logins with passwords to authenticate the user. How can the user's identity be established by a remote database server? Bear in mind that data travels over an exposed network. Security is such a big issue for distributed client/server computing systems that we devote a full chapter to it.

Resources need convenient names and they must be easy to locate.

Naming and location services allow clients and servers to easily find each other across a network. Most single-system operating systems provide an easy-to-use hierarchical file naming system. A framework must provide a similar naming system that allows you to name remote resources. A framework should also allow a client to name resources based on capability. For instance, suppose a client wants to access a matrix inverting server. You don't care which matrix inverting server your client program accesses; you just want the framework to select the best one available. The location service may also be required to handle location independence. For instance, a database may be moved from an old server machine to a newer, faster one. Nonetheless, client programs should continue to run without change, finding the new server transparently.

Server replication increases performance and reliability.

This brings up the problem of **replication**. Many services should be replicated consistently throughout the environment so there is always a server "close" (on the network) to every client, none of the servers are overloaded, and operation can continue even if a server fails or is unreachable due to network problems. For instance, many files are read-only (program executables, archival data, and so on) and can be placed on replicated file servers. Replication could be considered to be one strategy for achieving performance, availability, and reliability.

Many frameworks overlook **time synchronization**. The times on the system clocks of different computers are likely to be different (either through neglect or drifting, not to mention different time zones). Why should time be a problem? Well, consider that a file's time of last modification is used by file backup/restore systems to determine what files have changed since the last backup. With files distributed across numerous systems, there could be serious problems, such as failure to backup a changed file, if the system clocks differ significantly. Times are used for many other purposes, such as in transaction logs and for creating entries in database fields. Some frameworks provide *time services* to synchronize system clocks. This synchronization cannot be exact, of course, but can be within a fraction of a second in a medium-sized network.

It should be transparent and non-intrusive.

Finally, all of these problems must be solved as transparently as possible. In an RPC system, for instance, the client should only need to make a call to the server; the framework should do all of the hard location, security, and reliability work.

Some Important Client/Server Frameworks

There are many special-purpose products, but only a few general frameworks.

DCE and ONC are, arguably, the only two existing, widely available client/server frameworks that try to provide solutions to nearly all the issues raised in the previous section. Both of these client/server frameworks provide all manner of services including a complete RPC package and sophisticated naming and location services.

In addition to DCE and ONC, the marketplace offers a variety of specialized products. These products generally do not provide a complete range of services, but they still solve some of the issues named in the previous section. For example, Novell NetWare is a distributed file system that provides security services. Microsoft Windows NT Server also provides many client/server features.

SQL database servers, coupled with Microsoft ODBC clients, form a distributed database with TCP/IP (or other) IPC used to carry the SQL queries and responses. Many database servers provide replication and other advanced features.

New frameworks may appear.

There are some very promising technologies, in particular distributed object-oriented programming, that may become widely available in frameworks in the near future. At this time, however, such frameworks are not suitable for developing production systems, although they could be used for pilot projects.

The Operating System: Its Role and Requirements

Most operating systems are not distributed computing frameworks by themselves. Rather, a robust operating system can host a distributed client/server framework. In order to be a good operating system for hosting servers, the operating system should ideally provide or support the following features:

- Multiprocessing with interprocess communication.
- Thread support.
- Demand paged virtual memory.
- Network transport services; TCP/IP is the usual requirement.
- Security in the form of user login and file system permissions or other access control.

For example, UNIX and Microsoft Windows NT both provide all of the preceding features and are excellent hosts for servers.

To be a good operating system for hosting clients, the operating system need only provide the network transport services. For example, Microsoft Windows 3.1, when equipped with TCP/IP, is a common client host. Nonetheless, additional capabilities allow for the development of much more powerful applications. Microsoft's Windows 95 is the probable Windows replacement in the client role.

Summary

This chapter concludes by showing the architecture of a comprehensive distributed client/server framework with its applications. This architecture shows the different layers and how they relate. In the chapters that follow, we will "populate" this architecture with real solutions.

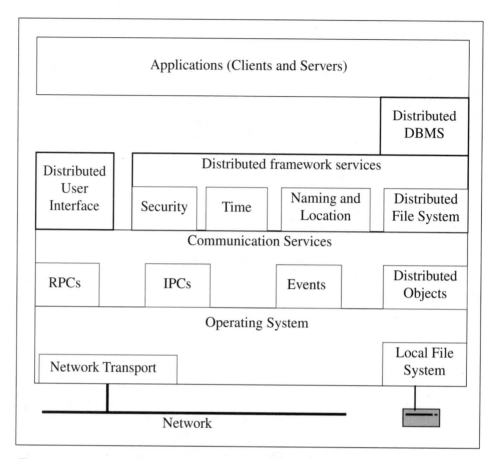

Figure 7   An Architecture for Distributed Client/Server Computing

Figure 7 shows a hierarchy of interdependent components, all presenting programming interfaces available to applications. RPCs use the host operating system, including its network transport. Applications, in turn, can use the features provided by any of the underlying layers. However, as a matter of policy, many applications use only RPCs or distributed objects and never use the network transport directly.

Figure 7 shows the hierarchy of services and how they depend on lower layers, in particular:

• The lower layers are available to applications. A typical application uses operating system services, communication services and framework services.

- The network transport and local file system are usually an integral part of the operating system and are accessed through the operating system.

Where are the features that we have said a framework must supply?

- Performance, scalability, and transparency must be addressed by all the components.
- There are separate framework services for security, naming and location, and time. All the other components and applications must, however, use those services properly. These services are also central to achieving the single-system view.
- Heterogeneity and reliability are addressed first in the communications services, but, in many cases, applications and other services have some responsibility in these areas.
- Data replication sometimes takes place in the DBMS. Logic replication is handled by the individual services, with support from the framework.

CHAPTER 3 # Standards and Open Systems

*Standards
define the
interfaces
between
systems and
the
components.*

Standards are critical in distributed client/server computing. Without standards, clients from one vendor would find it impossible to communicate with servers from other vendors. Standards let organizations interchange components from different suppliers. Furthermore, standard layers help define the boundaries between the components.

A cynical joke of the computer industry says that standards are nice because there are so many to choose from. This chapter attempts to sort out the dueling standards of client/server computing. We also take a quick look at where standards come from.

See Appendix A for a complete list of standards related to client/server computing along with information about the standards bodies.

Where Do Standards Come From?

Top-down standards from expert committees are one way to create standards.

In an ideal world, a qualified professional committee would meet in a mountain lodge just outside of Geneva to determine what standards were needed. These qualified professionals would then roll up their flannel sleeves and quickly produce magnificent, vendor-neutral standards. Vendors would immediately implement the standards and make their implementations available at reasonable cost. Then, the entire user community would bow to the superior wisdom of the qualified professional committee, applaud the superior quality of the standards-compliant implementations, and throw out now-obsolete proprietary products worth billions of dollars.

Committees can be slow, and their standards can be over-engineered.

Standards developed by committees are called **de jure** or **top-down standards**. Unfortunately, such standards are rarely successful; *de jure* standards often try to break too much new ground without the benefit of widespread experience or testing. Design by committee is a noble, but impractical idea. Vendor-neutral committee members are in short supply. Sometimes five or ten years elapses between the creation of a paper *de jure* specification and real widespread use. During this elapsed time, simpler solutions may have sprung up; many standards are simply abandoned.

Many important standards emerge from existing implementations.

De facto standards are not officially blessed by a standards body, but are established informally due to wide usage. A technology becomes a *de facto* standard simply by being popular. A *de jure* standard is like a movie that critics enjoy; a *de facto* standard is like a movie that lots of people go to see.

Of course, the ultimate movie is one that receives both critical and popular approval. Probably the best model for creating a standard is to start with a *de facto* standard and then evolve it and codify it into a *de jure* standard. Vendors are then ensured that they are implementing a popular technology, and customers are ensured of interchangeability. Here are some successful examples of this approach:

• TCP/IP
• SNMP (the Simple Network Management Protocol)
• The C programming language

Standards actually come from somewhere between classic *de jure* and classic *de facto*.

Proprietary products are sometimes "standard."

In the ***standardization by overwhelming numbers*** model, a single vendor provides a popular solution. Microsoft Windows 3.1 is probably the best example of a standard by overwhelming numbers, though the Apple Macintosh, Novell Net-Ware, and the Intel x86 processor family also belong in this category. These standards can be regarded as a variation of *de facto* standards where a vendor controls the standard and where source code is not available on reasonable terms.

Individual companies and consortia can create proprietary "standards."

In the ***standardization by fiat*** model, a vendor implements a solution, licenses the source code, and declares it to be a "standard." Sun Microsystems' NFS (Network File System) is a successful example of this approach.

In the ***standardization by consortium*** model, a consortium is assembled to integrate, enhance, and ultimately standardize an existing technology. Motif is a successful example of this approach. The Motif that some know and love evolved from older GUI implementations invented by Digital and Hewlett-Packard. The consortium, the Open Software Foundation, provided a mechanism for Motif to evolve from proprietary products to an open standard. OSF's Distributed Computing Environment (DCE) is also in this category.

What Is Open?

You often see the term open bandied about in marketing literature. What does it mean? Well, it usually means whatever a marketing executive wants it to mean. To us, ***open*** software means:

- Software that runs on systems from a wide variety of vendors.
- Software with a publicly documented API, from which any programmer can develop applications.
- Software whose future direction is not controlled by a single company.
- Software whose source code can be purchased by anyone.

Motif fits all four categories. Microsoft Windows NT, on the other hand, meets only the first two criteria.

Client/Server Standards

Table 1 describes several important categories of distributed client/server standards. In addition to the client/server software standards shown in the following table, there are numerous low-level standards that govern networking hardware, system buses, and other low-level protocols.

Category	Standards	*De Jure*?	*De Facto*?	Comments
Network Transport Layer	TCP/IP	Yes	Yes	TCP/IP is the only network transport protocol that is nearly universally available and interoperable.
	IPX/SPX	No	Yes	Used by Novell NetWare.
Server Operating Systems	POSIX 1003.1	Yes	Yes	Defines the API for operating systems. Most implementations of UNIX meet this standard as do OpenEdition/MVS and Open VMS. Windows/NT and Windows 95 also meet this specification.
Client Operating System	UNIX	Yes	Yes	
	DOS	No	Yes	
	Microsoft Windows	No	Yes	
	Windows/NT	No	Yes	
	Mac/OS	No	Yes	
Languages	C	Yes	Yes	Preferred languages, with libraries, for client/server application. Visual BASIC and COBOL are also popular.
	C++	Pending	Yes	

Table 1 Important Standards in Client/Server Computing

Category	Standards	*De Jure?*	*De Facto?*	Comments
RPC Packages	DCE	Yes	Yes	
	ONC	Yes	Yes	
Network Management	XMP	Yes	No	
	CMIP	Yes	No	
	CMIS	Yes	No	
	SNMP	Yes	Yes	
Distributed Databases	ODBC	No	Yes	A client API for database access, most commonly used in PCs running Microsoft Windows.
	SQL	Yes	Yes	Database access language used for both local and remote access.
Distributed Graphics	X	Yes	Yes	
	Motif	Yes	Yes	
Global Naming	DNS	Yes	Yes	Used by Internet and many others.
	X.500	Yes	Yes	Used by Novell NetWare.

Table 1 Important Standards in Client/Server Computing

Standards-based are often layered on one another. For instance, Motif is implemented in C and requires X.

Source Code Portability

Standards should support portable application source code.

Portable Source code can be compiled, linked, and executed on different machines, even if the machines run different operating systems or use different hardware instruction sets. For example, if the source code for a server program is truly portable, you can easily build it to run on a Sun workstation or on a Windows NT server. In turn, Windows NT servers are available on systems with a wide array of processor types (Intel, Digital Alpha AXP, Power PC, MIPS); truly portable source code works on all these processors.

Portability is difficult to achieve, especially for user interfaces.

For a variety of reasons, true source code portability is nearly impossible to achieve. For you to write portable code, every piece of software that your code relies on must be available on every important platform. For the following two reasons, writing portable client code is more difficult than writing portable server code:

- Most client operating systems are not POSIX 1003.1 compliant, but many server systems are. Therefore, servers can make portable operating system calls, but clients cannot.
- Clients almost always require GUI code, but servers do not. There is no single GUI standard for all client machines. For example, UNIX machines require Motif code, PCs require Microsoft Windows code, and Apple Macintosh computers require Mac/OS code.

Interoperability

Interoperability requires compatibility through multiple layers and must address machine differences.

Interoperability means that clients and servers on the network must be able to communicate. At the very minimum, the client and server must rely on the same network transport layer. The standard network transport layer is TCP/IP. Thus, any two systems running TCP/IP can almost always communicate and interoperate.

Even if the client and server rely on the same network transport layer, the client and server programs may still have trouble communicating if their host machines represent data differently. Different machines may represent characters differently (ASCII vs. EBCDIC) or integers differently (big endian vs. little endian, 16-bits vs. 32-bits). To avoid having to handle these details, many programmers use an RPC framework such as DCE or ONC.

Standards Can Be Better Than "Better"

Open standards create a level playing field. Users benefit from lower costs, wider availability, and known components. Vendors no longer compete on the basis of the bells and whistles in their proprietary products. Instead, vendors compete to sell a well-understood set of capabilities on the basis of price, performance, quality, and service. Furthermore, vendors benefit from not having to invest in proprietary product development.

These important advantages can outweigh technical superiority. Nearly everyone can think of some excellent product that became obsolete simply because a less capable, but adequate, standard replaced it. Better is not always better.

Summary

Standards bore most people. In fact, we are nodding off at the keyboard writing about them. Some people even suggest that standards squelch innovation and creativity.

Standards focus innovation where it is needed.

In fact, standards make the client/server industry possible. Standards take care of the nitty gritty groundwork, freeing programmers to focus on creativity and innovation in their applications. Without standards, the cost of developing and administering client/server applications would be unbearable.

Appendix A lists the standards and describes their roles in client/server computing.

CHAPTER 4   # Naming, Addressing, and Location Services

Human-readable symbolic names must be translated to numerical addresses.

Every distributed client/server system must provide a way to give a human-readable name to each service. Without a name, users would not be able to identify the service they are requesting. Computers, being heartless and logical, are more comfortable dealing with numbers rather than human-readable names. So, for each name, there must also be a corresponding numerical address. Finally, the system must provide some way to match up the name with the address. This matching is the responsibility of a *location service*.

This chapter explains the roles of naming, addressing, and location services in distributed systems. As we shall show, a good naming system goes a long way towards achieving the single-system view we were so excited about in Chapter 2.

Naming and Location Services

Any *naming and location service* must provide the following three capabilities:

Naming, addressing, and location capabilities.

- A unified scheme for *naming* distributed resources. The named resources may include host computers, users, files, servers, processes running on a server, and more. The naming scheme is usually hierarchical, which organizes complexity for users and systems alike.

- A consistent and unique mechanism for *addressing* resources; that is, for providing a numerical or quasi-numerical version of the name.

- A service (the *location service*) to map (resolve) names to addresses. A location service has a straightforward task: it must translate names to addresses and address to names. A location service does not obtain the actual named resource; it obtains only its address.

Implementation: Domain Name System (DNS)

The *Domain Name System* (*DNS*) has the most familiar naming, addressing, and location service in the client/server world. DNS identifies Internet sites and, with extensions, entities (such as people and servers) at an Internet site.

We now take a detailed look at DNS naming, addressing, and location services.

DNS Naming

The Internet's DNS uses hierarchical naming.

A DNS *domain* name identifies a particular site on the Internet. For example, `world.std.com` is a sample DNS domain name that identifies a company called Software Tool and Die. DNS domain names are also the basis of most email names. For example, the name `juggler@world.std.com` identifies an individual user at the `world.std.com` site.

DNS names are hierarchical. Each level of the hierarchy is called a *zone*. The part of the hierarchy that identifies a site name typically consists of two, three, or even four zones.

The highest zone in the hierarchy indicates one of two things:

- If the site is in the United States, the highest zone is a three-level abbreviation that indicates the category of enterprise. There are currently seven categories. For example, commercial enterprises (businesses) use a top-level of `.com`, educational institutions use a top-level of `.edu`, and government agencies use `.gov`.

- If the site is outside the United States, the highest zone is a two-letter abbreviation that indicates the country in which the site is located. For example, sites in France are designated with `.fr`, and sites from the United Kingdom are designated with `.uk`.

The next zone of the hierarchy in the United States[1] symbolizes the name of the enterprise itself. This zone is often called a ***second-level domain*** name. For example, Hewlett-Packard uses a second-level domain name of `hp`, and the Massachusetts Institute of Technology uses an enterprise name of `mit`.

The optional third zone specifies a subenterprise, which is a division of the enterprise.

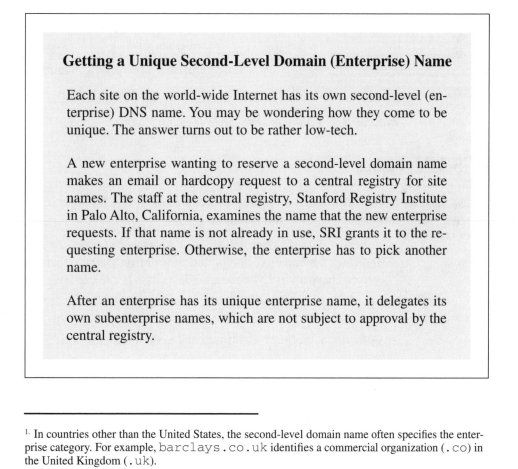

Getting a Unique Second-Level Domain (Enterprise) Name

Each site on the world-wide Internet has its own second-level (enterprise) DNS name. You may be wondering how they come to be unique. The answer turns out to be rather low-tech.

A new enterprise wanting to reserve a second-level domain name makes an email or hardcopy request to a central registry for site names. The staff at the central registry, Stanford Registry Institute in Palo Alto, California, examines the name that the new enterprise requests. If that name is not already in use, SRI grants it to the requesting enterprise. Otherwise, the enterprise has to pick another name.

After an enterprise has its unique enterprise name, it delegates its own subenterprise names, which are not subject to approval by the central registry.

[1.] In countries other than the United States, the second-level domain name often specifies the enterprise category. For example, `barclays.co.uk` identifies a commercial organization (`.co`) in the United Kingdom (`.uk`).

A DNS site name identifies all the levels of the hierarchy, with the highest level on the far right and the lowest level on the far left. A period separates each level. For example, Figure 8 shows a three-level DNS-style name for the old Apollo division of Hewlett-Packard. This site is in the United States, so the top-level indicates an enterprise category rather than a country.

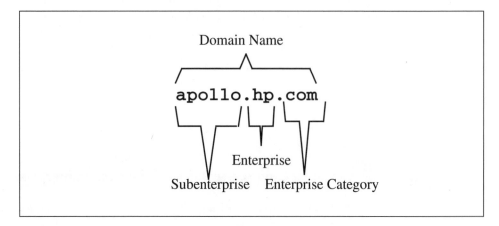

Figure 8   *A Sample DNS-Style Domain Name*

DNS Addressing

IP addresses are partitioned into several address classes.

DNS uses Internet IP addresses. Each Internet IP address is 32-bits long and contains three pieces of information:

- A header field that symbolizes the category or *class* of the DNS site. The class indicates how many different nodes can be on that site. For instance, a Class C site can have up to 254 nodes, while a Class B site can have up to 65534 nodes.

- An address field that uniquely identifies the DNS site from among all other DNS sites in the world.

- A field that uniquely identifies each node within the site.

By convention, people refer to IP numbers as four base-10 numbers separated by periods, for example, 192.74.137.5. Figure 9 illustrates this address.

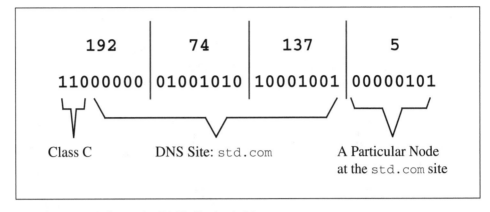

Figure 9   A Sample DNS-Style Address

Port Numbers

IP addresses identify nodes. Ports identify servers within a node.

IP addresses specify a physical system, such as a node or a network; other addressing schemes must identify particular resources, such as filenames or servers on the node or network. Thus, IP addressing must be supplemented with additional information. Most Internet applications use ***port numbers*** to identify a unique server on a host.

Some servers are on well-known ports.

IEach port number is a 16-bit integer. Some port numbers are ***well-known***, meaning that every server node in the world running TCP/IP reserves that port number for a particular service. For example, every server node reserves port number 21 for **ftp** servers and port number 23 for **telnet**. Of course, **ftp** and **telnet** are famous servers used all over the world. If you are trying to reach a server that is not well-known, you will find that the server's port number differs on each machine. For example, an obscure server named **FindMedian** might be contacted on port number 1352 on one machine and port number 2208 on another machine.

DNS Location Service

The DNS location service maps DNS names (such as `world.std.com`) to DNS addresses (such as `192.74.137.5`). Let's stop for a moment and consider what a Herculean task this is. The number of DNS names and addresses to be matched is astounding, currently in the tens of millions and rapidly increasing. If that were not bad enough, names and addresses are being added and removed every minute.

You may be wondering if DNS matches names to addresses by maintaining one central database of names and addresses. Fortunately, the answer is no. It would be just about impossible to keep that central database up to date. Instead, DNS performs a hierarchical search, delegating local searches to local DNS servers. Hierarchical naming not only reduces the complexity of naming, it also reduces the complexity of maintaining and searching the name database.

DNS location is hierarchical, delegating location within a zone to that zone.

The DNS location service is a hierarchical arrangement of servers; the hierarchical DNS name is resolved one step at a time. In this hierarchical search, no single entity manages the entire DNS name space. Instead, a location server has responsibility to know only about names and addresses one level underneath it. For example, to find the address associated with the name `apollo.hp.com`, the location service would first communicate with a root (top-level) server to locate the server responsible for the `hp.com` zone. The root server knows about all enterprise names; in particular, it knows where the `hp` enterprise is and can return the IP address of the authoritative name server for `hp.com`. In turn, the location service at the hpenterprise knows only location information for all the subenterprises in its zone. Thus, the location service at `hp` would know where the `apollo` subenterprise is.

Here are a few additional factoids about DNS:

- Location servers cache commonly used addresses. This method reduces lookup time.
- DNS location services communicate with each other by using Interprocess Communication (IPC) messaging
- DNS provides a simple API to convert between names and addresses. For example, a program with access to location service software can call **gethostbyname** or **gethostbyaddr** to get location information.
- World-wide, there are currently nine root (top-level) name servers.
- Enterprises are responsible for the administration of their zone's name servers. Enterprises usually have one primary name server and several secondary servers.

On most systems, the DNS location service software is in a suite called the Berkeley Internet Name Domain (***BIND***). The server program inside BIND is called **named** (pronounced name-dee, for "name daemon").

DNS is used by other frameworks.

DNS is so well-established and robust that it is used by most other distributed computing frameworks, including DCE and ONC, for wide-area naming and location.

By the way, Internet search systems, such as **archie** and **gopher**, are not location services in the sense used here. These tools can locate resources, such as **ftp** sites and directories, but they do not perform the name-to-address translation. Rather, they produce names that DNS can translate to addresses.

X.500 (XDS)

The X.500 Directory Services (XDS) is the only global naming and location service comparable to DNS. Naming on X.500 is very clear and easy to understand, although it is far more verbose than DNS naming. Novell NetWare uses X.500 for wide-area naming and location services, and DCE allows X.500 as an optional naming system.

The following fictitious X.500 name identifies the Art Acquisition department at the Louvre museum in France:

```
/C=FR/O=Louvre/OU=Art Acquisition
```

C is an abbreviation for Country, O for Organization, and OU for Organizational Unit. As you can see, X.500 naming is hierarchical, moving from the most general (Country) down to the more specific (Organizational Unit). X.500 supports additional lower levels in the hierarchy.The combination of a hierarchy identifier (such as C) and its value (such as FR) separated by an equal sign is known as an X.500 *attribute-value pair*.

Implementation: DCE Naming and Location

DCE is the most comprehensive of the client/server frameworks that we discuss in this book. We will now take a long look at naming and location in DCE.

DCE Naming

A DCE cell is the basic unit.

To understand DCE naming, you first have to understand cells. A *cell* is the basic administrative unit in DCE. One of the first things that a system administrator does in establishing a new DCE site is to organize nodes into one or more cells. A cell could be a building or campus network, an organizational subdivision, or a group of geographically dispersed networks.

Global Cell Naming

DCE names start at the global root. Cell names are DNS or X.500 names.

All DCE cells are located under the ***global root***. The DCE name for the global root is:

```
/...("slash triple dot")
```

The name of any DCE cell is the / . . . followed by the site's DNS or X.500 name. For instance, the following are all fictitious cell names:

```
/.../cs.bsu.org
/.../alphabeta.co.uk
/.../C=US/CO=DEXCO/ORG=RND
```

Of the three preceding global cell names, the first two are DNS names and the last one is an X.500 name. In the X.500 name, the attribute-value pairs specify the research and development organization at the Dexco company in the United States.

Naming within a Cell

CDS manages naming and location within a cell.

A cell has its own name space that includes all its distributed objects, such as servers, users, files, and hosts. This name space is managed by the Cell Directory Service (***CDS***). A global name is a fully-qualified name that is the concatenation of the cell name and the CDS name. The root of each cell is as follows:

```
/.:("slash dot colon")
```

All cells have a set of specialized top-level standard directories for locating hosts, participants in security operations, and distributed files. These directories serve as junctions to other DCE services. The standard junction directories are shown in Table 2.

Directory	What It Locates
/.:/cell-profile	Cell-wide application servers.
/.:/fs	The distributed file services junction for DFS.
/.:/hosts	All of the host machines in the cell.
/.:/lan-profile	The cell's application servers that are on the local network, used when server proximity is important.
/.:/sec	The junction to the Security Services name space.
/.:/subsys	Binding information for DCE services and application-specific servers.

Table 2 Standard DCE Junction Directories

Each cell has some standard directories.

Under the junctions directories are other standard directories. For example, the following directory contains all the security services principals:

`/.:/sec/principals`

A system administrator can create additional cell-wide directories and subdirectories as needed to hold files or resources that everyone in the cell might need. For example, Table 3 shows sample directories that a system administrator might create to hold information about all the printers accessible from a cell.

Directory	What It Holds
`/.:/printers`	All print servers in the cell.
`/.:/printers/Bldg1`	All print servers in Building 1.
`/.:/printers/Bldg1/PS`	All PostScript printers in Building 1.

Table 3 Sample Cell-Wide Print Server Directories

You can identify an object in a DCE cell in either of the following two ways:

- If the object is local to the host machine, you can specify a pathname that the host operating system would understand. This is called ***host-relative*** naming. For example, on a UNIX machine, a DCE cell understands UNIX-style pathnames such as:

  `/usr/jmhart/memos/todo.txt`

DCE supports cell-relative and host-relative names.

- If the object is local to the cell, then you can specify a ***cell-relative*** name by prefacing it with

  `/.:/fs`

  For example, if you want to access `todo.txt`, but do not know which node on the cell `todo.txt` is on, you can specify the following pathname:

  `/.:/fs/usr/jmhart/memos/todo.txt`

  The Distributed File System (**DFS**) is a component of DCE that is, well, a distributed file system that uses DCE naming. (See Chapter 7 for details on DFS.) At any rate, if you are using the DFS, then you can abbreviate the phrase

  `/.:/fs`

  to the much shorter

  `/:`

  Thus, under DFS, you can access todo.txt with the following pathname:

  `/:/usr/jmhart/memos/todo.txt`

Global and Local Naming

Absolute names allow access to any object in any other cell.

If you are in any DCE cell in the world, you can access any object in any other DCE cell in the world (assuming you have permission). To do so, you must concatenate the global cell name and the cell-relative name. For example, assuming that `todo.txt` was on a cell at the DNS site `rnd.lo.com`, you could access `todo.txt` from any DCE cell in the world as follows:

```
/.../rnd.lo.com/fs/usr/jmhart/memos/todo.txt
```

As you can see, DCE naming seamlessly joins global and cell-wide naming. DNS naming alone does not offer this feature; however, World Wide Web naming (Chapter 8) extends DNS naming to handle both server names and pathnames on that server.

DCE Addressing

DCE has a more sophisticated addressing scheme than DNS because DCE must identify more kinds of objects than DNS. DCE addressing must identify files, users, groups, and servers. DCE addressing must also support object replication (Chapter 10).

UIUDs identify objects within hosts.

DCE uses *universal unique identifiers* (*UUID*) for all addresses. All DCE systems provide a simple utility named **uuidgen** whose sole purpose is to create unique UUIDs.

UIUDs are guaranteed to be unique.

A UUID is true to its name; no two are ever the same.[1] There are enough bits in the UUID (128) to ensure that duplicates never occur. The **uuidgen** utility creates a UUID by concatenating a *media access control* (*MAC*) address with the current time. A MAC address is a 48-bit number stamped onto every network card by its manufacturer. Every network card vendor is responsible for ensuring that each network card has a unique MAC address.

In addition to identifying files and directories, UUIDs also identify many other DCE objects, such as servers, users, and RPC interfaces.

---

[1] Yes, as always, there are potential failures that could cause duplicates.

Are We Running Out of Addresses?

Internet IP addresses provide an interesting example of scale problems and what is meant by "large." (See the note in Chapter 1.)

A 32-bit address would seem to be large enough for all foreseeable needs. After all, 32-bits theoretically leads to over four billion unique addresses, which is nearly enough for everyone in the world to have his or her own address. However, 32-bits may not be enough. Consider that early enterprises on the Internet reserved large blocks of addresses based on unrealistic growth plans. Consequently, many of the four billion addresses are now inaccessible. Internet addresses are becoming a scarce enough resource that the Internet Engineering Task Force (IETF) is now proposing extension to 64-bit addressing. Will 64-bits be enough? It would seem so. However, if there is one lesson to be learned from computer history, it is never to underestimate the demand for address bits. It is possible that all sorts of devices will soon have IP addresses (fire alarm boxes, badge readers, vending machines, ATM machines, automobile control systems, and more).

We are less likely to run out of DCE UUIDs and MAC addresses than 32-bit Internet IP addresses. The 48-bit MAC addresses should be sufficient for quite a few years.

DCE Location Service

The *Directory Service* is DCE's location service. This service obtains attribute information in addition to network addresses.

The Directory Service consists of the following two components:

- The Cell Directory Service (*CDS*) provides location services within a cell.

- The Global Directory Service (***GDS***) locates cells that are outside the current cell.

GDS provides location services within a cell.

Each cell contains at least one CDS server. The primary responsibility of a CDS server is to locate servers and files in a particular cell. CDS locates all files in a cell except those under the `/.:/fs` or `/.:sec` directories. (DFS locates files under `/.:/fs`; the Security Service locate files under the `/.:sec` directory.) We explain how the CDS locates servers in Chapter 13.

GDS provides global location services.

GDS is quite versatile; it can locate cells based on either a DNS name or an X.500 name. To locate DNS names, GDS relies on the location services of the host's DNS implementation. To locate X.500 names, DCE provides an X.500 XDS location service implementation.

What Makes for a Good Naming System?

Naming systems should be hierarchical and able to combine existing naming systems.

DNS and DCE are both good naming systems. A good distributed client/server naming system has the following characteristics:

- The naming syntax is clear and unambiguous; a user should be able to look at a name and easily understand what is being accessed.
- The naming system is hierarchical, with clear separators between the hierarchy levels.
- The naming system allows you to specify both absolute names and relative names. For example, the following is an absolute DCE name:

      /.../rd.dexco.com/fs/usr/jmhart/memos/todo.txt

  and the following is a relative DCE name:

      /usr/jmhart/memos/todo.txt

- The naming system is a natural extension of familiar existing schemes. This familiarity helps users migrate to distributed computing. For example, many DCE users are familiar with hierarchical pathnames such as those used by UNIX and Windows. So, DCE naming allows UNIX users to specify DCE names in much the same way as they would specify UNIX names. ONC is also capable of a similar integration with DNS.
- The naming system allows you to join existing systems. For instance, DCE naming joins DNS with UNIX naming.

DCE naming provides a global convention for naming resources within cells. DCE naming has several notable features when compared to ONC and many other distributed client/server naming schemes:

- DCE names are independent of the host machines.
- DCE names have the same meaning everywhere within a cell and to any DCE system in the world. This uniform naming greatly simplifies administration and use. For example, if Marilyn emails Jacqueline a pathname, Jacqueline can access that pathname without having to "mount" directories the same way as Marilyn.
- A host's name space is attached to the cell name space.
- DCE naming supports junctions between different name domains (global, cell, individual hosts, cell Security Service, cell File Service).

Summary

Naming and location are essential for a robust, distributed, scalable, single-system view. DNS and DCE provide fully general, world-wide services. They both are robust and name resources uniformly. DCE extends the familiar UNIX naming syntax and integrates local naming with the global naming of DNS and X.500.

Other implementations, such as NFS and most PC systems, work well in smaller environments, but their limitations hinder large scale deployment. We take a much closer look at NFS and at Novell NetWare in Chapter 7.

CHAPTER 5

Client/Server Security

Distributed clients and servers make security difficult. Security is devilishly complicated on a networked system. You can expect an endless battle of wits between those who protect networked systems and those who attempt to violate their security. Security will always involve trade-offs among convenience, performance, and imperfect degrees of protection.

Throughout this book, we will explain how various client/server implementations provide security services. In this chapter, we will focus first on general security concepts and then look at Internet, ONC, and DCE security.

What Are the Security Threats?

Information must travel on an insecure network. A network is an inherently insecure communications channel; anyone can read and write network data. Networks cannot be secured physically. Furthermore, it is not practical to prevent physical access to most systems. We need to accept the fact that anyone can monitor network traffic or generate any data desired. All but the most secure networks also allow for external access via dial-in lines, the Internet, and other connections.

Network attackers have varying motives. Successful attacks can be costly and may go undetected.

Hackers abound. Their motives range from benign mischief to destructive maliciousness. The network attacks described in computer journals have the intrigue, sophistication, and double-dealing of a good spy novel. A successful attack against a distributed system can cost an enterprise untold amounts in money, inconvenience, and lost business. Even worse, security breaches may not be detected for a long time, if ever. Therefore, some level of security is often necessary, even though implementing security may come with a significant price tag.

We have heard it said that security is boring. We have to disagree. Security involves a fascinating mix of mathematical and computer science theory with real-world combat against unknown foes for large stakes.

Security can be expensive and difficult to achieve . Security must be carefully administered.

Many factors make it difficult to achieve high levels of security, including the following:

- Security software, like all other software, is imperfect (it has bugs). Attackers quickly learn to exploit these imperfections. The wide distribution of source code for many frameworks and operating systems helps hackers locate security defects.

- Security can be difficult to administer and enforce. For example, how do you force users to change their passwords frequently and yet still remember them?

- How do you publicize known security flaws to the good guys without tipping off the bad guys?

- If the stakes are high enough, hackers may try brute force attacks, such as guessing passwords or guessing the encryption key(s).

Imperfect security can still be very worthwhile and necessary.

Despite these daunting barriers to perfection, we must secure distributed client/server systems for the same reason that we lock doors or hire guards.

Security strategies involving encryption require an act of faith; namely that decryption is impossibly hard. That is, decryption, using the best known methods, takes large amounts of computing time beyond the practical capability of any foreseeable computers. Encryption and decryption are active areas of research. If any researchers have figured out how to decrypt the strong encryption schemes, they are not talking about it. Hence, the act of faith.

What Are the Security Services?

Single-system security models do not extend to networked systems.

Within non-networked, multi-user systems, the "Orange Book" defines security fairly precisely.[1] However, there is no such standard security model for distributed systems. So, we will have to content ourselves with explaining four security parameters:

- Authentication
- Authorization
- Data Integrity
- Privacy

Every security system can be attacked. Costs and benefits must be evaluated and traded off.

While the security mechanisms we describe may appear impressive at first sight, it pays to have a healthy respect for hackers.[2] Every security mechanism we describe can be attacked by devious hackers, and there are critiques in the literature showing potential weaknesses. In fact, announcing to the Internet community that you have a new hack-proof security system is like waving a red cape in front of a bull. Use of non-UNIX systems, such as mainframe operating system, is no guarantee of security either, despite the fact that UNIX and Internet breaches get the most publicity. You simply cannot be overly paranoid about security.

Well, perhaps you can be too paranoid. After all, security is expensive. It is not only expensive in terms of the cost of hardware and software, but also in terms of inconvenience, performance, and administration. Installing expensive security systems can even cause, dare we say it, a false sense of security that can lead to lapses. You always have to ask yourself if the security costs are justified. After all, vast amounts of useful data are currently stored on insecure networks across the Internet.

To examine the four security parameters, we will use various TCP/IP applications and services as examples.

---

[1] Although it defines security, the Department of Defense's 1985 "Orange Book" does not tell you how to achieve security. In fact, the higher levels of security described in the "Orange Book" are nearly impossible to achieve.

[2] Before the term "hacker" devolved to mean a pimply 14-year-old who knows how to steal atomic secrets from military networks, "hacker" had a completely different meaning. Nerds used this term to describe clever coding-by-the-seat-of-your-pants. "Aw, I'm just a hacker really," a nerd would say if someone tried to introduce him as a "software engineer."

Security Parameter: Authentication

Authentication means proving that you are who you claim to be. Both clients and human users must provide authentication in order to be granted services. For human users, the login name and password are the most common authentication mechanism. This is **authentication by what you know**.

All TCP/IP networks, whether LANs or the global Internet, require user authentication before they provide service. For example, to access another node with **telnet** or **ftp**, you typically must log in to that node and provide a password for the other system. This system has the following flaws:

- The system is inconvenient. Each user ends up with numerous accounts and passwords to be memorized.
- System administrators at each site must create and administer lots of login accounts.
- Users are slowed down by being forced to log in every time they **telnet** or **ftp** to another system.
- The system has lots of security holes. For example, the passwords that users type are sent over the network as plain, unencrypted text.
- The user may have entirely different account names and passwords on the two systems, and the group memberships will differ as well. In general, we want the client to be able to send requests containing authentication information to the server, and this information must have user and group identifications that have the same meaning to both client and server.

Authentication would be a lot easier for users if distributed systems could maintain a single-system view. In this view, each user would only have to prove his or her identity once, and that identity would be valid for all systems in the network, even if the network was world-wide. In other words, once a user logs in to one machine on the network, it would be as if that user has logged into every node on the entire network.

More advanced authentication strategies depend on **what you have**, such as a smart card. Future versions of "what you have" may involve voice, fingerprint, or retina recognition.

Authentication takes on a large role in a distributed client/server environment. Servers must be able to authenticate that requests actually came from a specific user and client system. Conversely, clients must be able to authenticate server responses to ensure that an attacker is not masquerading as a valid server. Finally, servers often communicate with other servers; in these situations, both servers need a way to authenticate each other.

Authentication guards against client spoofing attacks.

Authentication systems must prevent ***spoofing attacks***. In a spoofing attack, a client, server, or user pretends to be a different client, server, or user. For example, Figure 10 illustrates a spoofing attack in which a hacker creates a fake client that pretends to be a real client. In this scenario, the hacker intercepts a client's request to a server and prevents that request from ever reaching the server. The hacker's client steals the authentication information of the real client in order to masquerade as the real client. The hacker's client then reissues the real client's request but tells the server to return the results to the hacker's client rather than to the real client.

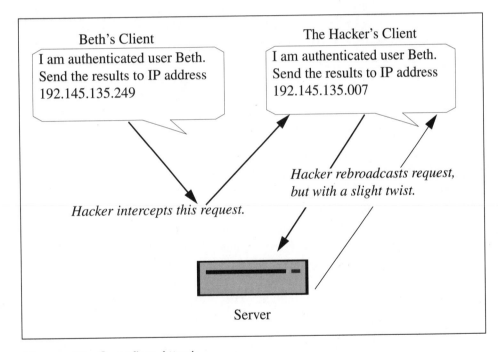

Figure 10 Spoofing Attack

Server spoofing can be just as bad.

In another kind of spoofing attack, a fake server advertises itself. Clients request the fake server, sending the fake server authentication information such as user passwords. The fake server collects this valuable authentication information and passes it on to the hacker.

Security Parameter: Authorization

What services is the client authorized to access?

A server must decide what services, if any, to provide to a requesting client. That is, the server must determine whether the client has the ***authorization*** to get the service it is requesting. For example, a user from the marketing department would not likely be authorized to access payroll information from an accounting server.

UNIX file permissions implement a form of authorization.

On many Internet sites, the server is running UNIX. On such sites, the server typically uses normal UNIX file permissions to determine authorization. The system authenticates most users when they use **telnet** or **ftp** to log in to the system. Once the user is authenticated, the server system knows the user's name and group membership. The system administrator controlling the server specifies read, write, and execute privileges for the owning user and group.

Some server sites need to make data or services publicly available. For example, some Internet sites offer a service called ***anonymous ftp***. A user logs in to any anonymous **ftp** site on the Internet by typing the login name `anonymous`; the user does not need an account on that machine. (Although it sounds a bit backwards, a user typically types his or her login name when asked for a password.) In short, the system bypasses authentication. Once logged in, a user can access files in the anonymous **ftp** tree. However, numerous protection schemes prevent the user from accessing any of the node's data that is outside the anonymous **ftp** tree.

Security Parameter: Privacy

How do you prevent hackers from reading your messages? Start with encryption.

Privacy means that a message can be read and understood only by the sender or receiver. Network traffic is easy to intercept and read. Internet mail, for instance, travels over exposed media and is routed through systems at unpredictable and not necessarily secure locations. Even within a small organization, you cannot regard network traffic as secure from interception. Simply put, a determined hacker can read your email and other data, such as file data being transferred to an authorized user or even an account name and password.

The obvious solution to this problem is to encrypt the data. There are numerous ways do this, but they all require that the reader be able to decrypt the message. Private key methods such as the ***Data Encryption Standard (DES)*** require that both the sender and receiver know the same encryption key. Many people on the Internet use a more flexible public key implementation called ***Pretty Good Privacy (PGP)***.

About Encryption and Decryption

Most encryption methods are well known, which may seem surprising in view of the need for security. You should just assume that all users know the exact encryption and decryption algorithms, or could find it out if they cared to. There is no advantage in trying to hide this information, although, in the United States, there are legal issues involved if you export such technology.

Encryption does not depend on a secret algorithm. A secret key and the encrypted message are both required as input to the matching well-known decryption algorithm. Anyone can intercept the encrypted message, but, without the key, cannot easily decrypt the message. The hacker's only hope is a brute force attack, which means trying every possible decryption key; when the message makes sense, the hacker determines that the message is decrypted. However, there are so many possible keys that the hacker cannot try them all in a reasonable time. All those researchers we mentioned try to figure out faster ways to do it, but, as far as anyone knows, there are no substantial improvements over brute force.

Consider the analogy to a combination lock. We can easily find out how a combination lock works, right down to the way the tumblers and other parts work inside and what kind of steel they are made of. We do not, however, know the combination of a particular lock. An expert safe cracker may be able to crack a locked safe, but, if so, that is a fault of the lock implementation. Alternatively, we can imitate the gangster movies and use a stick of dynamite (brute force).

We detail private and public key encryption algorithms a little later in this chapter.

Security Parameter: Data Integrity

How does the client (server) know that the message was not modified?

As privacy refers to read protection, **data integrity** refers to write protection. A client or server must be able to ensure that the data coming over the network has not been modified, either accidentally by a network or other failure or maliciously. For instance, if you could intercept and replace a message from my branch bank to the central bank, you could change a $1,000 deposit to a $1,000,000 deposit. An attacker could intercept a valid client request and replace the network address with that of the attacker's machine to create a spoofing attack. Countless other data modification attacks would be possible without provisions for data integrity.

If the data is private, it is hard to modify.

Data privacy is the first line of defense to ensure data integrity. If intruders cannot understand a message, they cannot modify it. This is the approach often used by Internet users, as the Internet does not provide an application-level data integrity service.

Data modification due to hardware failures is easily detected.

At a lower level, all network transport services guard against accidental data corruption due to network or system failure by using a conventional *cyclic redundancy code* (*CRC*). A CRC detects, but does not correct, nearly all data corruption errors so that the data can be retransmitted.

In a CRC scheme, the sender puts a message through a function[1] to yield a CRC value. The sender appends this value to the message. Upon receiving the message, the receiver runs the received message through the same function that the sender put it through. The receiver compares the function value that it calculates with the received CRC value. If the two are equal, the receiver assumes that received data was not corrupted. The probability of two messages having the same CRC value is negligible.

CRC is highly effective against failures. However, it is not effective against hatchers. A determined hacker could modify a message and compute a new CRC. This is another reason why encryption is often necessary.

---

[1] The function is usually a polynomial code checksum function designed to detect all errors of one, or even more, bits.

Implementation: Security on ONC

ONC is a distributed client/server framework developed by Sun Microsystems. ONC security starts with the Network Information Service (*NIS*). NIS maintains several weakly replicated databases representing standard UNIX administrative files such as /etc/services and /etc/passwd. (See Chapter 10 for details on weak replication.) All client/server communication on NIS uses ONC remote procedure calls (RPCs).

NIS is an administrative tool for managing ONC domains. An NIS domain could be the same as an Internet domain, but does not need to be.

Authenticating Users

Traditional UNIX systems maintain two authentication information files:

- /etc/passwd, which holds a login name, password, and group identifier for each user.
- /etc/group, which holds a list of all groups on the system.

NIS replaces single-system UNIX authentication.

By contrast, NIS maintains the following four maps:

- passwd.byname and passwd.byuid, which are basically the NIS versions of /etc/passwd.
- group.byname and group.bygid, which are basically the NIS versions of etc/group.

A system running NIS uses the following steps to authenticate a login name:

1. A user enters his or her login name.
2. If the host /etc/passwd file does not contain the user name, the login program queries the NIS server.
3. The NIS server looks in the appropriate NIS maps. If the login name is found in the maps, the NIS server returns the password, user IDs and set of group IDs back to the login program. This information is valid throughout the ONC domain.
4. The user enters his or her password.
5. The login program compares the entered password to the password information returned by the NIS server.

NIS helps provide a single-system view of the entire domain. From the user's perspective, logging into the domain isexactly the same as logging into a single node. However, any client that the user invokes can authenticate itself to any server on the domain.

Authenticating ONC Remote Procedure Calls (RPCs)

ONC also authenticates all remote procedure calls (RPCs). As we discussed in Chapter 2, a client uses an RPC to request a service from a server. Sun's Network File System (NFS) is the most popular application built from ONC RPCs.

Authentication takes place on NFS RPC file requests

An NFS client issues an RPC to request a file from an NFS server. NFS clients include a set of user credentials in every request. The user credentials tell the NFS server who the user is and which groups the user belongs to. The NFS server authenticates the request by checking the credentials against the normal UNIX file permissions. Since user IDs and group IDs are uniform throughout the NIS domain, any NIS server on the domain can authenticate any requester's credentials.

User-defined ONC servers can optionally use the same RPC authentication technique that NFS uses. That is, a client can elect to include user credentials in an RPC. The server (as written by the developer) must interpret those credentials in deciding whether to perform the service.

In older versions of NFS, user and RPC authentication were not terribly secure. NFS requests were prone to spoofing attacks. In a spoofing attack, a user pretends to be another (more privileged) user. Furthermore, ONC and NFS did not provide privacy support.

Secure RPC meets RPC authentication requirements.

These security shortcomings led Sun to add **Secure RPC** to recent versions of NFS. Secure RPC ensures privacy as follows:

1. The client and server decide on a conversation key, which is based on a combination of private and public keys.

2. The client encrypts the current time with the conversation key as the DES key and sends the request and timestamp to the server.

3. The server uses the same mutually agreed upon conversation key to decrypt the timestamp and ensures that it falls within a short interval before accepting the request.

Secure RPC is good, but points of attack remain. For example, the client and server must exchange a so-called *session key*, and, while it is only sent once in a session, it could be intercepted. Furthermore, the NIS master server maintains a key file which could be compromised.

Implementation: Security on DCE

DCE has a complete set of security services based on Kerberos.

The DCE *Security Services* provide authentication, authorization, privacy, and data integrity for DCE clients and servers. Furthermore, the DCE Security Services are flexible enough to allow users and system administrators to select the degree of security. The Security Services are a vital part of the DCE Distributed File System (DFS), and they are an implicit part of every application that runs on a DCE system.

Kerberos is the base architecture for DCE authentication. Kerberos authenticates user logins and RPCs.

In Kerberos, a *principal* is any participant in a secure communication. Users, clients, and servers are all Kerberos principals. One of the central tenets of Kerberos is that every principal must be able to authenticate itself whenever the security asks for authentication. All security principals have private keys derived from their passwords. (Yes, even servers have passwords.) Every principal and every group is uniquely identified by a UUID. A principal can belong to one or more groups.

Kerberos grants "tickets" to principals in a secure communication.

Kerberos operates by giving tickets for specific services to principals. A Kerberos ticket is analogous to a theatre ticket. When you present your credit card as authentication at a box office, the ticket vendor gives you a theatre ticket to a certain theatre performance. If you get a ticket to see "Cats," you cannot use that ticket to see "Hair."

A ticket encodes information about the principal and the groups it belongs to.

Instead of a box office, DCE provides a *Ticket Granting Server (TGS)*. When a principal authenticates itself at the TGS, the TGS grants a ticket. The ticket entitles the principal to get a service from a particular server. A ticket contains encrypted information identifying the principal and its credentials. The credentials consist of the user ID and all of the group IDs that the user belongs to. Servers use these credentials for authorization.

A ticket has a time limit.

A ticket for the September 26th performance of "Cats" will not get you into the September 27th performance. Similarly, a DCE ticket contains a timestamp and an expiration time. By the way, this is one reason that all DCE cells require a time service; if the server node and client node do not synchronize their clocks, then expiration times are meaningless.

A server, on receiving a ticket, must be able to decrypt it to obtain the user identification and credentials and to ensure that the ticket has not expired. Servers can also have authentication tickets so that a client can trust an RPC response. All of the hard work is done by DCE itself, making the operation transparent to the user. Of course, the programmer must be prepared to handle security violation errors and exceptions.

DCE Kerberos currently uses DES private key encryption.

Encryption is essential to this operation; otherwise, anyone could intercept and use the tickets. Kerberos works with either public or private key encryption. The DCE Kerberos implementation currently uses DES private keys, but public key encryption is a possible future enhancement.

DCE Security Service

DCE security consists of Registry, Authentication, and Privilege Services.

The DCE Security Service is responsible for a good part of authorization and authentication on a DCE system. In short, the Security Service takes care of implementing authentication and authorization so that application developers do not have to. The *Security Service* consists of the following three components:

- The *Registry Service*, which maintains a replicated database of users, groups, user accounts (with passwords), and more.
- The *Authentication Service*, which issues ticket granting tickets.
- The *Privilege Service*, which certifies a principal's credentials.

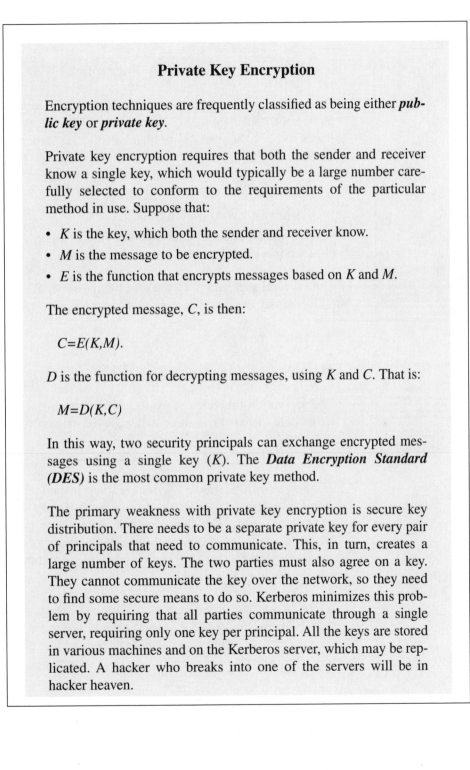

Private Key Encryption

Encryption techniques are frequently classified as being either *public key* or *private key*.

Private key encryption requires that both the sender and receiver know a single key, which would typically be a large number carefully selected to conform to the requirements of the particular method in use. Suppose that:

- K is the key, which both the sender and receiver know.
- M is the message to be encrypted.
- E is the function that encrypts messages based on K and M.

The encrypted message, C, is then:

$C=E(K,M)$.

D is the function for decrypting messages, using K and C. That is:

$M=D(K,C)$

In this way, two security principals can exchange encrypted messages using a single key (K). The *Data Encryption Standard (DES)* is the most common private key method.

The primary weakness with private key encryption is secure key distribution. There needs to be a separate private key for every pair of principals that need to communicate. This, in turn, creates a large number of keys. The two parties must also agree on a key. They cannot communicate the key over the network, so they need to find some secure means to do so. Kerberos minimizes this problem by requiring that all parties communicate through a single server, requiring only one key per principal. All the keys are stored in various machines and on the Kerberos server, which may be replicated. A hacker who breaks into one of the servers will be in hacker heaven.

Public Key Encryption

Public key encryption is becoming increasingly common with a number of implementations. Among other features, public key reduces the key distribution problem. Public key schemes work as follows.

Every principal has two keys:

- Pr, a private key, known to no one else.
- Pu, a public key that everyone knows. Pu might even be published in a directory.

The encryption function, E, requires the message, M, and the public key of the receiver. The encrypted message, C, is then:

$$C=E(Pu(Receiver),M)$$

Anyone can send an encrypted message to any receiver.

The decryption function, D, uses C and the receiver's private key, so only the intended receiver can decode the message. That is:

$$M=D(Pr(Receiver),C)$$

The best known public key system is RSA, named after its inventors. RSA cleverly uses results from number theory to create encryption and decryption functions with the property that the secret private key can only be figured out if you can factor a very large number that is the product of two large prime numbers. No one knows how to do this quickly.

While the key distribution problem has been minimized, there are still problems. For example, a hacker might figure out a method to masquerade as a public key database, giving out the public keys to requesting clients.

Security Services stand between the client and the server.

Conceptually, the Security Service lies between the client and the server as illustrated in Figure 11. The machine running the Security Service holds all of the passwords. Therefore, the Security Service machine should be physically secure, perhaps inside a locked room.

Security Services can extend across cell boundaries. For example, a server can authenticate a client located on a DCE cell in a different continent.

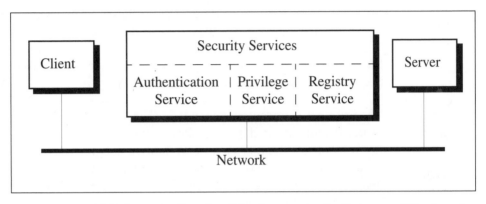

Figure 11 DCE Security Service Fits Conceptually Between Client and Server

DCE User Authentication

The three Security Service components are used in the multi-step user authentication process.

We now examine how the Authentication Service, Privilege Service, and Registry Service cooperate with a login program to verify a user's login name and password. The mechanism is based on secret keys held by various Security Service components. Figure 12 illustrates these interactions:

1. A login program (the client) prompts the user to log in.

2. The user types his or her login name. The user name is not a secret; anyone can easily find all the user names on a system.

3. The client sends the user name to the Authentication Service.

4. The Authentication Service sends the user name to the Registry Service. The Registry Service is on the same server as the Security Service.

5. The Registry Service maintains the user and password database. The Registry Service returns the unencrypted password to the Authentication Service.

6. The Authentication Service encrypts the password and passes it to the client. The encrypted password acts as the initial *ticket granting ticket* (*TGT*) returned to the client machine. The TGT is a Kerberos ticket to obtain additional tickets for specific purposes. The DES encryption key is based on the user's password.

7. The client then prompts the user to enter a password.

8. The user enters a password, which may or may not be correct.

The Registry Service and the user both know the password.

9. To determine if the password is correct, the client decrypts the password it received in Step 6 and compares it to the password the user entered. If the two match, the login is successful; the system has authenticated the user.

Success depends on secure encryption and the fact that the user and the Registry Service share a secret, namely, the user's password.

The PAC encodes all the credentials, using the principal and group UUIDs.

The Privilege Service is responsible for handing out a *privilege access certificate* (*PAC*) to authenticated users. A PAC is a user's credentials for authorization; a PAC completely identifies a user. You might imagine a PAC to be a kind of electronic birth certificate or passport. The Authentication Service creates a PAC by combining a user's user UUID and group UUIDs. Since UUIDs are unique, PACs are guaranteed to be unique.

So here are the final two steps in the authentication mechanism shown in Figure 12:

10. The client sends the ticket granting ticket (TGT), along with the user name, to the Privilege Service. The TGT is a Kerberos ticket to obtain additional tickets for specific purposes.

The PAC now contains certified credentials.

11. The Privilege Service can now access the user and group database because the ticket granting ticket authenticates the request. The Privilege Service can use the returned user and group information to create a privilege access certificate (PAC). The Privilege Service passes an encryption of the password and PAC back to the client. This encryption is returned as the ticket granting ticket, representing certified credentials, to the client.

The Authentication Service and Registry Service must be on the same machine so that the password is never passed over the network.

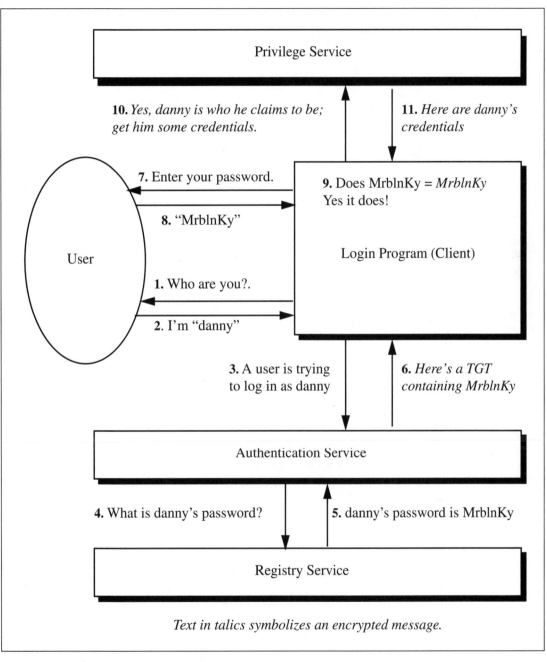

Figure 12 User Authentication in DCE

Notice that unencrypted passwords are never sent over the network; they are kept on individual computers. Furthermore, as mentioned previously, success depends on secure encryption and the fact that the user and the Registry Service share a secret, namely, the user's password.

It is only as secure as the encryption.

The security of this process depends on the encryption function. Can a hacker read a ticket granting ticket and decrypt it to obtain the password? Yes, it is possible if the attacker knows the encryption key. This is one reason why non-trivial passwords are important. Fortunately, there is no known *fast* method to break the Data Encryption Standard. Bear in mind that authentication information contains an expiration time. So, the attacker who intercepts the ticket granting ticket has to decrypt it quickly enough to beat the expiration time. As computers get faster, the encryption algorithms will have to become more sophisticated.

DCE Authorization

Access Control Lists determine what an authenticated client can do.

Authorization in DCE is based on Access Control Lists (*ACLs*[1]). ACLs define the permissions for every object in a DCE cell. They are similar to UNIX file permissions but are far more sophisticated. Consider that standard UNIX file permissions provide a way to identify permissions for only one user, only one group of users, and "others. " For example, the following rather cryptic UNIX file permissions entry shows user danny with read, write, and execute (rwx) permissions, the students group with read and execute permission (r-x), and all others with no permissions (---).

```
-rwxr-x---    1 danny students 832 Jan 26 17:52 page.html
```

ACLs are very specific.

By contrast, DCE ACLs can describe different file permissions for lots of individual users and lots of groups. Thus, ACLs give you pinpoint control to define who may do what to a file. For example, here is a sample ACL for a file:

```
<user     jmhart          read,write,delete,execute>
<user     danny           read,execute>
<user     rachel          read>
<group    accounting      read,execute>
<group    sysadmin        all>
<group    managers        deny all>
```

[1] Security gurus usually pronounce ACLs as "ackles" to rhyme with "tackles." ACLs are required for some Orange Book levels. Microsoft Windows NT uses ACLs for file access control.

Notice how the three individual users (`jmhart`, `danny`, and `rachel`) and the three different groups (`accounting`, `sysadmin`, and `managers`) each have a different set of permissions. This type of control is impossible with standard UNIX file permissions.

ACLs, while powerful, can be difficult to administer and understand.

The downside to ACLs is that they require more effort to create and maintain than do standard UNIX file permissions. Some users go wild with ACLs, creating all sorts of unnecessarily fancy permissions that are difficult to understand and manage and that may even lead to unintended security breaches. As a simple example, consider what happens when `danny` is promoted and any assumptions about what `managers` can do are no longer valid.

DCE Client Authentication and Authorization

Each server determines if an authenticated client is to be served.

Figure 13 illustrates how the Security Service authenticates a client's request. The steps the Security Service uses are as follows:

1. The client sends its TGT and the name of the service that it wants to the Authentication Service.

2. The Authentication Service grants a ticket allowing the client to request service from a particular server. This time, however, the encryption uses the server's password, which the Authentication Service also knows.

3. The client makes an RPC to the server. The request contains the identity of the service, all RPC parameters, and the ticket. The server knows its password, so it can decrypt the ticket to obtain the privilege access certificate and expiration time.

4. The server can now determine whether or not to provide the service. To determine this, the server compares the client's privilege access certificate to the server's access control ;ist. This is analogous to a border guard checking visas (PACs) against a list of who may be allowed into the country (ACLs) and how long they may stay (expiration time).

5. Depending on the outcome of the comparison, the server either goes to work processing the client's request or returns an authorization error to the client.

Authorization is transparent to users and programmers.

All of the preceding steps are transparent to the user or programmer, except that the client program must be prepared to recover from the "failure" of not obtaining service. Note that Figure 13 shows the case where access is denied, rather than the more typical case where the server grants the client's request.

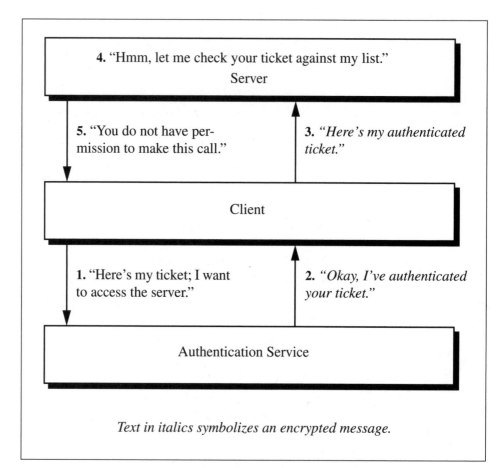

Figure 13 Client Authentication and Authorization in DCE

Varying Degrees of Authentication

Programmers can specify authentication "granularity."

DCE allows programmers to set varying degrees of RPC authentication. For instance, the client and server may agree that authentication be done on the first call only, or that authentication be performed on every call. Authenticating every call provides more security but reduces performance.

The client and server determine the security level jointly. The client requests the security level, and the server decides if this choice is sufficient. Clients can receive only the level of security supported by the server. If the level is not available, the server can be programmed to refuse the service or to give client something less.

For instance, suppose that the server requires per-call authentication. The client, however, requests first call authentication, so there is no match between what the server is willing to provide and what the client requests. The server should not allow the requested service as it is not sufficiently secure. The situation is reversed if the server does not support per-call authentication but the client requests it. The server can advise the client that it cannot provide that level of security, and the client can try again with a different RPC security level.

DFS (DCE's distributed file service; see Chapter 6) uses this DCE authorization and authentication in conjunction with ACLs.

DCE: Extra Levels of Privacy and Integrity

DCE also provides optional privacy and integrity.

As a privacy option, the client and server can encrypt data using a shared secret key, which can be obtained from the Authentication Service. Privacy contributes to data integrity as well, for an attacker cannot make undetected modifications. Data integrity is further ensured by computing a cyclic redundancy code (CRC) using shared secret keys. The client and server can verify and generate CRCs, but a hacker cannot.

Summary

DCE and ONC security can implement security for other systems, such as database management.

DCE offers a unified solution to the security requirements of distributed computing. The client can specify the RPC security level, ranging from nothing at all to authentication of every RPC. ONC also offers authentication, authorization, and privacy, but it is not as comprehensive as DCE and does not scale as easily to wide area networks.

Security services are easy to build into ONC or DCE RPC clients and servers; in fact, the programmer just binds in the appropriate routines. Security services can be added to existing client/server applications such as distributed DBMS applications.

The underlying Kerberos and encryption technologies have been used widely in various forms. While these technologies do have weaknesses, they will evolve to address the important security threats.

CHAPTER 6

Distributed File System Concepts

This chapter explains the central role that distributed file systems play in client/server computing.

What Is a Distributed File System?

Distributed file systems provide transparent access to remote files.

A file system is a basic component of modern operating systems. A *file system* maps human-readable names (such as `/usr/rachel/math`) to chunks of data stored on physical devices (such as track 5, section 4, head 2 on disk drive `sdg1`). The human-readable names are generally organized into some kind of hierarchy. Programmers use the file system to open, close, read from, or write to files. Users access the file system to create, rename, delete, read from, or edit files.

A *distributed file system* allows programmers and users to access files on another computer in the same way they access files on their own computer.

To explore this idea, let's first imagine a site without a distributed file system or without any sort of network altogether. Imagine two PCs at this site, one named

bird and the other named **magic**. Suppose that you are working at **bird** but you need to edit a text file named lion that is stored on **magic**. In order to edit lion, you'd have to do the following:

Manual file transfer is frustrating and error prone.

1. Walk over to **magic**.

2. Copy lion onto another storage device, say a floppy disk.

3. Walk back to **bird** and load the floppy.

4. On **bird**, edit lion.

5. Copy lion onto a floppy disk.

6. Bring the floppy disk over to **magic**.

7. Copy lion from the floppy disk to **magic**.

Not only is this painfully time-consuming, you also might end up asking yourself, "Which lion is the latest version?"

Networked file transfer is better, but it is not transparent, and version consistency is

After a few rounds of this sort of thing, you'd surely be looking into networking **bird** and **magic**. So, let's assume that you rush out to the store and install Ethernet boards and connect the computers with cable. You also install some sort of communications software with file transfer, such as **xmodem** or TCP/IP with **ftp**, on both nodes. Let's further assume that you still don't have software to set up a distributed file system. Therefore, you must do the following to edit lion:

1. From **bird**, log on to **magic**.

2. Use the file transfer utility to transfer a copy of lion from **magic** to **bird**.

3. On **bird**, edit lion.

4. Transfer the edited copy of lion back to **magic**.

The network has certainly reduced the number of steps; however, we can do a lot better still. Once we've set up a distributed file system, the steps to edit lion are as follows:

1. Edit lion.

Distributed file access makes it seem as if the file were local.

That's it! Clearly, our new distributed file system has really simplified matters for users. The resulting savings in time are well worth the nominal cost we paid for the software. But are we painting too rosy a picture of distributed file systems? Perhaps. We'll hit the issues in due time.

Distributed file systems have many advantages over nondistributed file systems, including the following:

- Users on separate clients can share a single file without making separate copies (and wasting disk space).

- Files can be modified serially by many users, without being copied. Sharing a single file ensures that there is only one version, helping to maintain consistency and control.

- All users can benefit from central management (backup and restore, for instance) of important data.

- Porting single-system programs to a distributed file system often requires very little program modification.

Two Major Kinds of Distributed File Systems

There might be one large file server.

The client/server cliche says that servers are big and beefy and that clients are anemic. Indeed, this cliche accurately describes *centralized distributed file system*. In this kind of file system, one powerful disk system holds most (or all) of the files on the network. In other words, the files are centralized onto one disk system. The disk system might be a single disk drive or might be a cluster of disks. We refer to this disk system as a *file server*. The other nodes on the network are all clients that ask the file server to access a particular file for them. Figure 14 illustrates a centralized distributed file system.

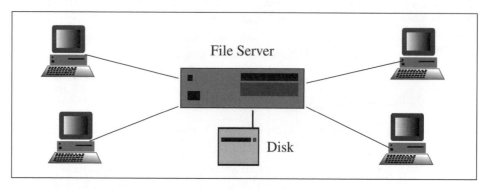

Figure 14   Centralized Distributed File System

Or, there might be numerous smaller file servers.

The client/server cliche does not do a good job of describing ***noncentralized distributed file systems***. Here, files are not centralized onto one disk drive. Rather, any or all of the disk drives on the network can act as file servers. Similarly, any node on the network can act as a client and request a particular file. In fact, as Figure 15shows, some nodes on a noncentralized distributed file system act as both a server and a client.

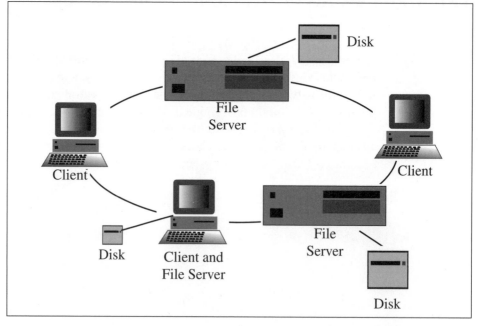

Figure 15   Noncentralized Distributed File System

Costs/Benefits of Distributed File Systems

This section examines the risks and rewards of distributed file systems.

Costs/Benefits for System Administrators

Everyone benefits after the start-up pain.

Setting up a distributed file system often places a significant burden on system administrators. However, once such a system is set up, system administrators generally are better off than before the distributed file system was available.

The big costs for a system administrator are as follows:

- Deciding which files should be shared and how they should be shared.
- Implementing and updating the file-sharing policies.
- Answering acute file-sharing questions from dazed users. This problem is particularly noticeable after a file server crashes as panicky users rush into the control room to ask if their work has survived the crash.

A distributed file system with one centralized file server is generally easier for a system administrator to maintain than a distributed file system with multiple servers. When you reduce the number of disks on the network, backups and software installations become much easier. Also, centralizing system software helps prevent version skew; that is, you don't end up with different versions of the same software roving around the network and causing incompatibility problems.

Costs/Benefits for Users

Users gain a lot by switching to a distributed file system. The primary advantage is easy access to any file on the network.

Users need to adjust to security controls.

One disadvantage for users, if indeed it can be called a disadvantage, is the presence of some sort of security system. Most PC and Mac users are accustomed to being able to access any file they want whenever they want. When a site switches over to a distributed file system, users suddenly run up against security constraints. ("What do you mean I can't read that file; I could read it before!") Conversely, they may not be used to having other people editing their files. All change, even change for the better, is troubling. Users will need some amount of instruction in using a new distributed file system.

Costs/Benefits for Programmers and Developers

Programmers need to be aware of the following two problems when users share distributed files:

- Concurrency control
- Unauthorized execution of application code

Programs may need modification to use concurrency control.

If a program contains data that multiple users will access simultaneously, then the programmer has to worry about locking and unlocking files and records. Record locking is not fully supported in all distributed file system implementations or in the client's own operating system. For example, UNIX file locking is only advisory. Advisory locking means that the program can test to see if a file is locked, but then the program can read or write to the locked file anyhow. Therefore, locking and concurrency control often have to be done by cooperating application programs. In any case, the programmer may need to make extensive code modifications.

Application code can be executed over the network.

Suppose that you develop a program and you want to make some money from it. This will, of course, strike some in our audience as pure heresy and others as pure folly, even though there are some well-known success stories. Nevertheless, pretend that you want each person who uses the program to pay you money. Suppose someone buys your program and installs it in the publicly accessible region of a file server. Sadly, there is nothing other than morality to prevent anyone on that network from using that program by executing it directly, just as if the program were in a local file system directory. As a software developer, you should be aware of this problem and make special note of it in your software licensing agreement. But let's face it, even with a well-worded agreement, enforcement is very difficult. This is a problem for system administrators as well, for they may need to create and enforce policies regarding sharing application code. There are a number of network licensing schemes in use to address just this problem, but network licensing imposes another burden on system administrators.

A Distributed File System Helping Programmers

The Oxymoron Corporation develops and maintains software for political organizations. A staff of twelve programmers maintains the source code, which is scattered across 200 source code files. All 200 source code files are stored on one central file server. A source code control system (not part of the distributed file system) hovers over the source code files.

Each member of the programming staff has a client workstation with a relatively small disk drive. On these disks, each programmer has a work area called a playpen. The playpen is a safe place for programmers to develop software. By safe, we mean that whatever coding a developer does in her playpen will have no adverse effect on the source code in the file server. The initial playpen consists of links to all 200 source code files, plus links to the extra files (such as a `Makefile`) necessary to build the source code into an executable binary.

When a developer wants to modify a source code file, she asks the source code control system for permission to make a revision. If granted, the system replaces a link in the programmer's playpen with a modifiable copy of the source code file. Thus, at this point, the playpen consists of 199 links plus one actual copy. The programmer may now edit, build, and debug to her heart's content. When she feels satisfied that her edits are worthy, she asks the source code control system to check the file back in. The source code control system copies the file from the programmer's playpen back to the file server; the source code control system removes the file from the programmer's playpen and leaves a link in its place.

Costs/Benefits for Managers and Architects

This section describes the features of distributed file systems that managers and architects should investigate when comparing products. Many of these issues apply to nondistributed file systems as well. You should also consider whether or not the client operating system can take advantage of the features provided by the distributed file system.

How much data can a file hold?

Purchasers should ask what the maximum supported size of a file is. A typical supported length at this time is for files to hold up to 4 gigabytes (2^{32}) of data. Some sites (those with extremely large databases) may bump up against that limit. If your site falls into that category, you will need to find a distributed file system that supports larger files. Some distributed file systems on the market today support files as large as 2^{64} bytes. Very few client operating systems will be able to exploit the larger files, however.

Does it provide concurrency control?

You should consider the distributed file system's ability to provide concurrency control. Concurrency control reduces conflicts when two or more parties try to change the same file at roughly the same time. For example, suppose that while user Per is editing a file, user Pascale asks to edit that same file. If the distributed file system has concurrency control, Pascale will probably be prevented from making changes until Per is through with the file. You should find out if a distributed file system provides this feature. If it does, find out the level of granularity for concurrency control. For example, if a file is divided into records, can the distributed file system lock individual records, or can it only lock an entire file?

Distributed file access can be almost as fast as local file access.

Performance is, of course, a key issue to consider. In large part, performance will be limited by the normal server system considerations such as disk access time, bus speeds, server load, and the server's ability to handle that load. The overall network load is also significant but is largely independent of the distributed file system itself. Experience shows that network file access can be competitive with local access.

Performance is a complex subject. Test it!

The distributed file system software may have far less influence on performance than the server system. Nevertheless, the distributed file system can do certain things to improve performance. For example, a distributed file system can cache all or part of a file on the client disk in order to reduce network access. Concurrency control can also influence performance; a system that can lock at the record level will probably have better performance than one that can lock only at the file level. Finally, some distributed file systems are implemented with client/server frameworks (such as DCE) that have special data structures for efficiently moving large blocks of data. So many factors go into performance that benchmark tests, rather than theoretical arguments, are the best way to determine distributed file system performance.

Security can be inconvenient. When investigating distributed file systems, you should factor in the security needs of your site. How much security is really necessary at your site? Security barriers designed to thwart outsiders often end up thwarting the people in your enterprise who genuinely need to use files. Before purchasing, you should make a careful analysis of the level of security you really need. Then, you should investigate how a distributed file system controls access to files. There are several parameters to consider.

How flexible are permissions? First, how many different kinds of permissions can you attach to a file? You would certainly expect all distributed file systems to provide read, write, and execute access to files, but what about additional kinds of controls? Are create, delete, and rename access control available?

How flexible is ownership? Second, how many different categories of people can you give access to? For example, some distributed file systems let you provide only three different categories of people (the owner of the file, a group, and anyone else). Other distributed file systems provide a much higher degree of granularity. For example, you could say that Jessica has certain privileges, Kalonymus has other privileges, the engineering group has a different set of privileges, and the marketing group has still a different set.

How easy is it to use? The third parameter is the ease with which the different access controls can be set and administered. Can system administrators and users set access controls with an easy-to-use graphical user interface, or do they have to rely on some clumsy command-line interface? Actually, if a distributed file system does not provide many different kinds of permissions or groups, then a command-line interface may be adequate.

How easy is security administration? The foundation of all security systems is a database of valid users and their passwords. On a centralized distributed file system, this database can easily be kept in one place on the network. On a noncentralized distributed file system, this database should be updated and/or replicated so that each server has access to the same list of users and passwords. If this database is not cared for, then the security system breaks down.

Common Implementation Requirements

How is distributed file access made transparent to the user and the programmer?

The major attraction of any distributed file system is its transparency to client users and applications. To the user, a file on a remote server is nearly indistinguishable from a local file. To a software developer, very little, if any, code needs modification to work with a distributed file system. We have seen how to set up and use distributed file systems; it is now time to see how distributed file systems are implemented.

Achieving transparency requires the distributed file system to provide *file access* through the normal operating system file system calls. File system calls that `open`, `read`, `write`, `seek` (position at an arbitrary location), `delete`, and otherwise access files must be modified, within the client operating system, so that they work the same way for files on both local and remote systems.

Client and Server Implementations

The client OS must distinguish local and remote file access.

The file system calls are part of the operating system. Therefore, in order for an operating system to provide this transparent service, it must be able to distinguish local and remote files. When the file is opened, the client operating system can use the name to make this distinction. Usually, the file handle returned by the `open` system call and used by subsequent operations contains information to distinguish local and remote files. The operating system then can take one of two actions:

- If the file is local, it exists on the same system that runs the operating system. The operating system simply invokes the local services that determine where a file exists on disk (or other random access storage) and performs the appropriate read, write, and other operations. That is, the file system call is passed through to the local file system.
- If the file is remote, then the operating system must convert the file system call into the appropriate client requests required by the distributed file system implementation.

The work is done in the client OS kernel.

At a high level, this is how all distributed file systems work. The important point is that the distributed file system must be supported within the client operating system kernel. Early distributed file system implementations required modifications to the existing operating systems, but, as would be expected, the support is increasingly designed and built into the operating system from the beginning.

Since the client operating system must direct file system calls to the correct file system, whether local or remote, the portion of the operating system that does this is named something like the "redirector" in MS-DOS and Windows and "DOS Requester" in Novell NetWare.

The server can be outside the OS kernel. The server accesses the local file system.

A distributed file system server can operate outside the operating system, as its role is to receive the remote file system requests, which generally map closely to the normal file system calls such as `open`, `read`, and `write`. The server, then, can just carry out the requested operation using its own operating system, making whatever adjustments are necessary to accommodate differences in file naming and in semantics between the server file system and the distributed file system protocol. Figure 16 shows this common distributed file system architecture.

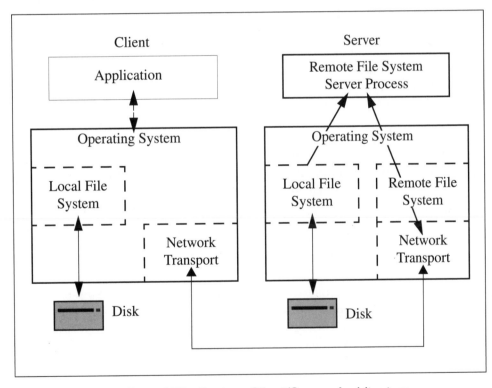

Figure 16   Distributed File System Client/Server Architecture

In many cases, a client must distinguish between operations on local and remote objects. In all these cases, it is worth noting how the objects are distinguished. For instance, remote procedure calls (RPCs) are able to make the procedure's remoteness seem almost inconsequential to the user or programmer. Similarly, distributed object-oriented programming implementations sometimes use "redirector" concepts, as we will see in Chapter 14.

The vendor changes the client operating system.   The actual client distributed file system implementation depends more on the client operating system than on the distributed file system itself. Within UNIX and many mainframe operating systems, the vendor must modify the operating system to act as a client, as shown in Figure 16. Windows 3.1, however, is a special case.

MS-DOS and Windows 3.1 Client Implementation

MS-DOS and Windows 3.1[1] do not have a protected kernel. The client file redirection is done outside of MS-DOS, which is slightly different from what Figure 16 shows. Microsoft LANManager clients, PC-NFS clients, and Novell NetWare clients all do client file redirection in a similar manner. We will use LANManager as an example.

MS-DOS and Windows use a Redirector TSR to extend the client OS.   An MS-DOS LANManager client, at startup, loads a Terminate and Stay Resident (***TSR***) program that initializes itself and then exits, but remains in memory. This client TSR, called the "Redirector," intercepts all MS-DOS operating system calls. It can do this because MS-DOS is not a protected system. All MS-DOS calls are performed using a known soft interrupt (INT X21 in the Intel x86 instruction set). The Redirector looks at the request and can take the following actions:

- If the request is not a file system request, it is passed on to MS-DOS for normal, local processing.
- If the requested file is local, the Redirector also passes the request on to MS-DOS.
- If the requested file is remote, the Redirector creates the LANManager request and communicates the request to the server using the network transport protocol. The server and Redirector cooperate, using the LANManager protocol, to carry out the remote file system operation and pass the results back to the client.

[1.] Windows 3.1 uses the MS-DOS file system.

This architecture differs from that in Figure 16 only in that you consider the Redirector and the network protocol stack as part of the operating system, and MS-DOS as another part.

File Access Protocols

The actual file access protocols that the client and server use in Figure 16 can be divided according to three broad designs.

There are three different designs.

- The *stateless* protocols, of which NFS is the prime example, use network datagrams to communicate. The client and server do not share any information about the state of the file access. For example, the server does not keep track of which clients have specific files open. NFS uses Sun's ONC and its stateless RPCs, which we will see more of in Chapter 12.

- The *connection-oriented, stateful* protocols, such as Microsoft's LANManager, use network transport virtual circuits to establish the client/server communication channel. The server also keeps track of the state of each open file, by client, as well as lock and current position information. The network virtual circuit also contains considerable state information, but at a lower level.

- The *connectionless, stateful* protocols, such as DFS, use datagrams or RPCs to communicate without the need for a network transport connection. Nonetheless, the client and server contain file access state information that must be maintained in a consistent state.

All three designs work well.

A lot of ink has been spilled debating the relative merits of the three architectures, but NFS, LANManager, and DFS illustrate that all three can be successful. The arguments center around factors such as:

- The simplicity and robustness of stateless protocols are significant. With NFS, a server could crash and be rebooted in the middle of a file access. Barring client time-outs, the clients would not fail even though they would experience file access delays.

- State is, inevitably, necessary for full functionality. For instance, a server that maintains file locks for each client is maintaining state information.

You will hear more about stateful and stateless servers and protocols when we discuss RPCs and Internet client/server services in later chapters.

Summary

Distributed file systems make it easy for users to share data and programs. However, sharing brings on a raft of naming and security issues. The next chapter explains several popular distributed file system implementations and explains how these implementations address naming and security issues.

CHAPTER 7

Distributed File System Implementations

This chapter details four of the most popular distributed file system implementations and concludes by showing the architectural design that all these systems share.

Implementation Overview

There is no shortage of products for creating distributed file systems on local area networks.

NFS is the prime UNIX choice. If your network consists of multiple UNIX machines, then you are probably going to use NFS. However, DFS (a component of DCE) may someday become popular so we will take a short look at it.

Novell NetWare is very popular on PCs. If your network consists of PCs, then you are probably going to use Novell NetWare. That's no slight against other distributed file system products (such as Banyan Vines); it's just that NetWare currently has an amazingly high share of this market. If you don't use NetWare, then you are probably going to use a distributed file system based on Microsoft's LANManager protocols. For example, the following distributed file system products use these protocols:

- Digital PATHWORKS
- IBM LAN Server
- Microsoft Windows NT Server

Macintoshes have a built-in system.

If your network consists of Macintosh computers, then you may not need to layer on additional distributed file system software. Every Macintosh has file-sharing support built into the Macintosh operating system.

If your network is heterogeneous–that is, if your network supports a mixture of hardware and/or operating systems–then you will run into some interesting problems in creating distributed file systems. We will describe those problems and some solutions at the end of this chapter.

Implementation: NFS

NFS source is licensed. It is available on a wide range of systems.

The **Network File System (NFS)** was developed by Sun Microsystems in the mid-1980s. Sun decided to license NFS freely. This strategy paid off handsomely as it is now difficult to find a UNIX system that does not support NFS. NFS has become the *de facto* standard for distributed file systems.

The domain of NFS now extends far beyond UNIX. NFS is now implemented on everything from PCs to mainframes and is used with such operating systems as OS/2 and Microsoft Windows NT.

How It Works

Any machine can be a client, a server, or both.

NFS is an example of a noncentralized distributed file system. Any machine on an NFS network can be a server; any machine can be a client. At many sites, some machines act as both servers and clients.

Servers export of their local file system.

To be an NFS server, a node must announce (**export**) the names of the directories it is willing to make available to clients. To be an NFS client, a machine must attach (**mount**) a remote directory.

A System Administrator's View

Ongoing administration is required.

Before users can get anything useful out of NFS, a system administrator has to do a fair amount of setup. "Setup" is perhaps a misleading term because the activities that we describe in this section might be better considered ongoing.

Server Side Setup

Every machine on the network is a potential server. Some sites decide to make only one machine, probably the one with the fastest or largest disk, into an NFS server. However, at most NFS sites, many machines act as NFS file servers.

Export the files that others can access.

Each server machine holds a list of the files and directories that it will make available to requesters (clients). This list is stored in an ASCII text file stored at pathname `/etc/exports`. Only a superuser is allowed to edit this file. The superuser thus has complete control over whether a machine can serve a particular file or directory to a client.

For example, the following is a sample `/etc/exports` file:

```
/latest/sources/release2.0
/usr/man
```

The preceding `/etc/exports` file makes two directories (and all their subdirectories) available to potential clients. UNIX systems typically store online documentation (`man` pages) inside the `/usr/man` directory. By placing all online documentation on one NFS server machine, we can eliminate the need for each machine to store separate copies.

Servers can specify access rights to exported directories.

NFS allows a system administrator to exert all sorts of control over the kinds of access that a client can make on a particular directory. For example, a system administrator can mark a particular directory (such as `/usr/man`) as read-only. Therefore, NFS would prevent any client from modifying any online documentation files stored in `/usr/man`.

Client Side Setup

A client's machine must explicitly "mount" an exported directory or file before a client process can access them. A client machine at an NFS site can mount any number of exported directories. Note that a single client machine can mount exported directories from multiple servers on the network.

Clients must "mount" the exported server directories before accessing them, often at startup time.

The term "mount" has several related meanings in the UNIX world. Basically, mounting is a way of introducing your machine to peripherals and external files that it may encounter. NFS provides the following two ways to mount exported files:

- Through a startup file
- Through the **mount** command

The first way to mount external files is to store a list of them in a certain startup file, usually `/etc/fstab`. When the machine is booted, NFS automatically reads this startup file and mounts all the entries. The entries remain mounted for as long as the machine is running. (A system administrator can unmount an entry without bringing down the machine.) For example, suppose that a node named **jordan** contains the following `/etc/fstab` file:

```
bird:/usr/man          /usr/man nfs rw,bg,hard 0 0
magic:/latest/facts /ripley  nfs rw,bg,hard 0 0
```

Clients request access rights.

The first line mounts the `/usr/man` directory of server **bird**. The second line mounts a directory named `/latest/facts` stored on server **magic**. The information at the end of the lines specifies various options associated with the mount. For example, the phrase `rw` signifies that clients can have both read and write access to the mounted files. If the phrase `ro` had appeared instead of `rw`, then clients would have read-only access.

A second way for a client node to mount external files is via the UNIX **mount** command. For example, the command-line equivalent of the first line in our example `/etc/fstab` file would look as follows:

```
$ mount bird:/usr/man /usr/man
```

The directories or files remain mounted as long as the system stays up or until the system receives an unmount request, whichever comes first.

NFS can access files outside the local area network.

All the examples we have shown so far assume that the client is mounting a node on the local area network. In fact, a client can also mount server directories on nodes outside the local area network. At mount time, the client host uses DNS to determine the network address of the server host. The client caches this address.

Automounters

If setting up all those NFS clients sounds like a nightmare, then you might consider using an *automounter* program instead. Before starting an automounter, you must create a map of all exported objects on the network. Then, any time a client tries to access an unmounted directory, the automounter reads this map and issues the appropriate mount calls. In short, the automounter figures out what you need mounted and goes ahead and mounts it for you. The user or system administrator never has to issue a **mount** command.

Two popular automounter programs **are amd** and **automount**.

A User's View

After setup is complete, a user may access files or directories on other nodes exactly as a user would access them locally.

When a client node mounts an external object, the mount indicates not only the external object but also its local porthole. For example, consider the following mount command issued from node **magic**:

```
$ mount bird:/usr/man /usr/man
```

The client sees the remote file system as being part of its own file system.
In this example, the mounted object (`/usr/man` on **bird**) has a local porthole of `/usr/man`. Therefore, whenever a user on **magic** specifies a pathname that starts with `/usr/man`, NFS automatically translates that pathname into the `/usr/man` directory on **bird**. For example, if a user on **magic** issues the following command:

```
$ cd /usr/man/cat3
```

then NFS will automatically change directories to `/usr/man/cat3` on **bird** as illustrated in Figure 17 .

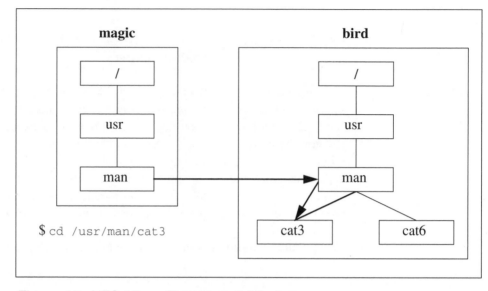

Figure 17 NFS Allows Transparent File Access

Pathnames are not uniform from one client to another. Some conventions help solve this.

A file's pathname may vary from client to client. For example, consider a file named `frisbee`. Ramesh might view `frisbee` as being in directory `/games/ultimate`, while Tom might view `frisbee` as being in directory `/park/nuisances`. This is all part of the charm of NFS and its solution to the distributed naming problem (Chapter 4); each user can create his or her own personalized view of the same object. However, this flexibility makes it hard for coworkers to communicate the location of a particular object. If Ramesh tells Elizabeth to read `/games/ultimate/frisbee`, Elizabeth will only be able to find `frisbee` if her node uses the same mount commands as Ramesh's node.

To get around the problem of different names for the same object and to simplify administration, there are some commonly used naming conventions. For example, by convention, `/home` is the directory for distributed objects, with subdirectories such as `/home/hostname` and `/home/username`.

Security Services

NFS uses UNIX file permissions.

Most implementations of NFS rely on the security services of the host operating system. In most cases, this means that file access is controlled by the UNIX operating system model. Unfortunately, UNIX is limited to file permissions, rather than ACLs, for file access control.

The Network Information Service (NIS)

NIS is necessary for a uniform user and group database.

The Network Information Service (***NIS***) runs on some implementations of NFS. NIS provides a convenient way for sites to synchronize certain network databases. For example, consider how a site registers its users. Prior to NIS, this database of users was stored at pathname /etc/passwd on each node in the network. Since each node was keeping its own copy, it was very easy for the copies to get out of synch. By using NIS, the system keeps one central registry of logins and passwords. With only one master registry, there is nothing to get out of synch.

NIS provides a server daemon (process), **ypserv**, to handle client requests. The server maintains maps (name to address and port) for multiple domains, but it does not query other servers if it fails to find a requested domain. Therefore, the administrator must take care to ensure a complete set of maps. The **ypbind** daemon is the NIS client that client programs use to communicate with **ypserv**; it returns the binding information (network address and port) to the client program. The client program can rebind (locate another server) at any time.

NFS is implemented with ONC RPCs. For more information on RPCs, see Chapter 12.

Implementation: DFS

DFS is an ambitious world-wide distributed file system.

The Distributed File System (***DFS***) is not currently a major player in the distributed file system market. However, it is important to look into DFS for two reasons:

- The DFS design is ambitious. Some of its features may be incorporated into future products.
- DFS was designed from the very beginning to act as a world-wide distributed file system.

Although DFS ships under the OSF banner, the coding was primarily done by Transarc, which based many of its ideas on the Andrew File System (AFS) developed at Carnegie-Mellon University.

The primary goal of DFS is to create a world-wide distributed file system that allows any users, security permitting, to access any remote file just as easily as a local file.

How It Works

DFS is decentralized.

DFS is a noncentralized distributed file system. Any node on a DCE cell can be a server and any node can be a client.

Explicit mounting is unnecessary.

Under NFS, you always have to mount a directory before you can access it remotely. Under DFS, there is no mounting. In other words, under DFS, the system administrator does not have to set up mount tables. Once a system administrator sets up a cell, the user can access any file.

Naming and Location

DFS uses DCE naming.

DFS uses the very rich DCE naming and location services described in Chapter 4. For example, the following command invokes the **emacs** editor to edit a particular file on the local cell:

```
$ emacs /:/usr/jmhart/memos/todo.txt
```

DCE naming makes it fairly easy for users to access files outside the cell. To edit a file on a remote cell, we merely add the cell name to the pathname. For example, the following command edits a file on a cell named rnd.lo.com:

```
$ emacs /.../rnd.lo.com/fs/usr/jmhart/memos/todo.txt
```

Security Services

DFS uses DCE security, with the server using ACLs for file authorization.

DFS naming and location services make it possible for any user on any DCE cell to name any file on any other DCE cell. DFS uses the DCE Security Services (Chapter 5). In particular, DFS servers support file ACLs, which extend the normal UNIX-style file permissions. A DFS server, after authenticating a client file request, can use the client privilege access certificate to determine if the client can perform the requested operation (read, write, delete, etc.) on the file.

Implementation: Novell NetWare

Novell NetWare supports PC networks.

Novell NetWare provides distributed file system services to networks of PCs. It does not matter whether the networked PCs are running DOS, OS/2, or some variant of Windows.

It usually runs on department-sized networks.

Novell NetWare does have some capabilities for handling large numbers of nodes across wide area networks. However, it is far more typical for NetWare to provide a distributed file system on a department-level local area network consisting of a few nodes.

How It Works

File servers are centralized.

Novell NetWare is an example of a centralized distributed file system. Novell NetWare expects your site to dedicate a node with a big disk system to act as a file server. Larger sites may have to dedicate several powerful file servers. Then you build a network of workstations (client nodes) that can access files from the file server.

Novell NetWare provides a 32-bit operating system on the server.

You must install the Novell NetWare operating system on the server machine. The NetWare operating system is a full 32-bit operating system, supporting advanced features such as multitasking and threading. This operating system even comes with its own scripting language for creating sophisticated login scripts. In short, the Novell NetWare operating system is far better equipped than MS-DOS or Microsoft Windows to handle the rigors of distributed file systems. By providing its own operating system, NetWare is not limited by the inherent deficiencies of MS-DOS or Microsoft Windows.

A System Administrator's View

Let us assume that your site has obtained a server machine and a bunch of PC workstations and that you have networked them all. Your next step is to set up Novell NetWare on the server and on the clients.

Server Side Setup

Some familiar start-up files are used.

Your next step is to install the NetWare operating system on the server machine. You should not expect that installing the Novell NetWare operating system is as easy as installing MS-DOS or Windows. In fact, you should expect a certain amount of pain. Novell NetWare has so many more features than MS-DOS or Windows that the installation is necessarily more complicated. Nevertheless, Windows gurus setting up the server will end up working with familiar configuration files such as CONFIG.SYS and AUTOEXEC.BAT. NetWare comes with several programs such as SERVMAN and MONITOR for checking on the status of the server from the server console.

The server maintains a registry.

The system administrator maintains a central registry of eligible users on the server. The registry holds a login name and password for each user. A system administrator can easily create groups; each group is a different subset of registered users. A user may belong to more than one group at a time.

Client Side Setup

Client startup uses the existing startup files.

You must also install software on the client nodes. Installing the client-side software is far less time-consuming than installing the server-side software. In fact, the client-side installation requires the system administrator to answer only a few simple questions. The client-side installation program takes care of updating the client node's startup files (CONFIG.SYS and AUTOEXEC.BAT).

Naming and Location Services

The drive name indicates a virtual file system.

In the MS-DOS and Windows world, all disk drives have simple one-character labels followed by a colon. For example, the label for a floppy disk is typically A: or B:, while the label for a hard disk is usually C: or D:. Novell extends this comfortable naming convention. The Novell NetWare file servers have labels beginning at letter F:. A MS-DOS user can switch to the file server simply by typing F: and switch back to the local hard drive by typing C:. A Windows user simply selects F: or C: in the File Manager. NetWare can automatically figure out where the C: or F: drive is and can also select directories on the network drive.

Note that MS-DOS labels (like C:) symbolize a physical device, but the Novell NetWare labels (such as F:) symbolize a virtual device. For example, a system administrator can map the F: label to the \WINDOWS\SYS directory on a file server named **MAMMOTH**, and map the G: label to the \PROGRAM\DEVELOP direc-tory on **MAMMOTH**. In other words, F: and G: are part of the *same* physical device.

File servers such as **MAMMOTH** advertise their presence with Novell NetWare's Service Advertising Protocol (*SAP*). SAP is the location service of Novell Net-Ware. SAP periodically (normally, every 60 seconds) broadcasts its name, ad-dress, and other related information. This advertising allows the client to locate the server.

Security Services

When users switch directories to a file server, Novell NetWare prompts for a login and password.

Novell NetWare has more sophisticated access controls than NFS.

Novell NetWare provides fine degrees of access control for files and directories on the server. For example, the following is a partial list of the kinds of rights that a user can control on a file:

- Read
- Create
- Write
- Erase
- Modify
- Scan

Novell NetWare also provides users with a fine degree of control in describing which individuals and groups can access files and directories.

Implementation: Macintosh

The Macintosh has a built-in distributed file system.

Support for a distributed file system is built into the Apple Macintosh operating system. In other words, you do not have to buy extra software in order to imple-ment a distributed file system. Just unpack the Macintosh box, plug in a few net-work cables, turn on your Macintosh, point and click the mouse a few times, and *voila*, an instant distributed file system.

Sound easy? Yes, it is easy to set up and reasonably easy to use. For example, to create a user group, you simply drag the appropriate user icons into a group icon. If you get lost while doing the set up, you can refer to the well-designed Hypercard documentation that also comes free on every modern Macintosh.

How It Works

Clients can also be servers.

The Macintosh distributed file system is noncentralized; any node can be a server and any node can be a client. However, in practice, it is more common for a site to designate only one central node as a Macintosh file server.

A System Administrator's View

On a Macintosh file server, a system administrator can specify that the entire disk or just an individual folder is sharable. (A folder is Apple's term for a directory.)

Server Side Set-Up

Administrative tools are also built in.

Setting up a node as a Macintosh file server is easy enough for the average user to attempt. The procedure is mainly a matter of clicking through a few menus in the Control Panels. In order to designate a folder or disk for sharing, you must do the following:

- Specify the folder or disk that the node is willing to share.
- Specify the individual and group that can access the folder or file. A "group" can be a named set of registered users on the network or a single registered user. Anyone who is not specified as an individual or group falls under the catchall category, "Everyone."
- Specify the access permissions for each individual, group, and everyone. The Macintosh system supports the following three permission categories: See Folders, See Files, and Make Changes.

Client Side Set-Up

The Macintosh offers a variety of ways for a client to access a shared directory or file.

*There is no
centralized
registry.*

One way is for users to connect to a server machine by specifying their login names and passwords. (The Macintosh distributed file system does not provide a centralized registry of login names and passwords. Thus, it is possible for passwords on different file servers to get out of synch.) After login, users may access shared regions of the server in exactly the same way as they would access local folders and files.

Users can also connect to a shared disk by creating an ***alias***. An alias is analogous to a link in UNIX. An alias can point to a local file (or folder) or to a remote file or folder object on a Macintosh file server. If the alias points to a remote object, the file sharing software automatically and transparently accesses it.

Heterogeneous Distributed File Systems

*Heterogeneous
systems need to
account for
naming
differences.*

Most large enterprises have all sorts of hardware and operating systems floating around. ("The UNIX workstations sounded like a good deal, so we bought some of them. Then, the Macintoshes and PCs sounded like a good deal, so we bought some of them, too. Now we want them all to talk to each other.")

Distributed file systems on heterogeneous networks run into the following sorts of problems:

- Pathname conventions differ across operating systems. For example, Mac users are accustomed to accessing files through a pleasant point-and-click graphical user interface; Mac users should not be forced to type UNIX-style pathnames.

- Filenaming conventions differ across operating systems. For example, UNIX systems support long, case-sensitive filenames; DOS systems support short, case-insensitive filenames.

- Operating systems represent data differently. For example, Macintosh computers and PCs have different ways to mark the end of data on a line.

These different conventions make it tricky for a distributed file system to provide users with true transparent access to files.

Implementation: PC-NFS

PC-NFS must map UNIX and DOS file systems.

SunSoft provides a version of NFS that allows PCs to access files on UNIX systems. This version of NFS is called, appropriately enough, PC-NFS. PC-NFS provides distributed file system services for a mixed network of PCs and UNIX machines.

PC-NFS servers currently run on UNIX, Open/VMS, Windows NT and many other systems. PCs running MS-DOS or Windows cannot act as servers. The client nodes access files from the server machines. As in all NFS implementations, the client must mount the desired directories or files before accessing them. The appropriate **mount** commands are normally placed inside PC start-up files.

Suppose that a UNIX server contains an exported file named `AccountsReceivableMiami`. Consider the obstacles that PC-NFS must overcome in making this file accessible to a PC client running MS-DOS. First, the file name is too long for MS-DOS, so PC-NFS must scale it down to the 8.3 (maximum of 8 characters, then an optional dot, then a maximum of 3 more characters) filenaming conventions of MS-DOS. Second, the filename must be presented to the MS-DOS user in all uppercase letters. Note that PC-NFS must perform this sleight of hand without actually changing the filename on the server.

A final interesting feature is PC-NFS's ability to convert between the UNIX end-of-line character (linefeed) and the MS-DOS end-of-line (carriage return followed by linefeed) for text files.

Implementation: Novell NetWare

NetWare allows non-PC clients.

Earlier in this chapter, we described a network of PC clients talking to a PC server running Novell NetWare. In fact, with supplementary software, the PC server can handle Macintosh clients, UNIX clients, or VMS clients.

For example, you can install a powerful NetWare PC server and a bunch of Macintosh clients.

You can install a supplementary product called NetWare for Macintosh in order to make the server files accessible to Macintosh computers. With NetWare for Macintosh, objects on the user's Macintosh appear as familiar folder and file icons. In other words, NetWare for Macintosh hides the fact that the server files are actually stored on a PC.

Summary

This chapter described three important distributed file systems (NFS, Novell Net-Ware, and the Macintosh). It also described various ways to provide distributed file system services on heterogeneous networks.

The following table summarizes the features of several distributed file systems.

Feature	NFS V2	Novell NetWare 4	Mac/OS V7.0
Maximum Filename Length	256	8.3	32
Maximum File Capacity	2^{32} Bytes	2^{32} Bytes	2^{32} Bytes
Access Controls	Same as UNIX	Sophisticated	Similar to UNIX
Auditing	None	Full	Some
Locking Granularity	File level	Record level	Record level
GUI for Administration	Yes, on some implementations	Yes	Yes
Ability to access remote peripherals other than hard disk drives	Yes	No	No
Central Registry of Users	Yes (with NIS)	Yes	No

Table 4 Summary of Distributed File System Features

As you read this table, keep in mind that all three systems will no doubt be updated. For example, the listing for NFS shows the parameters for Version 2, the most commonly used version at this writing. However, NFS Version 3 is now available, and this later version offers superior functionality to Version 2, including support for a maximum file capacity of 2^{64} bytes.

CHAPTER 8   Client/Server on the Internet

The Internet is the largest data orchard in the world. Until recently, the harvesting of that orchard has been reserved for the few techies who knew where and how to pick. Today, though, there are plenty of client/server applications on the Internet that dramatically simplify data gathering. These applications are essential because the Internet is no longer dominated by the computer elite. Millions of just plain folks use the Internet every day.

Internet is the world's largest client/server system.

The biggest upside of the Internet for client/server applications is that millions of people world-wide have access to it. Unfortunately, this is also the biggest downside to the Internet. On such a gargantuan network, how can you restrict access to some information and services while permitting public access to other information and services?

This chapter examines client/server implementations on the Internet. We look at how clients and servers find each other, how security works, and how to program Internet applications.

An Internet Overview

The Internet is a loose confederation of many smaller networks spread out across the entire globe.

The Internet is more than just UNIX systems; all you need is TCP/IP.

The Internet was originally dominated by UNIX machines. Now, though, just about every kind of machine is hooked into the Internet. The only real requirement for connection is the TCP/IP communication protocol and utilities. That is, every machine on the Internet must know how to speak TCP/IP. It does not matter if the client is in Kenya on a Macintosh and the server is in Canada on a VAX; as long as the client and server nodes can make a TCP/IP connection, then the client can make requests and the server can provide the services.

Since any two nodes on the Internet can find each other, the Internet provides a phenomenal infrastructure for client/server applications.

Security on the Internet

Many Internet applications offer security mechanisms.

You can use either or both of the following approaches to implement Internet server security:

- You can use the security features that come with some of the more advanced client/server applications such as the World Wide Web.
- You can build a firewall around your local area network.

The first approach gives you very fine degrees of access control. However, the cost of all that control is that you will have to learn how to use the differing security features of each application.

A firewall can secure an entire Internet site.

The latter approach, building a firewall, has recently become very popular. A *firewall* is a combination of hardware, software, and network controllers that controls the way clients from the Internet can access servers on your local area network. Basically, the firewall filters all requests to a certain port that originated outside the firewall. For example, you might set up a firewall that prevents any outside clients from accessing **ftp** servers inside your local area network. The firewall permits clients inside the local area network to access the **ftp** server as shown in Figure 18.

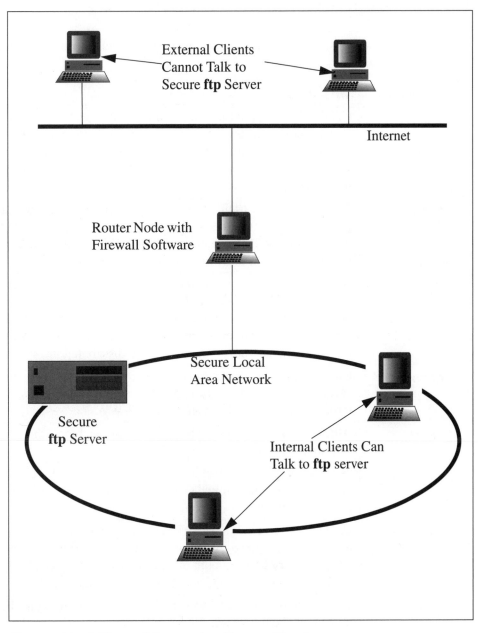

Figure 18 A Firewall Preventing External **ftp** *Access*

Internet Implementation Overview

Table 5 summarizes some of the more popular client/server applications and utilities on the Internet.

Application	What It Does
archie	Client asks server to find a list of all publicly accessible files on a particular topic. (Publicly accessible files are found in ***anonymous ftp*** sites. A user does not need a login account in order to access files from an anonymous ftp site.) Server returns list to client. User can then try to obtain files from the list using **ftp** or WWW.
finger	Client asks server to find information on a particular user at a particular site. Information returned by server can include the date and time that the user last logged in. In addition, a **finger** server can return any specific information that a user wants to convey to other users.
ftp	Allows users to log in remotely to a server machine. Once logged in, users can transfer files between their nodes (the clients) and the server node. (**ftp** does the same kinds of things as **kermit** or **xmodem.**) Implementations of **ftp** run on just about every operating system. In addition, **ftp** is widely used on local area networks that do not have distributed file systems.
gopher	Client displays a simple graphical user interface through which users can access data and services from a server node. **gopher** is a step above **ftp** in terms of ease of use, but a step below WWW.
telnet	Allows users to log in remotely to a server machine. Once logged in, users can run programs on the remote CPU.
veronica	**veronica** is similar to **archie**, except that **veronica** searches through publicly accessible **gopher** sites, whereas **archie** searches through publicly accessible **ftp** sites.
wais	Client asks server to do key word or key phrase search through vast databases maintained by the Wide Area Information Service, or **wais**. If a site has a very large amount of data such as an online encyclopedia or dictionary, **wais** is a good way to serve that data to clients.
WWW	Clients ask servers for all sorts of data, server returns data, client figures out how to invoke the served data. WWW is the current superstar of Internet client/server applications, and we detail it in the next section.

Table 5 Some Popular Client/Server Internet Applications

Implementation: World Wide Web

The *World Wide Web* (*WWW*, or more informally, "The Web") is a global, read-only, noncentralized, distributed information system.

WWW is a multimedia client/server system.

Unfortunately, the preceding description makes the WWW sound like a weak, read-only cousin of NFS. In fact, the WWW might be the most spectacular of all client/server enabling technologies because it can serve all sorts of information including audio, graphics, video, and hypertext. The WWW is so exciting that productivity often drops to near nothing when workers discover a new and interesting WWW server site. As economic and performance barriers drop, the WWW might actually compete as an amusement, dare we say it, with television itself.

WWW did not require a standards body.

Back in Chapter 3, we described august standards bodies, making important-sounding pronouncements, mandating this and that. Often, the only things these standards bodies end up producing are fancy press releases, unread standards documents, and frequent flyer coupons. The invention of the WWW is a refreshing change from all that. Standards bodies had absolutely nothing to do with its invention. Rather, the European research laboratory, CERN, invented the WWW in 1989 simply to solve some of its own information distribution problems. In 1992, CERN shared its invention with the Internet community and WWW use has exploded ever since.

WWW software is free, but you can pay if you want to.

Today, no one owns the WWW. You can still get good quality WWW client-side and server-side software for free. However, commercial client-side software is starting to sprout up, and some of it offers superior quality to the freeware roaming around the network.

The Server Side

Server sites must provide a server program, config files, a home page, and the data to be served.

Any node on the Internet with its own TCP/IP address may act as a WWW server. In fact, any file at a WWW server site can theoretically be served to any WWW client.

Each server site has the following software:

- Each server site must run a *WWW server* program. The most popular WWW server for UNIX systems is a daemon named **httpd** developed by the *National*

Center for Supercomputer Applications (NSCA). You can obtain a free copy of **httpd** on many sites around the Internet.

- Each WWW server program has an associated group of configuration files. These configuration files allow a system administrator to fine-tune the server.

Did We Say "World Wide"?

It is common to use such phrases as "the world-wide Internet." You might be thinking that we should not have such a limited vision. While no one (to our knowledge) is seriously suggesting Internet domains at the University of Mars (`umars.edu.ma`, perhaps), space stations and deep space probes have computer systems with the same communications needs as their Earth-bound counterparts. It should not come as a surprise, then, to learn that there is an international *Consultative Committee for Space Data Systems (CCSDS)*. The CCSDS specifies OSI-like communication standards. These standards are being designed into new systems, such as the Cassini Jupiter probe. At a recent presentation, a slide showed Cassini, orbiting Jupiter, as an "Internet site." In all likelihood, future space stations will be on the Internet.

The problems faced in designing reliable OSI-like protocols reveal how many implicit assumption we make when discussing distributed systems. The CCSDS must overcome new problems, including round-trip communication times that are measured in hours (not fractions of seconds), communication links available only a few hours a day, difficult synchronization issues, and scarce communication bandwidth.

- Each server site must provide a *home page*. A home page is a starting point for clients who want to explore the server site. Most home pages are hypertext documents that point to interesting data and services available at that server site and possibly at other server sites.

- Finally, each server site provides the goodies themselves, that is, the data and services that this server site is providing.

So, what are the goodies? At the bottom rung of the goodies ladder is plain old text. Moving up a rung, server sites can jazz up plain old text and make it into hypertext. With hypertext, each document provides portholes to all sorts of related documents.

Home pages offer pictures, motion, and sound.

Moving beyond words, we find pictures, both moving and still. For example, The Louvre in Paris has a WWW server site that provides digitized images of many famous paintings. For a different sort of cultural experience, the International Jugglers' Association provides a WWW server site that dispenses video sequences of famous jugglers plying their trade. Audio rounds out the multimedia experience. Of course, to play an audio or video file, the client node has to have suitable hardware and software. For example, to play audio files, the client node should have a sound card, speakers, and an audio playback program.

The Client Side

WWW clients are called **browsers**. Browsers abound. In fact, if you do not find one to your liking, you can write your own.

Mosaic is the most popular free browser.

The most popular free browser is named **Mosaic**. This program provides a pleasant graphical user interface for wandering through the wonders of the WWW. **Mosaic** is simple enough that a novice can began net surfing almost immediately, but sophisticated enough for an experienced user to create complex hyperlinks between servers. Several educational and research institutes are currently working on improvements to **Mosaic**. For example, Figure 19 shows **Mosaic** displaying the public home page of a software company named The MathWorks, Inc. Every underlined expression is a hyperlink to some other piece of information. A user can click on any expression or graphic that is underlined. For example, clicking on the term "Welcome to MathWorks" brings up another hypertext document (containing more clickable items). Other clickable items are end points. For example, clicking on certain boxes causes a picture to appear; however, there is nothing on the picture that can be clicked.

Special section: The Pentium Papers

Information about the much–publicized Intel Pentium Floating Point Divide (FDIV) bug is available in the Pentium Papers as compiled by MathWorks Chief Scientist Cleve Moler. Read the original electronic documents that spawned the controversy and judge for yourself.

Welcome to The MathWorks homepage!

You can request information using our simple on–line form; browse through our quarterly newletter, MATLAB News & Notes; get a listing of available MATLAB–Based books and more. Have your frequently asked questions (FAQ) and detailed technical questions about MATLAB answered immediately. Browse our index of user–contributed M/MEX files on ftp.mathworks.com, and get a listing of our available network services (FTP, news, etc.). See a list of tradeshows that The MathWorks will attend in 1995 and look at the MATLAB Conference proceedings from 1993.

Keep watch for information on The MATLAB Conference going on this year...

Figure 19   Mosaic Displaying a Sample Home Page

Some of **Mosaic**'s inventors have gone off and formed their own company called Netscape to make a commercial browser. Some commercial browsers offer superior performance and functionality to the freeware version of **Mosaic**.

Mosaic gets all the data before displaying anything; Lynx is a popular low-end browser .

You need a fairly high-speed network link to get some enjoyment out of **Mosaic**. **Mosaic** does not display its data until the server has finished transferring it. When the server sends graphics, video, or audio, the wait on a slow network can be annoying. Many users do not have the necessary hardware or a fast enough network connection to run **Mosaic**. For these users, the **Lynx** browser program is appropriate. **Lynx** is a text-based browser. The **Lynx** interface is not nearly as sophisticated as the **Mosaic** interface, yet it does insulate users from the brutalities of the Internet. In order to run **Lynx** on a machine, the machine must be able to do VT100 emulation and must be connected to a machine running TCP/IP. Nearly every machine has a VT100 emulator; for instance, VT100 emulation is built into Microsoft Windows 3.1.

How Does It Work?

To understand how the WWW works, you must become familiar with the following three things:

- The WWW naming and location services, which are based on Universal Resource Locators (*URLs*).
- HyperText Markup Language (*HTML*), which is an interpreted language that humans use to describe the data that a WWW server is making available to the outside world.
- HyperText Transfer Protocol (*HTTP*), which is the protocol that WWW servers and clients use to negotiate requests.

We next examine each of these things.

Public and Private WWW Servers

The MathWorks, Inc. uses two WWW servers to distribute information about its line of software products.

One server, the public server, is available to anyone on the Internet. This server provides net surfers with information about the company and its products. Users can take an online tour, complete with demos. Since a lot of the company's products are graphical, the Web provides a much better way to demonstrate what the products do than a simple text-only forum could. Interested customers can even use the public server to contact sales people at the company for more information about products.

The other server, a private server, is accessible only to employees of The MathWorks. This server provides employees with a variety of information about company benefits, holidays, who-is-working-on-what, etc. It also provides a sort of hypertext bulletin board for anyone in the company who wants to communicate an idea to everyone else in the company. Engineers and writers use the private server to distribute specifications detailing upcoming MathWorks products.

The private server is behind a firewall. Even if outsiders know the URL (next section) of the private server, they still cannot access it.

Naming and Location

WWW uses URLs for naming.

The WWW naming and location services are based on *Universal Resource Locators (URLs)*. A URL is like a very sophisticated pathname that uniquely identifies any servable object on any WWW server. URLs come in a few different flavors including absolute URLs and relative URLs, which are analogous to the absolute and relative pathnames found on UNIX or DOS. That is, absolute URLs identify any servable object anywhere on the WWW; relative URLs identify only those servable objects at the current server site.

A URL contains a domain name, a protocol, a port, and a local pathname.

An absolute URL contains the following information:

- The protocol with which the client and server exchange information. This is typically the special Web protocol called **http**, but may also be any other TCP/IP protocol such as **ftp**, **telnet**, **archie**, **veronica**, or **gopher**.
- Optionally, the port on which the server is listening for requests.
- The domain name of the server site.
- The pathname of the file within the server site itself.

For example, consider the URL shown in Figure 20.

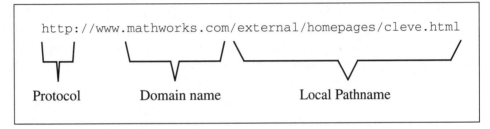

```
http://www.mathworks.com/external/homepages/cleve.html
```

Protocol   Domain name   Local Pathname

Figure 20 A Sample URL

The URL shown in Figure 21 points to a particular hypertext document being offered by the WWW server of The MathWorks, Inc. The DNS domain name of The MathWorks is `mathworks.com`. By convention, the phrase `www.` prefixes the DNS name. Thus, `www.mathworks.com` appears right after the double slash (*//*). Since no port number is specified in the URL, port number 80 is assumed. (By default, **httpd** listens for client requests at port 80.)

The remainder of the URL, `/external/homepages/cleve.html`, is the pathname on the server site itself. Since WWW servers provide a local pathname aliasing mechanism, it is possible that `/external` is actually an alias (or link) to a directory named something other than `/external` on the server site.

URL identifies the protocol between the client and the server.

URLs identify not only a location but a protocol (or service) as well. For example, the sample URL in Figure 21 identifies an **ftp** server running at a site named

`ftp.uu.net`; on this server, the URL identifies a local pathname of `/pub/`
`shells`:

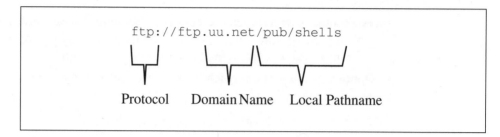

Figure 21 Another Sample URL

You may be wondering what the difference is between accessing an **ftp** site
through a WWW browser and accessing the same site through the **ftp** utility itself.
One difference is that the WWW provides authentication services. Thus, a WWW
browser takes care of identifying you to the server, so there is no need for you to
type a login name (such as `anonymous`) and a password. Another difference is
that the URL identifies a particular local directory, whereas old-fashioned **ftp**
forces you to log in to the server site and then navigate to the local directory.

HTML

HTML specifies how the client browser should interpret the data.

All home pages are written in a special Web language called ***HTML***. You also use
HTML to create other hypertext documents that the home page might ultimately
point to. It is not uncommon for one server site to provide hundreds of HTML
files. You could describe HTML as a programming language or you could describe it as a markup language such as SGML or troff. For example, the following
is a simple HTML file:

```
<HEAD>
<TITLE>Home Page for Barry Rosenberg</TITLE>
</HEAD>

<BODY>
<H1>Barry Rosenberg's Home Page</H1>
<P>
Professionally, I'm very interested in client/server applications
and in ksh.
</P>
<P>
But the WWW is too much fun to waste on professional stuff.
</P>

<H2>Tropical Weather</H2>
<UL>
<LI>Visible and Infrared images of
<A HREF="ftp://wx.research.att.com/wx/"> North America</A>
</LI>
<LI><AREF="gopher://metlab1.met.fsu.edu/11/images/vis/tropical">
Caribbean Sea</A> and vicinity.
</LI>
<LI>High-resolution images of
<A HREF="gopher://metlab1.met.fsu.edu/11/images/vis/florida">
Florida</A> (excellent detail here)
</UL>

<H2>Fun and Games</H2>
<UL>
<IMG SRC="./juggling2.gif">
<LI>Here is some nifty stuff about
<A HREF="http://www.hal.com/services/juggle/"> Juggling </A>
including some movies.
</UL>
</BODY>
```

Figure 22 shows the home page generated by this HTML file.

Barry Rosenberg's Home Page

Professionally, I'm very interested in client/server applications and in ksh.

But the WWW is too much fun to waste on professional stuff.

Tropical Weather

- Visible and Infrared images of <u>North America</u>
- <u>Caribbean Sea</u> and vicinity.
- High-resolution images of <u>Florida</u> (excellent detail here)

Fun and Games

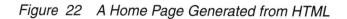

- Here is some nifty stuff about <u>Juggling</u> including some movies.

Figure 22   A Home Page Generated from HTML

A complete description of the HTML language is beyond the scope of this book. However, we can point out a few things that will help you get started:

- All HTML directives are encased inside a pair of angle brackets (< and >).

- All HTML directives have both a start component and a stop component. (The stop component contains a slash /.) These form syntactic bookends for the directive. For example, the directive that starts the title is `<Title>`, and the directive that ends the title is `</Title>`.

- HTML directives are hierarchical. For example, the phrase "Barry Rosenberg's Home Page" is a first-level head, marked as `<H1>`. The phrase "Tropical Weather" is a second-level head, marked as `<H2>`. You can also specify deeper head levels (`<H3>`, `<H4>`, and so on) as required.

- The <A> directive denotes a hyperlink.
- HTML files typically contain a liberal sprinkling of URLs. Our example featured quite a few absolute URLs and one relative URL.

HTML files do not contain font directives. In fact, HTML expects the client to map HTML directives to whatever font the client wants to use for a particular directive. For example, if an HTML file specifies <H3>, some browsers might display an <H3> as 12-point boldface, while others might display that same head as 14-point italic.

HTTP

The client and server use HTTP to communicate.

The server and the client negotiate through a special Web protocol named the ***Hypertext Transfer Protocol (HTTP)***. This protocol provides a mutually agreed upon way for a WWW client to request certain objects and for a WWW server to grant them to the client. This protocol also governs the object content that will be served.

A typical conversation between a WWW client and server proceeds as follows:

1. Client displays the home page of some server site.
2. User selects one of the highlighted passages in the home page, such as North America in Figure 22.
3. The client examines the HTML file to determine what URL the user has selected.
4. The client connects to the server specified in the URL. The client passes several pieces of information about itself; for example, the identity of the requester.
5. The server tries to find the local pathname identified by the URL. If this local pathname exists and if the client has permission to access it, the server sends the file to the client.
6. The client receives the file and tries to display it.

A server can provide many different sorts of object files (audio, graphics, video, hypertext). The server figures out what kind of data is in a particular file based on the suffix of the filename. For example, if a file has the suffix .gif then it is a graphics file in the GIF format. The server maintains a database that maps file suffix to object content type. All object content types in HTTP must be expressed in ***Multipurpose Internet Mail Extension (MIME)*** format.

The server puts the file type before the data so the client can interpret the data.

When a server sends a file to a client, HTTP forces the server to write a little preface to the file that indicates the file's MIME type. For example, if the server is sending the client a GIF file, the server places a little note at the front of the file indicating that it is indeed a graphics file in GIF format. The client browser reads the note and then decides how to display it.

When a browser receives a file from a server, the browser can either display the file itself inside its own browser window or ask another program to display the file. For example, suppose a server sends a video in *QuickTime* format. If the client does not know how to display QuickTime videos, the client invokes a QuickTime viewing program that does. The browser program refers to a configuration file that maps received MIME types to external viewer programs.

Clients can be extended to interpret new data types.

Since browsers do not have to be smart enough to display every conceivable MIME type, a browser can be both lightweight and extensible. For example, suppose Web servers should one day start providing hologram files. In this case, an existing browser would not have to be rewritten to accommodate holograms. Rather, the client would merely need to invoke a hologram reader program.

Reliability

WANs have a higher failure rates than LANs.

In a lot of the client/server implementations discussed in this book, the client and server are on the same LAN. The connection over a LAN is relatively reliable. By contrast, clients and servers on the Internet do not typically have the same level of reliability. Clients and servers on the Internet are often separated by great physical distances and great numbers of network hops. In other words, the routing between client and server often passes through several network hubs. Thus, as anyone who has played around with the WWW can confirm, there is a higher probability of connection failure on the WWW than on most LAN-based client/server applications.

WWW uses a connection-oriented protocol and must restart failed connections.

When the user requests a particular URL, the client makes a connection request to the server site specified in the URL. If the connection cannot be made, the client will continue trying until it either connects with the server or until it times out. If the connection request can be made, the client and server remain connected until the server finishes fulfilling the request.

If, for some reason, the connection collapses before the server finishes transferring the data, the user must redo the request. In other words, if the connection collapses in the middle, the server is not smart enough (not "stateful" enough) to retransmit only the remainder of the message. This can be frustrating if your network connection fails 95% of the way through a large file transfer. WWW uses a "stateless" protocol; see Chapters 11 and 12 for details on stateless protocols.

Security

Security is decent on the WWW right now and will likely get a lot stronger in the future. We now examine current security measures.

WWW servers log clients.

Most WWW servers automatically keep logs of everyone accessing the server. (The log file is likely to be named `access_log`.) So, in theory, if someone did hack illegally onto a WWW server, the perpetrator would leave his or her electronic fingerprint. However, even though the perpetrator's name is in the log file, it still might be difficult or impossible to figure out who did something illegal. Furthermore, clever hackers can disguise their identity or edit the log file.

Current Security

By default, WWW servers are accessible to anyone on the Internet. Indeed, many WWW servers should be publicly accessible. Obviously though, access to some servers containing private or sensitive information should be restricted.

WWW servers provide two authorization mechanisms for controlling access:

* Through configuration files.
* Through a login registry.

The ACF is a from of ACL.

The configuration file that controls security at a given site is called an ***Access Control File*** (***ACF***). The ACF is usually located at filename `access.conf`. Unfortunately, the information you provide to an ACF, which is similar to an ACL, requires a rather bizarre syntax. You can use the ACF to deny or admit clients based on their site. For example, you might say that clients from Sun are allowed to use a server site but that clients from Silicon Graphics are not. A typical use for an ACF is to keep a server site private to only those clients from the same site as the server. The following sample ACF shows a slightly more interesting case in which a server site denies requests from everyone except those clients originating from the Open Software Foundation (`osf.org`), the X Consortium (`x.org`) and the Object Management Group (`omg.org`):

```
<Directory /extern/www/consortium>
   <Limit Get>
      order deny, allow
      deny from all
      allow from osf.org x.org omg.org
   </Limit>
</Directory>
```

You can protect individual directories. There is a registry for users and groups.

In addition to controlling access to the site as a whole, you can also control access to specific directories at the site. That is, you can put an ACF in every directory to control access for that directory. On UNIX, directory ACFs are typically located at filename `.htaccess`.

A system administrator can lump a bunch of WWW users into a named group for additional authorization. An ACF can also control services based on the group a user is in. For example, the `professor` group might be allowed access to grades information, but anyone in the `student` group would be denied.

As mentioned earlier, WWW server sites can also control access through a special WWW login registry. The WWW login registry has a similar design to the login registries found on UNIX systems. A system administrator typically uses a utility called **htpasswd** to create the special Web login accounts. Then, when a client attempts to access a WWW server site, the WWW server demands that the user enter a login name and password. ACFs control what the server can serve to that user.

WWW users do not want to be delayed by typing login information, so WWW login accounts are rarely used. Some purists say that if you're going to start requiring net surfers to login into WWW servers, you might as well go back to **ftp** servers.

Future Security

The have-your-cake-and-eat-it-too security scenario is for WWW servers to provide very concise control over who can be served but to implement security without requiring that users actually log in. At the time of this writing, various groups are working on implementing this scenario.

A specification called *Secure HTTP* should one day supplement HTTP by providing extra encryption and authentication information.

Costs/Benefits for Programmers

We refer to anyone who authors WWW server data as a WWW "programmer," although it is just as likely that the "programmer" is actually a writer, an artist, or a system administrator. WWW programmers are often referred to as ***authors***.

There are several ways to generate HTML code.

As we mentioned earlier, WWW servers are written in the HTML language. As a programmer, you can enter an HTML program in one of the following two ways:

- You can type HTML codes directly into a text file with some sort of old-fashioned ASCII text editor (such as **vi** or **TeachText**).
- You can write text in some publishing program (such as **FrameMaker**) and then run a filter that converts your word processor files to HTML code. In fact, some word processing tools are springing up that specialize in producing HTML code.

HTML is an interpreted (as opposed to compiled) language. It is remarkably forgiving, but paradoxically, it is also rather tricky to perfect.

Good WWW server sites are hard to create.

Beyond learning the syntax of HTML, writing Web servers requires skills that are fairly rare. For instance, most technical people are comfortable presenting information hierarchically. However, good Web authors must design circularly. That is, good Web servers provide useful hyperlinks that allow users to navigate in any direction through the server and to easily find their way back to useful information.

The ideal WWW author must master several different media. The required combination of skills is hard to come by. For instance, the writer who is good with words is not necessarily good with pictures.

Costs/Benefits for Users

*Users do not need to know **ftp** and other protocols.*

The browser programs hide a lot of the complexity that used to make net surfing so hazardous. No longer does the average Internet user have to master the vagaries of **ftp** in order to grab an enticing graphics file. The only downside for users is that is very easy to waste a day chasing interesting hyperlinks.

Costs/Benefits for System Administrators

*Home pages
need
maintenance.*

Large server sites often designate one system administrator to be the so-called **Webmaster**, in charge of administering the WWW server and servable data. Getting a WWW server going is generally not too consuming; most sites can become a WWW server site in half a day. The Webmaster is responsible not only for ensuring that the WWW server is up and running, but also for ensuring that the home page is maintained.

Costs/Benefits for Vendors

Enterprises are beginning to make money from the WWW. These money-making enterprises fall into the following categories:

- Using the WWW to advertise products.
- Using the WWW to sell information.

It is relatively easy for vendors to set up a shopping mall WWW server. However, successful online purchases are still very tricky because HTTP currently does not provide many security features. For example, suppose a guy named Norm uses Mosaic to browse an online shopping mall server. If Norm decides that he really needs to buy 12 cubic zirconium rings, he can fill out a form provided by the server. The form would probably ask Norm to provide his credit card number. In an ideal world, Norm would enter his credit card number, a server would run a credit card check, and 12 cubic zirconium rings would show up at Norm's house the next day.

*WWW has
great
commercial
appeal, but
security needs
work.*

Now, we know what you're thinking. The previous transaction sounded as if it had just as many security holes as any purchase made over a telephone from Norm to a human operator. For example, there is little to prevent Norm from entering a stolen credit card number. Yes, the security holes are theoretically identical, but in real life, there is something about a computer that makes otherwise honest people throw their scruples on the trash heap. Perhaps it is the relative anonymity of computers (no human operator to hear you lying) or perhaps it is the challenge of the hack. Whatever the reason, online shopping through the WWW has to be significantly more secure than traditional catalog shopping. (See the "Security" section earlier in this chapter for more information.) However, the promise of Internet commerce is so inviting that there will certainly be products and services to address these authentication problems.

Summary

By the early 21st century, people without an Internet jack in their house will feel as isolated as 20th century people who do not have a telephone jack in their house. The Internet, or its successor, will change the mail system, the telephone system, the entertainment system, and the way companies do business. Client/server computing will be at the heart of most Internet commercial applications.

CHAPTER 9   Distributed DBMS

Distributed database systems can integrate the desktop and the data center.

Client/server computing for many people is nothing more or less than distributed database management. The connection is so tight that there is even a trade show called *Database & Client/Server World*. It is easy to see why database management systems (DBMSs) are so important in distributed computing. Inexpensive personal computers and high-speed networking now allow integration of the best aspects of personal computing and centralized computing.

This chapter describes the role of DBMSs in distributed computing. It also shows how the client/server architecture enhances and extends the usefulness of DBMSs. We pay particular attention to the role that personal computers play as clients. We also focus on the most important distributed DBMS standards (SQL and ODBC), and briefly describe alternatives to the standards.

What Is a Database Management System?

The purpose of a DBMS is to store, maintain, and provide access to information. A DBMS has many characteristics of a file system. However, a DBMS is different in that it uses higher level access methods, provides for data consistency and other important properties, and may be layered on a file system.

Database access is at a higher level than file access, but the advantages of distribution are the same.

The differing levels of access are the biggest difference from a user's perspective. In a file system, data access is by a physical record number or key value. For instance, a programmer would read the twentieth record or read the personnel record of employee number 03214. By comparison, database access is by record properties or contents, and the number of records returned may not be known ahead of time. Thus, if you make a database request for the records of customers who are book authors and also have phone numbers starting with the six digits 617-237, you may get zero, one, ten, or more records in response. A DBMS also maintains consistency, ensuring, perhaps, that there is only one employee with number 03214 and that all references to that employee number refer to the same person.

Distributed databases have the same advantages as distributed file systems. These advantages include centralized management, security, data integrity, shared data, minimal redundancy, and minimal inconsistency. In fact, the same cost/benefits for system administrators, users, programmers, managers, and architects cited in Chapter 6 for distributed file systems also apply to distributed DBMSs.

What is distributed in a distributed DBMS? Primarily, we mean that the actual data storage and database queries are performed by servers, and the clients make the requests and process and present the responses. Additional distribution is possible but not as central to this discussion. For example, the server could access a remote file system.

DBMSs and the Client/Server Model

Distributed DBMSs fit the client/server model perfectly for two reasons:

- Most large databases need to be accessed by multiple users.
- Information returned by databases often needs to be integrated into other applications.

Personal computers need to integrate database information into desktop applications.

A large database is typically shared by many users. It does not make sense for each user to have a personal copy of a large database, but it does makes sense to keep one copy of a large database under central control. By itself, this is not a sufficient reason to create a client/server DBMS. After all, users on dumb terminals can share a central DBMS. Nevertheless, PCs and Macs make for much better platforms for DBMS clients than do dumb terminals. PCs and Macs support numerous low-cost "personal productivity applications" with spreadsheets and document processors being the simplest examples. These applications work with DBMSs in ways such as the following:

- Data obtained from a DBMS query can be placed into a spreadsheet and integrated with other data. For instance, parts prices could be obtained from the DBMS and integrated into a product costing plan.

- A departmental budget, produced in a spreadsheet, could be entered into a database and integrated there with all other departmental budgets.

- A user-developed PC application could query a database to obtain information on all delinquent accounts. The returned information could be integrated into form letters requesting payment.

Distributed DBMSs have all the client/ server requirements. RPCs are a good implementation mechanism.

Distributed DBMSs require all the client/server features (performance, scalability, reliability, security, naming and location, replication, time, and a single system view) provided by a good distributed client/server framework. For example, database queries are synchronous operations. That is, the client makes a query and waits for the server to respond. RPCs are the easiest way to make distributed synchronous queries. Therefore, it makes sense to build a distributed database on top of a distributed framework that provides RPCs. In many cases, the server response may come before the request, such as a record update or deletion, is actually complete. The response simply means that the server has received the request and has queued it for processing.

Many systems bypass RPCs.

Despite the advantages of distributed client/server frameworks, not all distributed DBMSs are built on top of them. Figure 23shows required and optional layers underneath a distributed DBMS server. For example, instead of using a client/server RPC framework for client communication, some distributed DBMS servers implement a request-response protocol directly over the network transport layer.

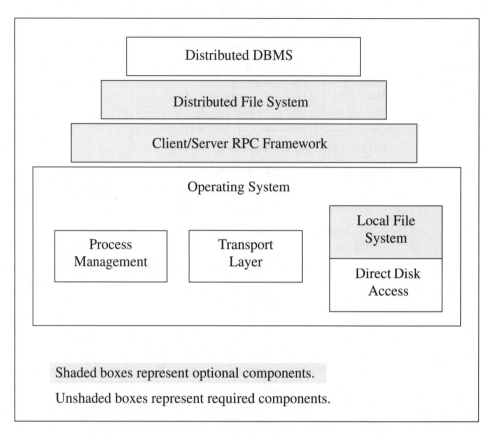

Figure 23   A Distributed DBMS Server Can Be Built on Top of Different
Components

Servers use the local file system or access the disk directly.

As shown in Figure 23, a distributed DBMS server can access data for a remote client in several different ways. For example, some servers access data through the file system. Other DBMS servers gain a performance advantage by accessing data directly from the raw disk at the block level.

Servers can also access remote files.

Some distributed computing frameworks themselves can even act as distributed DBMS with limited capability. For example, NIS is essentially a database built on top of ONC, Sun's distributed client/server RPC framework.

Figure 24 shows partitioning in a typical client/server distributed DBMS. The client software provides a pleasant user interface for accessing the database. In addition, the client software integrates data from the database with a spreadsheet

application. The role of the database server is to maintain the database and process client queries and updates.

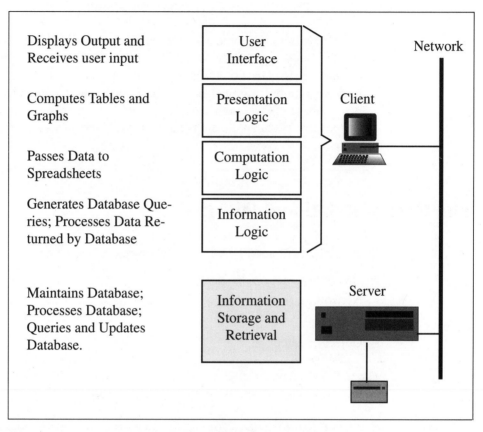

Figure 24   A Typical Client/Server DBMS Architecture

Servers can be
replicated.   At a typical site, client software runs on many different computers, typically PCs
or Apple Macintoshes. The server must be able to process multiple concurrent client requests, and it must do so securely and reliably. To improve performance and
increase reliability, some sites provide multiple database servers.

> ### Turnkey Solutions
>
> Many users are content with **turnkey** distributed DBMS solutions. That is, they purchase all of the client software and use the database as an extension of their normal applications. For example, users might buy a spreadsheet that is already integrated with a certain database. Other users will go beyond these turnkey solutions and develop client applications that make direct database queries.

The Role of Relational DBMSs

There are four common DBMS architectures:

- Hierarchical
- Network
- Relational
- Object-oriented

The first three have been used for decades and are heavily standardized. The last category, object-oriented, is not yet as mature as the others.

Relational databases are the most popular. **Relational DBMSs (RDBMSs)** are far and away the most popular architecture for client/server systems. Because of their popularity, we will concentrate on them. Hierarchical and network DBMSs are still in use, particularly in mainframe environments. This dominant position took a long time to come about; RDBMS sales did not exceed sales of other types of DBMSs until 1992, more than 20 years after development of the basic theory.

RDBMSs have many well-established advantages over hierarchical and network database architectures. Many readers are already familiar with RDBMSs, and a RDBMS tutorial is not appropriate. Nonetheless, we now introduce a small sample relational database, which will be useful for discussing distributed RDBMSs in the rest of the chapter.

RDBMS Example: Manufacturing Database

This is a sample RDBMS schema to be used for examples.

A relational database *schema* for a small manufacturing operation consists of the following relations, where we name the relation (in uppercase) and its fixed-size fields (inside the parentheses):

```
PARTS (PartNum, PartName)
PRODUCTS (ProdNum, ProdName)
BILL-OF-MATERIALS (ProdNum, PartNum, Quantity)
VENDOR (VendNum, VendName, VendAddress)
SUPPLIER (PartNum, VendNum, Price, VendPN)
```

This is only the schema for the relational database; there is no actual data. Several organizations could use the same schema, but with different data. Schema definition languages also describe the field data types, but we omit those here.

A specific database fills in the relations with data "tuples" or rows. For instance, the BILL-OF-MATERIALS relation will show all of the parts that are required to make a particular product (or, we could regard it as showing all of the products requiring a specific part). The SUPPLIER relation will tell us who supplies what parts and at what cost. It also maps our company's part number to the vendor's part number.

The client and server both know the schema.

Both the client and the server need to be aware of the database schema. The client will create database queries and updates and will display results. The server must be able to store and retrieve data to respond to client requests, so it also needs to know how the database is arranged. This shared knowledge of data structuring is common in many client/server systems, and we will see it again, but in different forms, in our discussions of RPCs, distributed objects, and system management.

Beyond Relational Databases

Database clients are becoming increasingly more powerful and are placing greater demands on the server and on the way in which data is represented. The demand for multimedia sound and images is but one example. RDBMSs and emerging *object-oriented DBMSs (OO-DBMSs)* are addressing this demand and are changing the way in which clients and servers model and interpret data.

Most commercial RDBMSs extend the pure relational model somewhat to satisfy these additional requirements. The fixed-size fields are an immediate limitation if you need to include text strings and become an even bigger problem if you want to include hypertext and graphics images, such as copies of credit card transactions. This need is addressed by providing for *BLOBs* (Binary Large Objects). Normally, the BLOBs are not processed by the RDBMS; you cannot, for instance, search for all records with specified contents in a BLOB field.

OO-DBMSs extend the benefits of object-oriented programming to DBMSs, and they can directly store and retrieve BLOB-like objects and objects with complex structures.

OO-DBMSs are unlikely to replace RDBMSs quickly. After all, companies have already invested buckets of money in RDBMSs. Change is slow; consider that it took nearly 20 years for companies to migrate from hierarchical and network DBMSs to RDBMSs. The more likely outcome is that OO features will work their way into RDBMSs.

SQL

SQL is the standard access language.

The Structured Query Language (SQL) is the standard language for accessing RDBMSs. IBM developed SQL in the mid-1970s. *SQL* refers to the language that users enter to access a database; *Embedded SQL* refers to the language that programmers use to access a database from a program. Therefore, Embedded SQL is the API for a RDBMS. In a client/server application, the client uses Embedded SQL to invoke functions that call the server.

SQL Is Both Standard and Proprietary

SQL is a standard supported by ANSI, X/Open, and the SQL Access Group (SAG). However, most implementations do not follow the standard exactly; in other words, there are many proprietary variations of SQL.

Some of the enhancements in proprietary versions of SQL are very valuable. For example, some proprietary versions provide procedural language extensions. These extensions allow SQL statements to be included in loops, conditional statements, and procedures. Furthermore, error status codes and result message formatting are not standardized. Nor are there standards (yet) for stored procedures (series of SQL statements) or events (called *triggers*).

One of the main reasons that Microsoft's Open Database Connectivity (ODBC) has been so successful is that it provides a common interface that hides the proprietary differences.

The next sections provide some examples of simple SQL commands using our sample manufacturing database introduced earlier.

SQL commands generally return relations, and the lengths are not known ahead of time. Notice how easily these results would fit into a client spreadsheet or other document.

Simple Qualified Retrieval

The following SQL command finds the vendor number and price for all vendors who supply part number 40235:

```
SELECT VendNum, Price
    FROM SUPPLIER
    WHERE PartNum = 40235
```

Retrieval from More Than One Table

For each part with a price less than $15, get the name and address of each supplier, along with the part number and price.

```
SELECT PartNum, Price, VendName, VendAddress
    FROM SUPPLIER, VENDOR
    WHERE SUPPLIER.VendNum = VENDOR.VendNum
        AND Price < 15
```

Update

The following example increases the cost of all products from Los Angeles by 20%:

```
UPDATE SUPPLIER SET Price = 1.2 * Price
    WHERE VendAddress = 'Los Angeles'
```

Database Views and Security

Database security usually consists of controlling access at the level of individual relations. In this way, users have different database views. For example, a buyer might have both read and write access to the VENDOR and SUPPLIER relations, but only have read access to the BILL-OF-MATERIALS. A product manager, however, might have both read and write access to BILL-OF-MATERIALS.

SQL in Client/Server Protocols

We previously mentioned how database operations (queries, updates, insertions, deletions) are naturally request-response operations. That is, a user or client issues an operation and waits for a server response. The response indicates that an operation is being processed or, as in the case of a query, is complete. When an RDBMS is distributed, the client can send a SQL statement to the server and, again, wait for the response. The client must also process the result and handle faults. There are two natural programming models for this:

Clients can use IPCs or RPCs to talk to a remote DBMS server.

- Distributed interprocess communication. The SQL statement, as a text string, is sent using a network transport (typically, a socket interface to TCP/IP), and the response is received the same way. The client and server can either establish a connection or use datagrams. In any case, the distributed IPC is used in a request-response mode.

- RPCs. The SQL statement text is used a parameter to an RPC. The resulting relation is returned. RPCs represent a straightforward mechanism for implementing a reliable request-response protocol.

DBMS Server Hardware and Software

Database servers run on a wide range of systems, including PCs.

Historically, DBMSs ran on mainframes or minicomputer systems. Big computer systems were required to meet the speed and capacity requirements of large DBMSs. Furthermore, big computers were the only ones that had enough disk capacity for large DBMSs. Today, however, a Windows NT or UNIX workstation or even a fast PC is powerful enough to be an RDBMS server in small organizations, though they would not be powerful enough to handle a large life insurance company with a 10-terabyte database.

The major DBMS server software vendors in the UNIX market include Oracle, Sybase, Informix, and Ingres. These vendors, and many others, are also making their servers available on non-UNIX operating systems, such as IBM OS/2 and Microsoft Windows NT. IBM and Computer Associates International, Inc. are major mainframe DBMS suppliers. The Pick system, while not purely relational, is widely used, particularly on mission-critical, fail-safe systems.

Servers will exploit advances in system performance and scale.

The market for DBMS servers will continue to be significant. To support performance demands, vendors will exploit operating system and hardware for symmetric multiprocessing (SMP), multithreading of servers, and larger file systems (with 64-bit file addresses for very large file lengths).

We still expect some degree of centralized control over the database. A corporate department, such as Management Information Services (MIS), is expected to coordinate with individual departments, which, increasingly, are managing their own databases. These tasks include the following:

Distribution of management tasks.

- Manage the corporate database.
- Determine the access rights (views) available to different classes of user, including views to departmental databases.
- Define the RDBMS schema.
- Take care of important day-to-day administrative details.

Database Facelifting

Many database users are still stuck in the seventies. Oppressed users access old-fashioned databases from old-fashioned dumb terminals instead of through modern PCs and X terminals. The dumb terminals cannot display pleasing GUIs. Users interact with these systems through the keyboard rather than with a mouse.

Many of these old-fashioned systems are now undergoing database *facelifts*. That is, these old-fashioned systems are now taking the first step into the client/server world.

The first step in facelifting is to replace the dumb terminals with smart client PCs, Macintoshes, or workstations with an advanced *Graphical User Interface (GUI)*.

Facelifting updates tired applications with shiny new GUIs.

The next step is to build client software to interact with the DBMS and to take advantage of the processing power and advanced GUI of the new client system. The client assists the user in creating queries, shields the user from SQL details, and displays the data, creates reports, and helps to integrate the data into other client applications.

For example, the client PC in Figure 25 displays a form for the user to fill out. After the user fills out the form, the client examines the choices that the user has made in order to compose a SQL query for the DBMS. Thus, the clever GUI insulates the user from the vagaries of SQL. Finally, the client sends the request to the server as if the request had come from a dumb terminal.

The server side of the application is essentially the old DBMS application. The server side takes SQL queries as input just as it did before the application was facelifted. In addition, the server side does the DBMS operation and returns results just as it did before the facelift.

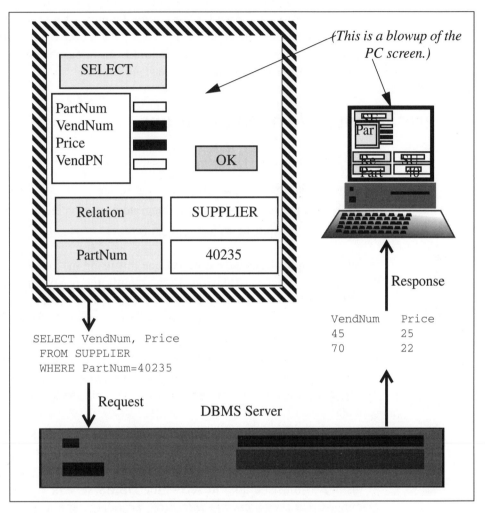

Figure 25 GUI Facelift to a PC-Based Terminal Emulation

Facelifting is simple but is not complete integration. This sort of facelifting is widely and productively practiced. It has the advantage of being simple; recoding is relatively straight forward. Facelifting generally does not require RPCs; rather it is often done with IPCs. Therefore, a complete client/ server framework such as DCE is not required in order to facelift. However, the application programmer writing the client side must be aware of the database schema.

Notice that the client and server are still not fully integrated. In particular, client applications must still consider the unique features of a particular DBMS. Furthermore, the client programmer does not have a convenient API. This lack of openness discourages application vendors from integrating the database access into their PC applications (such as spreadsheets).

Integration into Client Applications

Client applications need to do the following processing:

- Generate database queries to pass to the server.
- Grab what the server returns and integrate it into the client application.
- Create reports specific to the application.

How can client applications build in transparent, vendor-independent database access?

Mainframe applications have always done this using mechanisms such as Embedded SQL, which act as extensions to the mainframe programming languages and systems. Clients need an equivalent to embedded SQL that is compatible with PCs and can use a client/server framework. The requirements for such a solution include the following:

- The client must be shielded from the differences between servers from different vendors. This is called *vendor independence*. Yet, the client must still be able to access a wide variety of servers, possibly including non-relational systems.
- The database server could be on a local or remote network, or it could even be on the client machine. This is called *location independence*.
- PC applications (for instance, spreadsheets such as Excel, QuattroPro, or Lotus 1-2-3) must be able to access the DBMS servers without user programming. *Open programming interfaces* encourage application vendors to build in the database integration.
- Users must be able to access, combine, and integrate data from multiple databases simultaneously.

The Role of ODBC

In order to integrate DBMS servers into PC client applications, it is necessary to have a standard interface between the applications and the servers, and this interface must meet the requirements of the previous section. Microsoft's Open Database Connectivity (***ODBC***) specification has quickly filled this niche. ODBC is based on standard SQL. ODBC defines:

- The methods for data type representation; this is necessary for interoperability.
- Connection and login management; this is necessary for authentication.
- Error processing.

ODBC allows client integration. DBMS vendors provide drivers. But, you need a separate driver for each server type.

ODBC requires a ***client driver*** for every database server type. The client driver is the interface between the ODBC API and the actual database server. Normally, the database vendor supplies the drivers. The driver must account for the server characteristics. It is even possible to have drivers for non-relational database servers by converting the API commands into the server's query language. Vendor-supplied client drivers for Sybase, Ingres, Oracle, and so on, allow ODBC to achieve vendor independence. The server itself does not change; the driver accommodates the server. A client driver must manage details such as:

- The differences in each server's SQL implementation.
- The format which the server requires for its requests and the format of the responses. The request and responses are typically encapsulated in TCP or UDP packets.
- ODBC is independent of the actual communications protocol; the drivers need to support the server's protocol.
- Differences in the way that different servers encode data. For example, ODBC manages data alignment, packing, byte ordering, and such.
- Naming and location, through a mapping from data source name to driver.
- Connection management between the client and server.

As with any other standardized software layer between an application and a service, ODBC requires a trade-off between the advantages of standardization and the potential advantages of custom interfaces. These trade-offs can involve performance, resource use, and the amount of access to specialized features of a specific service. Each user must balance these trade-offs based on specific needs. Figure 26 shows the advantages of standardization. Performance becomes less of an issue as PC and other client systems evolve.

Spreadsheet integration as an ODBC example.

Many PC applications are now integrated with ODBC. Figure 26 shows the architecture, with Microsoft Excel and BrandZ SS as representative spreadsheet applications. In the figure, any number of clients can connect to multiple servers. One PC has two client applications (one of which is custom), and there are several

server types. Figure 26 shows servers from three different vendors; one server
contains the sample manufacturing database, while the other two contain accounting and human resource databases. This separation of databases onto distinct machines is not always necessary. An individual database can be a confederation of
databases on separate machines, or, conversely, several databases can be on the
same system.

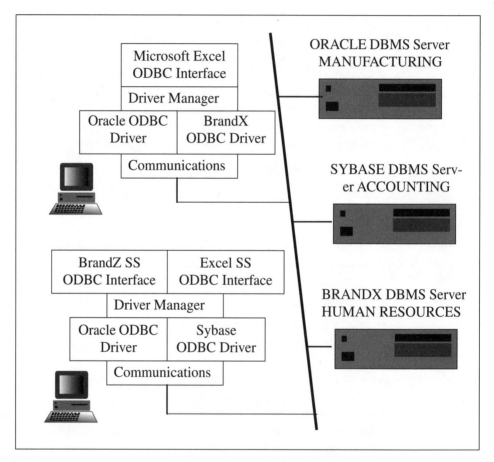

Figure 26   Clients and Servers in an ODBC Environment

An Excel Example

As we have already mentioned, Microsoft Excel is a example of a spreadsheet integrated with ODBC. We can now summarize how an Excel user would access a

database and integrate the result. It is not necessary to be an Excel user to follow the short narration, and nearly any other spreadsheet could operate in a similar manner.

The client application uses ODBC to access the database.

Suppose that you want Excel to list the supplier name and address and the part number and price for each part with a price less than $15. The steps are roughly as follows:

1. From the **Data** menu, select **Get External Data.**

2. Select the data source named *MANUFACTURING*.

3. Add the "tables" (relations) that you are selecting from. The two tables for this example are *SUPPLIER* and *VENDOR*.

4. Select the fields in the order they should appear, adding tables as needed. The fields for this query are *PartNum*, *Price*, *VendName*, and *VendAddress*. Excel constructs a display of the tables and fields to aid this process. This completes the query construction.

5. Excel now sends the following string to the driver:

```
SELECT PartNum, Price, VendName, VendAddress
    FROM SUPPLIER, VENDOR
    WHERE SUPPLIER.PartNum = VENDOR.VendNum
        AND Price < 15
```

The server does not even have to be aware that the query came from a PC spreadsheet.

6. From the **File** menu, select **Return Data to Microsoft Excel**.

7. You make choices for the destination cells, inclusion of field names, and retaining the query for future use.

8. The query response then appears in the selected cells, essentially as we showed it before. From there, you can do anything you want with it. Typically, you could use the parts prices to compute product costs and then include the result in some other report.

As you might expect, Excel provides ways to combine some of these steps into a macro, assign the macro to a menu button, or specify automatic execution.

Data composed within the spreadsheet can also be used to update the database.

ODBC Summary

ODBC provides a strong and successful client-based framework for DBMSs, but it does not form a complete distributed client/server framework by itself. ODBC is integrated with numerous desktop applications. PowerBuilder and Visual Basic are two of the many available application development environments. The drivers are flexible and can incorporate the services of any client/server framework. For example, it is feasible to consider ODBC drivers built on DCE that take advantage or DCE's rich location, security, and reliability features.

Distributed RDBMSs, ODBC, and the Framework Requirements

How well, and in what manner, do RDBMS servers and ODBC clients meet the Chapter 2 requirements for a distributed computing framework? First, of course, such a configuration is not a general-purpose framework, but is designed for database applications only.

For most requirements, the answer is, "it depends." Certainly, the ODBC/RDMS architecture shown in Figure 26 is very powerful and useful. Nonetheless, there are a number of open issues. Some issues simply stem from the fact that a lot of data has to move over the network.

ODBC uses the services of an underlying framework for naming and security. ODBC and SQL do not specify the communication framework; they only specify an application protocol. Therefore, ODBC/SQL inherit the features of the underlying framework. TCP/IP and NetWare's SPX/IPX are common communication mechanisms, but reliability depends on how the SQL server and corresponding ODBC driver implement their request-response protocol.

Likewise, naming and location depend on name-to-location mappings required by the client. These mappings could be configured manually, or, at the other extreme, the ODBC driver could invoke the DCE naming service. Similarly, the degree of security can vary widely. A lot can happen in the driver and communications layers of Figure 26.

The client performs much of the work to compensate for differences between the client and different server systems. Having the client do this is an impediment to scaling and is an acknowledgment that servers are not sufficiently standardized.

Thus, each client maintains its own drivers, naming tables, and macros, which could complicate management at a large site. Furthermore, developers often experience problems getting multiple ODBC drivers to work together on a single client machine.

Some issues are inherent to distribution.

Distributing databases over local and wide area networks introduces inherent performance and scaling problems when the amount of data (primarily from long query responses) are transferred. ODBC itself is not a significant factor, but the distribution is. Performance, then, depends on the total system power of the servers, the size of the responses, and network performance.

Transactions and Databases

A *transaction* is an atomic operation, usually on a database. The operation must be completed correctly or not be done at all. Furthermore, the operation cannot be interrupted by other operations on the same data.

Banks DBMS applications require transactional integrity.

Bank account management provides a favorite example of transaction processing. Imagine a bank with a large account database and multiple branches. Two people share a joint account. At about the same time, one makes a deposit and the other makes a withdrawal. The deposit and withdrawal are separate individual transactions, and it typically does not matter in what order the DBMS performs these transactions.[1] However, in order to make the balance correct at completion, one transaction must be completed before the other starts. Likewise, if the network between the branch and central office fails in the middle of a transaction, the transaction must be rolled back as if it had never been started.

Increasingly, this sort of "transactional integrity" is a feature of DBMSs, and there are fewer stand-alone transaction processing systems. In fact, RDBMS performance is usually benchmarked by measuring "transactions per second."

Another trend is to extend the distributed client/server framework by adding transaction support. Transarc Corporation's Encina (which uses DCE) and Tuxedo from UNIX System Laboratories are the two most prominent open transaction processing systems. Chapter 17 describes Encina.

---

[1] Transaction order would become important if the withdrawal came first and the withdrawal amount exceeded the account balance.

Architecturally, the X/Open has specified the ***Distributed Transaction Processing (DTP)*** model. DTP defines how applications, transaction managers, resource managers, and communications managers interact.

Summary

Databases play an important role in distributed client/server computing. Large centralized databases already exist, and making them available to distributed clients exposes all of the major problems and issues that we introduced in Chapter 2.

Currently, database vendors provide their own distribution, security, reliability, and other mechanisms, generally using SQL as the application-level protocol. ODBC is the most common platform for PC integration. In the future, vendors may implement ODBC drivers using distributed computing frameworks such as DCE to provide integrated, secure, and reliable client/server communications.

CHAPTER 10   Data Replication

We have mentioned the concept of server replication several times, and it is now appropriate to discuss both the general concept and how it applies to DBMSs.

Replicate servers for performance, reliability, and availability.

Server replication means that several identical servers are available. Client/server applications replicate servers for the following two reasons:

- Performance. Multiple servers can spread the load so that each individual server can be more responsive. Furthermore, replicated servers can be placed close to clients so as to minimize network delays.

- Reliability and availability. If one server fails or cannot be reached due to network failures, then an alternative server can be used.

How do replicas stay identical?

The major problem is to ensure that the replicated servers are indeed identical, or nearly so. This is not a trivial problem. Consider replicating the manufacturing database server of the example in the previous chapter. An update operation, such as the one to change the prices of parts from Los Angeles, will change the database. How can we ensure that all the servers receive the update simultaneously? Is it possible for a client to get different prices of the Los Angeles parts depending on

147

which server it uses during and after the update interval? And, is it really necessary for all the servers to be absolutely consistent, especially if the consistency comes at a price?

We will take a brief look at two kinds of replication. Then, we will see how replication applies to distributed DBMS. We will conclude with a look at the role that replicated servers play in other areas of distributed computing.

Strongly Consistent Replication

Replicated servers can be *strongly* or *weakly consistent*.

Strongly consistent servers must either produce the exact same results at any time or else not be available. It is permissible for Server A to return results and for B to be unavailable. If they are both available, however, they must give the same result. Figure 27 illustrates how this can be achieved.

Strong replication ensures the servers really are the same, but at a cost.

In Figure 27, Server A receives the update request. Before doing anything else, Server A makes itself unavailable and sends a message to Server B telling it also to make itself unavailable except to receive commands from Server A. The rest of the dialog can be traced in the figure. This update protocol can be extended to multiple servers. Notice that Figure 27 is optimistic; it assumes that nothing breaks during this transaction.

Challenge: What can go wrong during this strong replication update, and how should A and B respond?

This sort of replication protocol is not the sort of thing that most application developers would implement themselves; it is provided as part of the DBMS implementation. Those implementations, in turn, can use a *online transaction processing system (OLTP)* to implement this logic.

The following two OLTP systems are commonly used in open systems:

- Tuxedo, developed by AT&T, is a transaction monitor and database system.
- Encina, from Transarc Corporation, is layered on DCE and provides for transactional integrity to the RPCs. We describe Encina in Chapter 17.

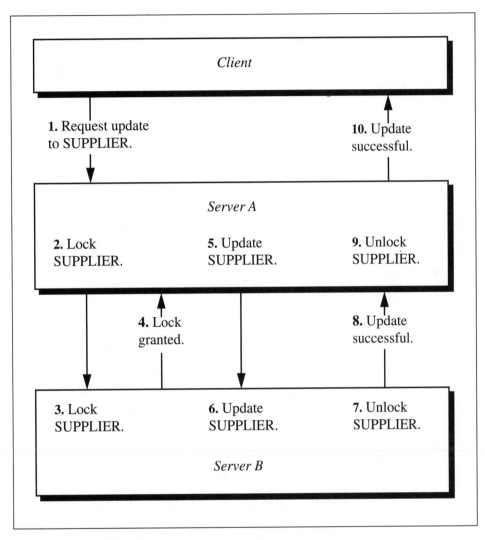

Figure 27 A Strongly Consistent Update

Some applications require strong consistency.

This strong, synchronous, replication is expensive; the database becomes unavailable for a relatively long time. Nevertheless, strong consistency is sometimes required. For example, a ticket agency does not want to reserve the same concert seat twice, so any replicated ticket reservation databases should be strongly consistent.

Strongly consistent servers may be configured so that there is one ***master*** server that can be updated. In this configuration, all of the replicas are read-only, except that they will accept updates from the master. In this way, performance and availability are improved. Alternatively, the strong consistency protocol can be applied between peers. These master-slave and peer-peer distinctions are similar to those discussed in Chapter 1.

Weakly Consistent Replication

Many applications can use weak consistency, which is easier to implement and has less impact on performance.

Frequently, it is sufficient to provide ***weakly consistent*** updates. The data might not be updated very often and may not have an urgent nature, or there may only be a small cost associated with occasionally sending obsolete data to a client. The Domain Name Service (DNS), for instance, is weakly consistent, and a client can recover from receiving an incorrect address. Alternatively, consider a library database. Acquisitions and deacquisition updates might be performed only once a day. The changes can be sent out to other servers during the night, and the impact of slight inconsistencies is minimal.

For another example of weak consistency, consider the case of a customer database at a company with numerous branch offices, which receive customer orders and enter the orders into the branch databases. The orders can then be sent to the central database. While it is essential that the order be entered consistently within a few hours, it is not necessary to keep the databases absolutely consistent.

An example with a different flavor is provided by a database that maintains records of stock market trades to provide the latest prices. The master server could send update request to all replicas, but all servers would remain available continuously. High availability would take precedence over absolute consistency. The worst case would be that a server might not have the latest trades, but this is preferable to making the server totally unavailable.

Weak consistency can be achieved with asynchronous updates. In Figure 27, we would eliminate the locking messages and the waiting. Server A would probably send the update command to Server B as soon as it completed its own update. It would return a "success" to the client at the same time. In the case of failure at Server B, Server A would send the request again until it succeeded.

Replication in Distributed Databases

Replication services are becoming an expected and standard option with distributed database servers. Most replication services do their updates with SQL statements. Many of them are heterogeneous; that is, they can maintain consistency among servers from different vendors.

DBMS servers can be expected to offer replication, now or in the near future.

Strongly consistent replication is sometimes called *decision-support replication (DSS-R)*. Usually, the master performs the client update commands, and the slaves get their updates from the master. There are various performance improvement schemes that cascade the updates through a hierarchy of masters and slaves. Some vendors provide peer-to-peer strong consistency whereby any server can receive an update.

Transaction processing replication (TP-R) provides weak consistency. Both master-slave and peer-to-peer architectures are available. Note the problem with potential collisions if two replicas update the same database record simultaneously.

There is a third possibility; namely, that the data is archival or is constant for a long period of time. Nonetheless, it may be needed at many locations, so multiple read-only replicas are required. Old financial records, mail order catalogs and price lists, and quarterly airline schedules are examples. Such situations are sometimes called *data warehousing*.

Summary

File servers, location servers, and other framework services are commonly replicated.

This chapter focused on database replication. However, all the issues and solutions we described for database replication are also relevant for many other kinds of replication, including the following:

- Some distributed file systems (for instance, DFS) provide facilities that allow ordinary files to be replicated.
- Some location services are essentially replicated databases. DNS location service databases are weakly replicated databases with a twist. Instead of waiting for a master server to send a list of changes, the replicas actively query the master server for changes.

Distributed Programming Concepts

How do partitions communicate? RPCs are a good way.

In Chapter 2, we said that it often makes sense to divide up a program so that separate parts (modules) run on separate systems. Subsequent chapters showed how databases, naming, and security systems can be partitioned. Here in Chapter 11, we'll explain various ways to partition programs and we'll look at how the partitions communicate. We'll tip our hand early and tell you that we'll use Remote Procedure Calls (RPCs) for implementing the distributed computing examples.

Categorizing Procedure Calls

We can separate module-to-module communication into the following three categories:

- Local procedure calls (LPC)
- Interprocess communication messages (IPC)
- Remote procedure calls (RPC)

Local procedures are linked together in the same address space.

A *local procedure call (LPC)* is a call in a typical nondistributed program. In an LPC, the caller, or calling procedure, and called procedure are in the same address space. With LPCs, the flow of control through the program is *synchronous*. That is, when the caller invokes an LPC, the caller stops running and does not resume running until the called procedure is finished. The caller and called procedure typically use parameter passing to transfer data.

IPCs can be within a system or between network nodes. Normally, the processes run asynchronously.

An in*terprocess communication (IPC)* is a message from one running program (process) to another. In an IPC, the sender (or caller) and receiver (or called process) generally do not share the same address space. All communication is through data in the message itself, although it is sometimes possible for processes to share memory.[1] A local IPC communicates between processes on the same node; a distributed IPC communicates between processes on different nodes. With IPCs, the calling and called processes run *asynchronously*. In other words, after the caller invokes an IPC, the caller can continue running and does not necessarily wait for the called process to complete. Furthermore, the called process might *never* send a response message to the caller. Finally, a caller can send an IPC to multiple receivers at the same time. IPCs are usually implemented on top of a network transport layer (TCP/IP, for instance) using programming interfaces such as Berkeley sockets (for UNIX systems) and WinSockets (for Microsoft Windows-based systems).

RPCs allow client/server communication using familiar, synchronous, procedures.

A *remote procedure call (RPC)* is a hybrid between an LPC and an IPC. Like an IPC, an RPC connects processes running on the same node or on different nodes. Like an LPC, an RPC is synchronous. That is, when the calling procedure invokes an RPC, the calling process suspends execution and the called process resumes execution. When the called process finishes its part of the RPC, the called process stops running and the original calling process resumes execution. In short, RPCs extend to distributed computing the well-known LPC metaphors of nondistributed programming.

Messaging is sometimes regarded as a fourth category of model-to-model communication. However, we view messaging as a form of IPC in which one system

---

[1] Processes on the same machine sometimes do share memory. Processes on different machines can sometimes share memory, although this feature is not available in any common implementations. We will continue to make the assumption that processes on separate machines have distinct memory spaces, as this is the more typical case.

does not need to respond to the other. Furthermore, messages can be sent simultaneously to many receivers.

Objects are another important model for creating communicating program modules, and we will discuss them in Chapter 14.

Local Programming vs. Distributed Programming

Programs are organized into procedures.

Procedures are the most common organizing unit in both local and distributed programming. In local programming, all the procedures are combined into one program. In distributed programming with RPCs, some of the procedures run on the client node, and some procedures run on the server node. This section compares local programming with LPCs to distributed programming with RPCs.

RPC programming is intentionally similar to LPC programming.

Programming with RPCs was designed to be similar to programming with traditional LPCs. Nevertheless, programming with RPCs brings up some interesting issues. Let's examine a program and see what kinds of problems we run into by dividing it up into a client part and server part through RPC calls.

Consider a C program that takes in two integers and returns the number of prime numbers between them. So, for example, if you run the program, the input and output might look something like this:

```
$ CountPrimes
Enter the lower integer: 10
Enter the upper integer: 20
There are 4 prime numbers between 10 and 20.
```

The following code shows one way of implementing this program with LPCs. Chapter 12 shows the same program implemented with RPCs.

```
/* Necessary "include" files to support I/O and math
   functions                                          */
#include <stdio.h>
#include <math.h>

/* Definitions of external functions.                 */
extern void UserInterface(void);
extern long int FindNumberOfPrimes(long int, long int);

void main(void)
```

```
{
  UserInterface();
}


/* This routine is the user interface for the program. */
void UserInterface(void)
{
 unsigned long int lower, upper, NumberOfPrimes;

  printf("Enter the lower integer: ");
  scanf("%d", &lower);
  printf("Enter the upper integer: ");
  scanf("%d", &upper);
  NumberOfPrimes = FindNumberOfPrimes(lower, upper);
  printf("There are %d prime numbers between %d and %d.\n",
  NumberOfPrimes, lower, upper);
}


/* This routine returns the number of prime numbers between
   lower and upper inclusive. */
long int FindPrimes(long int lower,
                               long int upper)
{
#define PRIME 1
#define COMPOSITE 2
  int    NumberIs;
  long int   current, terminator, NumberOfPrimes=0, i;

   for (current = lower; current <= upper; current++)  {
      terminator = (long int)sqrt((double)current);
      NumberIs=PRIME;
      for (i=2; i<= terminator; i++)  {
          if ( (current % i) == 0 )  {
            NumberIs=COMPOSITE;
            break;  /* Composite */
          }
        }
      if (NumberIs == PRIME)
         NumberOfPrimes++;
   }
 return(NumberOfPrimes);
}
```

The sample program has three procedure modules.

As you can see, this program consists of the following three procedures (which are actually referred to as "functions" in the C language):

- A trivial **main** routine.

- A routine named **UserInterface** that reads in two data points, a lower bound and an upper bound. A better **UserInterface** routine would check the input data for errors. A much better **UserInterface** routine would display a graphical user interface.

- A routine named **FindPrimes** that calculates the number of prime numbers between the upper and lower bounds. We do not claim that this routine is optimal, and, for serious computing, a programmer might want to modify the routine to use extended precision arithmetic.

What are the differences between local and remote procedures?

We use this program to examine some of the distinctions between LPC programming and RPC programming. Chapter 12 explains the steps necessary to divide this program into an RPC-based client/server application. For now, we focus on the big picture; that is, we look at how distributed programs differ from nondistributed programs. As we convert this program to RPCs in the next chapter, observe what sort of changes need to be made and what parts of the program stay the same.

Where Do the Procedures and Data End Up?

As a local program, all three procedures (**main**, **UserInterface**, and **FindPrimes**) end up in the same executable file. Along with the data, they occupy the same address space at run time as shown in Figure 28.

The remote procedures will run as separate processes in separate address spaces.

To create the distributed version of the program, we divide up the routines so that they run on two separate machines. Computationally intensive routines are the likeliest candidates for server nodes. Figure 28 shows such a configuration. In this figure, **main** and **UserInterface** share the same address space and run as one process, but **FindPrimes** runs as part of a different process.

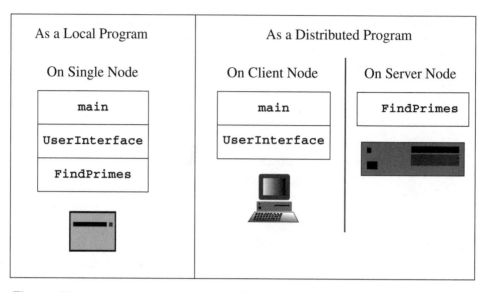

Figure 28 FindPrimes *As a Local Prorgram and a Distributed Program*

A C program cannot execute without a main routine. So, we must somehow code and link in a main routine with the version of FindPrimes that runs on the server node. We show how to do this in Chapter 12.

Flow of Control

The flow of control through a local program is synchronous. That is, only one routine of the program can run at any one time. Figure 29 illustrates this flow.

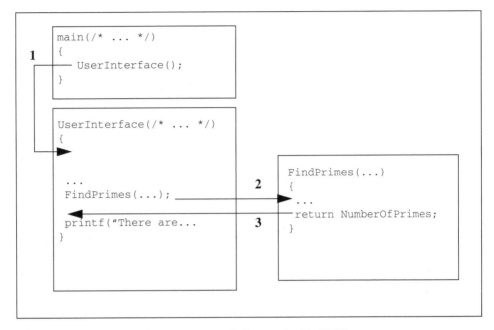

Figure 29 Flow of Control with LPCs and with RPCs

The middleware works hard in an RPC-based application.

The flow of control through a distributed RPC program is virtually identical to the flow of control through the local program. We say "virtually" because there is a layer of software standing between the client and server processes. In other words, behind-the-scenes code (supplied by the middleware) creates the illusion that **UserInterface** calls **FindPrimes** as if it were on the same machine. In reality, the intervening code performs the hard work to deal with network communication, security, reliability, transparency, and so on as required for distributed client/server operation. From the programmer's point of view, the flow of data and control transparently passes from **UserInterface** to **FindPrimes**.

How Does UserInterface Locate FindPrimes?

Local procedures are linked at build or run time.

In a local program, the caller and the called procedure have little trouble finding each other. At link time (or possibly run time on some systems), the linker calculates the address of the procedure and supplies it to the caller. At run time, the caller executes commands that ultimately cause the program counter to end up with the address of the called procedure. It is rather easy to do this in a local program because the caller and the called procedure share the same address space.

The client must locate and bind to the server. In a distributed program, it is much harder for the client caller to find the remote procedure. Not only are the client and remote procedure not sharing the same address space, they're not even on the same machine. At link time, the client typically does not know and does not care where the server is.

In a distributed program, the mechanism by which a caller (the client) finds the called procedure (the server) is called **binding**. Binding is the subject of Chapter 13. For now, we can say that the caller typically finds the remote procedure by asking a third party, perhaps a daemon process or location server, for the remote procedure's location.

Passing Parameters and Returning Values

The client often passes one or more parameters for the procedure to analyze. For example, `UserInterface` passes two parameters to `FindPrimes`. Similarly, the procedure often passes answers back to the client. All procedure calls, whether LPCs or RPCs, incur some expense.

Costs of Passing Parameters and Returning Values

Local procedures can use addresses in the common memory. To perform an LPC, the caller must push state information and call parameters on the stack or place them in registers. After the LPC completes, the caller must pop various values off the stack in order to refresh state information and to examine values returned by the called procedure. This procedure initialization and return incurs a small amount of overhead for every LPC, but the overhead cost of making an LPC is almost negligible compared to the cost of making an RPC.

Remote procedures need all the data directly. In an RPC, the caller (client) and remote procedure (server) cannot pass information via the stack. After all, the client and server no longer have access to the same stack. In place of a stack, the client and server must pass parameters and return values via the network. Various layers of run-time software must negotiate the passing of parameters and return values.

Passing Pointers

In an LPC, the caller can pass a pointer as a parameter. For example, in C, the caller typically does not pass an entire array to the called procedure. Rather, as shown in Figure 30, the caller merely uses the stack to pass the address of the first element of the array. Since the caller and called procedure share the same address space, the called procedure can easily dereference the pointer to obtain the actual array elements.

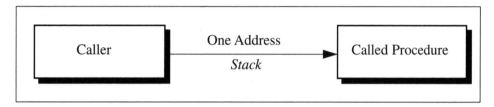

Figure 30 Passing a Million-Element Array with an LPC

In an RPC, by contrast, the caller (client) cannot pass a pointer to the remote procedure (server). Since the client and server do not share the same address space, there is no way for the server to dereference an address on the client. Therefore, when the client uses an RPC, the entire array must be passed to the server. If the amount of data is large, as shown in Figure 31, then the cost of passing that array will be significant.

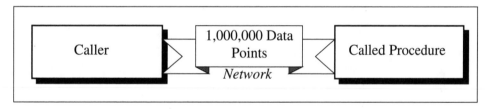

Figure 31 Passing a Million-Element Array with an RPC

Data Representations

The client and server may represent data differently.

Different machines define different ways to represent data. For example, some machines insist that the leftmost byte of an integer is the most significant and others insist that it is the rightmost byte. Similarly, some machines encode character data in ASCII, while others encode characters in EBCDIC. Some machines represent integers in 16 bits; others represent them in 32 or even 64 bits. You get the idea.

In an LPC, the caller and procedure are on the same machine. So, there are no disagreements over how data should be represented.

In an RPC, the caller (client) and remote procedure (server) are on different machines and there is a decent chance that the two machines do not use the same data representation schemes. An RPC package can solve this mismatch in one of two ways:

- Through a canonical or generic data representation protocol
- Through a receiver-makes-it-right protocol

The two RPC systems that we discuss, Sun's Open Network Computing (ONC) and OSF's Distributed Computing Environment (DCE), have different data representation strategies. ONC uses a canonical data representation, and DCE uses receiver-makes-it-right.

In generic representation, all passed data must be converted to a standard format.

Figure 32 illustrates the **generic data representation** protocol. In this protocol, all data passed between client and server, in either direction, must first be converted to an agreed-upon data representation. The generic data representation protocol requires up to four data conversions for each RPC:

1. RPC software on client must convert call parameters from client's native format to generic data representation.
2. RPC software on server must convert received call parameters from generic data representation to server's native format.
3. RPC software on server must convert any results from server's native format to generic data representation.
4. RPC software on client must convert results from generic data representation to client's native format.

In receiver-makes-it-right, the receiver of the passed data must convert the data.

The **receiver-makes-it-right** protocol does not involve conversion to a generic data representation. Instead, the client passes its call parameters in the client's native format and forces RPC software on the server to translate the data into the server's native format. Similarly, if the server passes results back to the client, RPC software on the client must translate the results into the client's native format. This mechanism requires some information from the sender as to what kind of data it is passing.

Both techniques have been used successfully.

Which protocol is better? Both protocols have ardant supporters, and we don't want to get caught in the middle of this battle. However, we will mention that the client and server sometimes run on nodes having the same architecture. (For instance, client and server might both run on HP workstations.) In such situations, receiver-makes-it-right is less expensive. However, if both the client and the server happen to use the generic data representation, then the generic data representation is less expensive. Life and RPC implementations are full of trade-offs.

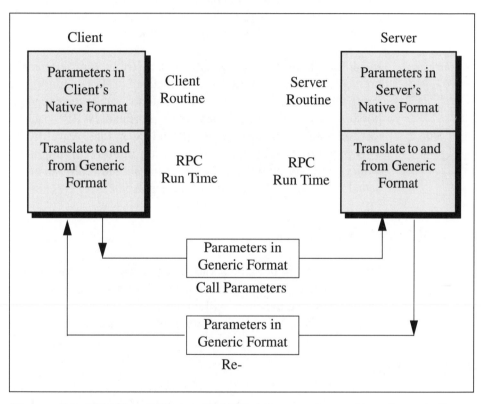

Figure 32 Handling Different Data Representations with a Generic Data Format

Marshalling and Unmarshalling

The RPC run time prepares data for transmission.

As you probably noticed, one of the tasks performed by the underlying RPC run-time software is to package parameters for a call from client to server. This preparation of parameters for transmission is called *marshalling*.

On the receiving end, the underlying RPC run-time software in the server must decode the marshalled parameters and present them to the server in a palatable fashion. This unwrapping of parameters is called ***unmarshalling***.

Errors and Exceptions

In any program, whether LPC-based or RPC-based, a variety of things can go wrong while the program is running. For example, the caller could pass unacceptable arguments to the procedure, or the procedure could fail by addressing out of bounds with an illegal pointer or array index.

Clients should be prepared to deal with procedure failures.
In addition to these common ailments, distributed programs run into all sorts of problems that local programs never dreamed of. For example, in a distributed program, the caller (client) might not be able to contact the called procedure (server), possibly as a result of a network failure. Fortunately, RPC packages are able to detect and report many different errors and exceptions. A well-written client or server is prepared to take appropriate action upon receiving an error notification. Notice, however, that the server run time should return an error indication if the actual server code fails for any of these reasons.

Global Variables

Get rid of global variables.
Programmers can put global variables inside a nondistributed program. However, in a distributed program, the server part will not be able to see "global" variables on the client and the client will not be able to see "global" variables on the server. Consequently, you cannot have truly global variables in a distributed program.

Holding State

Client must know whether a server is stateless or stateful.
All procedures, whether remote or local, fit into one of the following categories:

- Idempotent, or stateless
- Stateful

Suppose a client calls a procedure more than once, each time passing the same arguments. If the called procedure is guaranteed to return the same results to the client, then the called procedure is ***stateless*** or ***idempotent*** or ***at least once*** (because correct operation requires one or more server executions). If the called procedure does not guarantee the same results each time it is called with the same arguments, the called procedure is ***stateful*** or ***at most once*** (because the server RPC run time must ensure that the procedure is performed exactly one time or not at all).

Error recovery is easier with stateless procedures.

Idempotent routines recover easily from failure because there is no state to reconstruct. For instance, suppose `UserInterface` calls `FindPrimes`, but the node that `FindPrimes` is running on crashes or the network connection fails. Since `FindPrimes` cannot respond to `UserInterface`'s initial request, `UserInterface`'s run-time support will retransmit its request. Suppose the system administrator restarts the server node on which `FindPrimes` is running. When `FindPrimes` starts running again, `FindPrimes` is guaranteed to return the same results that it would have before the server node crashed. If `FindPrimes` had been stateful, then recovering from the crash would have been difficult. On the other hand, the client run time must be prepared to reject duplicate server responses when, for instance, the client makes several requests due to transmission delays.

Stateful procedures may be necessary.

In C, stateful procedures typically access `static` variables or global variables. For example, the following procedure is stateful because variables *RunningTotal* and *RunningNumberOfValues* will increase each time `RunningAverage` is called:

```c
int RunningAverage(int NewValue)
{   /* stateful routine */
 static int   RunningTotal;
 static int   RunningNumberOfValues;

    RunningTotal = RunningTotal + NewValue;
    RunningNumberOfValues = RunningNumberOfValues + 1;
    RunningAverage = RunningTotal / RunningNumberOfValues;
    return(RunningAverage)
}
```

The run time software ensures that stateful procedures are not executed twice.

Because of such factors as network delays or failures and delays on a heavily loaded server, there are instances where a client run time retransmits the same RPC to a server. If the server routine is idempotent, then executing the same RPC twice does not cause problems. If the server routine is stateful, then the server's RPC run time package must recognize the duplicate call and not call the server procedure a second time.

ONC supports stateless procedures; DCE supports both types.

Some RPC packages (such as DCE) allow the programmer to designate remote procedures as either idempotent or stateful. By contrast, other RPC packages, such as ONC, only support idempotent remote procedures. For example, NFS, the most famous ONC application, is always idempotent. Therefore, an NFS client can make the same RPC to an NFS server multiple times. If an NFS server happens to respond multiple times to the same request from an NFS client, RPC code running at the NFS client will suppress duplicate responses.

"Stateless" procedures may actually contain state.

In reality, NFS file system calls are not truly idempotent. For instance, multiple calls to delete a file will give different return codes. The first call may delete the file successfully, but the second call will return an error code indicating that there was no file to delete. Furthermore, the server maintains the files and their contents, and the files are inherently stateful. Other problems could occur with sequences of calls to position at the end of a file to append data. Concurrent access to the same remote file from multiple clients complicates matters even more. Nonetheless, NFS's stateless design is quite robust, and NFS is widely and successfully deployed.

When Should You Distribute an Application?

Data transmission and RPC overhead are expensive. When is an RPC worthwhile?

As the previous section suggested, an RPC incurs a lot more overhead than an LPC. So, you may be wondering when this overhead expense is justified. You may also be wondering what routines should go on a server node and what routines should stay on a client node. Furthermore, where should the data reside so as to improve performance?

Any of the following characteristics of a routine makes it a good candidate for being partitioned on to a server node:

- The routine does a lot of computation. For example, the **FindPrimes** routine does a lot of computation if the spread between *lower* and *upper* is great, or if the values of *lower* and *upper* are relatively high.
- The routine requires large amounts of memory or disk.
- The routine accesses a shared resource (files or databases, for instance).
- The routine performs some other unique or specialized service, such as printing.

Not all routines that require a lot of computation are ideal servers. For example, some routines require a lot of computation just because there is a lot of data to chew on. However, remember that if there is a lot of data to chew on, it is generally very expensive to deliver that data to the server. You have to ask if this expense is worth the benefit. In an ideal server routine, the amount of computation goes up faster than the amount of data passed to it.

Computation time frequently increases faster than the amount of data.

For example, consider a routine that sorts N numbers. The best algorithms sort data as a factor of $N*\log_2 N$. So, a routine that sorts 20,000 numbers should take about 2.3 times longer to sort than a routine that sorts 10,000 numbers. In other words, computation time increases slightly faster than the amount of data passed. It may only be worthwhile to put a sort routine on a server when the value of N is high.

Client routines tend not to be compute-intensive. Routines that interact directly with the user should typically stay on the client side. (We look at an exception in Chapter 15, where we see how the user interface is sometimes referred to as a "server.")

Data Shipping and Function Shipping

When designing a distributed application, you must consider where to keep the data. In some applications, the server stores the data; in other applications, the client feeds the data to the server.

You can move the data to the function or the function to the data.

For example, consider a client that gathers data into a matrix and a server that calculates the eigenvalues of a matrix. In this application, the client transmits the entire matrix to the server, and the server chews on the data. This application is an example of ***data shipping*** or ***moving the data to the function***. Most Internet services involve data shipping.

Client/server DBMSs generally keep data on the server. This is an example of ***function shipping*** or ***moving the function to the data.*** Function shipping is appropriate when the cost of shipping the data to the server is too high. For example, consider a DBMS application in which many of the client's requests rely on sorted data. It makes no sense for the client to repeatedly ship large amounts of data to the server for sorting. Anyhow, the server needs to share the data with numerous clients. It does make sense, however, for the server to sort the data once and then store the sorted data inside the server process.

We realize that the term "function shipping" is somewhat counterintuitive; the client does not actually transmit code to the server. From the client's perspective, the part of the program that does the processing is moved to the server system.

A distributed file system is a form of ***data sharing***. The client's simple file access request is not complex enough to be considered a function.

Finally, sending a file to a print server would be pure data shipping if the file is simple text. However, if the file is in PostScript format, some function shipping is involved because the printer must convert the file to a graphics display.

The relative amounts of data and computation enter into function vs. data shipping trade-offs, as do security and other considerations. The following examples illustrate several possibilities.

Case Study 1: The Wily Law Enforcer

A very small amount of data can cause a very large amount of specialized computation.

Frieda is a law enforcement officer[1] with a court warrant to read Evil Ed's encrypted email messages to his evil henchpersons. She has a copy of Ed's public key but does not know the private key. To read the mail messages, Frieda will need to factor a large number into two primes, requiring some major computing resources.

Frieda has calculated that it will take between one and three years to break the code on her PC. However, Frieda has a very powerful multiprocessor server on her local area network. This server system has a password-cracking routine already installed, which uses a powerful prime factoring algorithm. By passing the encrypted password to the server, Frieda found the encryption key in a matter of hours. Thanks to Frieda, Ed is now behind bars at a minimum security prison where he enjoys golf, tennis, and maniacal cackling.

Case Study 1 is an ideal example of RPC and function shipping. The amount of data passed to the server was negligible compared to the amount of computation the server performed. In other words, the benefit of using a powerful server outweighed the overhead of the RPC by a tremendous margin.

[1.] Please, no hate mail on this example. This is just an example of client/server technology in action; we are not endorsing computer snooping.

Case Study 2: The Traveling Fertilizer Salesman

The data may be secret and the processing complex. Ship the function to the data.

Tom is a traveling sales representative for the Fernbuster Fertilizer Company. In a typical quarter, Tom has to drive to 50 of 250 different cities spread across a vast geographic territory. In order to plan his sales calls, Tom dials up from his laptop and enters the names of the cities he needs to visit.

Back at Fernbuster headquarters, a database holds all the data for a 250x250 matrix giving the distance and best routes for travel between all pairs of cities. This list also contains the customers in each city along with projected sales for the coming year. This information is very secret and is not shared with Tom. This database server node is also particularly adept at optimizing expected sales. In fact, it can solve such problems much faster than Tom's laptop can, even if Tom had the secret sales projections. Tom quickly has his optimal itinerary.

In this example, the server performs extensive calculations and also has unique access to data necessary to perform the calculation. This is also an example of function shipping.

Case Study 3: The Chip Simulator

You may need to ship some data and the function to a location where there is even more data.

Li designs computer CPU chips from her new Windows 95 workstation. She downloads the latest chip design to her workstation from a large design database. As she makes modifications, she displays the updated designs on her workstation. The workstation has a nice monitor and good graphics capabilities. However, when Li wants to simulate the operation of the entire chip, she will need a lot more computing horsepower than her workstation can provide. She will also need access to the database library containing circuit component specifications. As it happens, her department owns a multiprocessor Windows NT Server running a chip simulator program. By turning over the compute-intensive simulation to the compute engine, Li performed the simulation overnight instead of over the course of a week. Consequently, Li found a bug in the chip's floating-point unit, fixed the bug quickly, and then ran the simulation again to validate the new design before the chip went into production. Notice that if all chip designers in Li's department tried to use the simulator simultaneously, there might not be a performance gain. However, the simulator is a shared resource that each designer uses infrequently.

In this case, there was a lot of data representing the chip design. However, the size of the input data was eclipsed by the enormity of the calculations. The simulation requires a large amount of computing time due to the number of components in the chip and the fact that the simulation needs to model chip behavior over a long period of time. Furthermore, the server requires a large physical memory to hold data about all the chip components. There were both data shipping and function shipping.

Case Study 4: The Deficit-Chomping Politician

Simulations can be very compute-intensive. And they always want more computing power.

The President of Parador needs to chop taxes quickly or he's history. Unfortunately, chopping taxes raises the deficit, although some contend that tax decreases will increase tax revenues. The President's three leading economists offer various tax reduction proposals. In order to determine which proposal is the most politically expedient and how the conflicting predictions actually work out, the President's data entry team feeds the tax cut parameters to the client portion of the program. The client portion passes these parameters to the server, which runs on a super-computer. The server models the deficit for the next ten years, accounting for all economic effects of the various tax cuts. Armed with the results, the President presents the optimal tax bill to his Congress, which passes it quickly with little controversy. Once more, function shipping has saved the day.

In this case, the only data are the tax cut parameters (the other economic contexts are fixed), but the computing task is huge. This is an ideal situation for distributing logic.

Simulations such as the economic and chip models have a never-ending appetite for computing power. Users will want to refine the models, improve numerical approximations, run the simulation for longer time periods (simulation time, that is), or do any number of other things to consume newer and faster computing resources.

Do You Need RPCs? Are IPCs Sufficient?

RPCs are layered on IPCs.

Application programmers have made heavy use of IPCs for years. Many old-time programming gurus already feel comfortable programming with IPCs and wonder why RPCs are needed at all. Well, as Figure 33 illustrates, RPCs are typically layered on top of IPCs. In a very real sense, RPCs add value to what IPCs already provide.

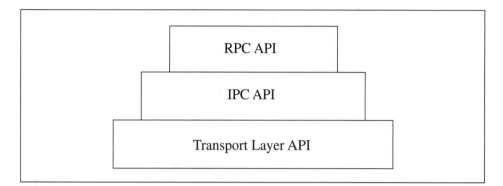

Figure 33 Typical Distributed Programming Call Hierarchy

IPCs are still appropriate for some applications.

We do not want to give you the impression that RPCs will make IPCs obsolete. In fact, IPCs are useful for programs requiring the client and server to execute asynchronously. For example, the very popular **telnet** utility requires constant bidirectional, full-duplex, data flow. That is, data must flow simultaneously from client to server and from server to client, both of which transmit asynchronously without being specifically requested to do so. Therefore, **telnet** is implemented as an IPC program rather than an RPC program.

RPCs distribute the familiar procedure programming model.

Most applications, though, are better off using RPCs than IPCs. The primary reason is that RPCs use the same synchronous programming model that most LPC programmers are already accustomed to. In addition, RPCs solve the data representation problem; IPCs do not. RPCs also solve the reliability problem (retransmitting requests, preventing multiple calls to stateful procedures, and so on); IPCs do not. Most RPC packages provide security and naming and location services transparently to the programmer; IPC packages do not. Finally, using threads, clients can actually create an asynchronous program model. We discuss this use of threads at the end of Chapter 13.

Of course, a clever IPC programmer can layer extra code on top of an IPC package in order to overcome the limitations of IPC. But why bother? RPCs have taken care of this extra code for you. Furthermore, any extra code you layer on top of IPC will not necessarily interoperate with another programmer's extra layer of code.

Programming with an RPC Package

Most RPC packages use the same programming model, which is the one illustrated in Figure 34. In this model, the following three entities provide elements of the program:

- The programmer
- An IDL compiler
- The RPC run-time package itself, typically by ensuring that certain library routines are linked into both the client and the server

We explore this model in greater detail.

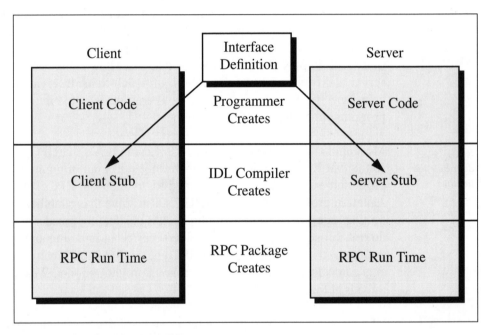

Figure 34   Generic RPC Programming Mode

What the Programmer Provides

In most RPC packages, the application programmer provides the following three separate pieces of code:

- The client code
- The server code
- An interface definition

As we mentioned earlier, the client code and the server code look pretty much like regular code in a nondistributed application. For some applications, the code will be written in some procedural language (such as C), and in other applications the code will be written in some object-oriented language (such as C++). For procedural languages, the client code and server code will consist of separate routines. For object-oriented languages, the client code will instantiate some objects, and the server code will instantiate other objects.

The interface definition specifies the following sorts of information:

- The parameters that the client will pass to the server
- The values that the server will return to the client

Specify the interfaces with a special language, the IDL.

A C programmer who thinks that the interface definition sounds an awful lot like a glorified header file is not far off the mark. However, unlike a header file, an interface definition is not written in the same language that was used to code the client and server. In fact, the programmer writes the interface definition in something called an ***Interface Definition Language (IDL)***.

IDLs are declarative languages.

There are many different IDLs available. Programmers who write client and server code in a procedural language (such as C) will probably use a popular IDL that looks a lot like C. For programmers working with object-oriented languages, there are several IDLs that look a lot like C++. When we say "look a lot like..." we do not mean to imply that IDLs are full programming languages; in fact, IDLs do not contain flow constructs (such as `for` loops or `if/then/else` statements.) IDLs are declarative languages that usually support only data type constructs and object declaration constructs. We will see several examples of IDL code later on in the next chapter.

Although not shown in Figure 34, some RPC implementations also require a programmer to write a ***server initialization routine***. The code in this routine provides information that helps the client find the server at run time.

Some RPC programming environments are sophisticated enough that they actually write the IDL file for the programmer. Similarly, some products may take care of writing any server initialization routine.

What the IDL Compiler Provides

The IDL compiler generates stub files.

To convert the IDL file into something useful, you must invoke the IDL compiler. Unlike other compilers, IDL compilers do not generate object code. Rather, an IDL compiler generates *stub files* in source form. From one IDL source file, the IDL compiler creates the following two stub files:

- A client stub file
- A server stub file

The stub files encapsulate many of the gory details of the RPC. The stub code, working with the run-time code, typically handles reliability, naming and location services, security, and marshalling. The stub file hides much of the underlying complexity of the RPC so that the programmer does not have to worry about them.

What the RPC Run-Time Package Provides

The RPC run time talks with the network transport.

A stub file contains code specific to a particular call from a client to a server. However, all RPCs require more general services. For example, all distributed RPCs need to travel over the network from the client node to the server node. In most RPC packages, TCP/IP takes care of the transport of the RPC from client to server. Nevertheless, there needs to be some code that interfaces to the transport layer. Rather than ask the application programmer to write that code, the code is typically linked in from an RPC library. This code is typically referred to as *RPC run -time code*.

The RPC Model and the OSI Reference Model

The RPC model maps into the OSI 7-layer model.

The *Open Systems Interconnect (OSI)* model describes seven separate layers of communication. In the OSI model, each layer on a sending machine knows how to communicate with its peer on a receiving machine. Furthermore, each layer communicates with the two adjacent layers on the same machine. For example, suppose the sending machine encodes information at the transport layer. The encoded message is processed in the receiving node by its own transport layer.

Like the OSI model, the RPC model also uses layering for peer-to-peer communication between the layers. Figure 35 maps the upper OSI layers to the RPC components. At the top level, application programmers can code the client and server, remaining oblivious to all the complexities required to transfer data from client to server. Similarly, the stubs talk only to each other. The RPC run-time code on the client communicates with the RPC run-time code on the server. At the bottom of Figure 35, we see the familiar bottom four layers of the OSI model.

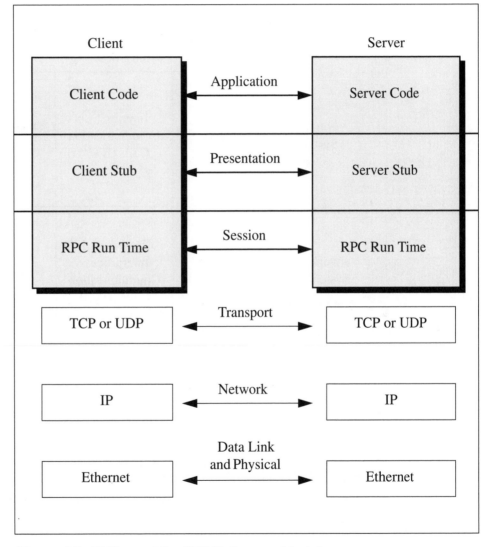

Figure 35 RPCs and the OSI Reference Model

Summary

Figure 36 shows our six-step evolution of computing. The six boxes are numbered to show the approximate historical order in which these methods have become popular.

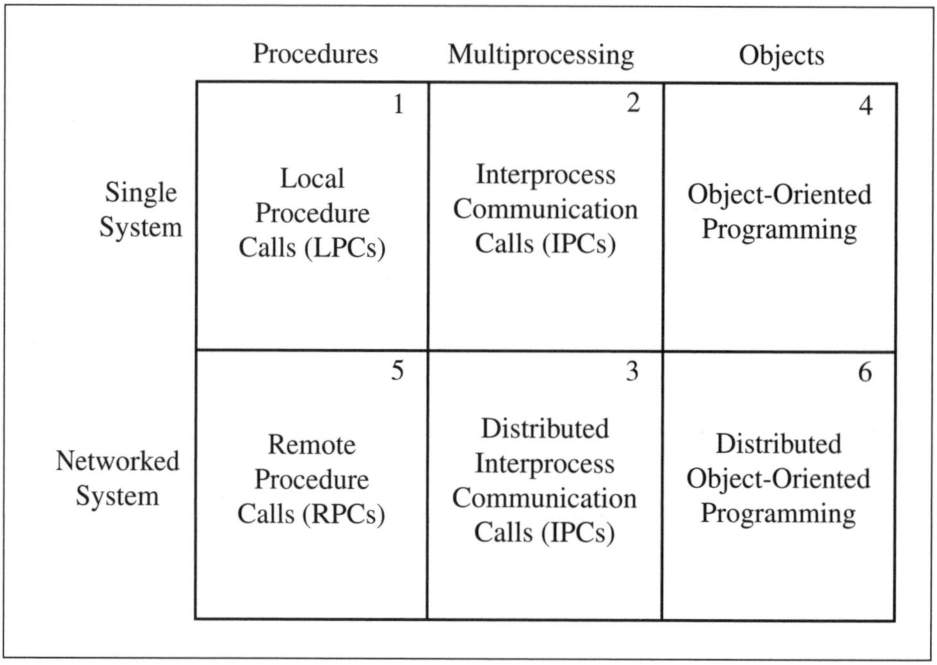

	Procedures	Multiprocessing	Objects
Single System	1 Local Procedure Calls (LPCs)	2 Interprocess Communication Calls (IPCs)	4 Object-Oriented Programming
Networked System	5 Remote Procedure Calls (RPCs)	3 Distributed Interprocess Communication Calls (IPCs)	6 Distributed Object-Oriented Programming

Figure 36 The Evolution of Computing

The evolution of program modularization and distribution is one of many ways to trace computer history.

The order we picked is quite subjective (many readers will find exceptions to the order), but it does suggest two trends:

- Single-system programming concepts have migrated to networked systems. For example, programming is moving from LPCs to RPCs.

- Object-oriented programming is slowly replacing procedural programming.

These three distributed computing models are not entirely independent; rather they are hierarchical, one being built on the other. RPC implementations require IPC, and some distributed OOP implementations use RPCs for object-to-object communication.

CHAPTER 12 Distributed Programming Implementations

Chapter 11 described the theory of RPC-based programming. Here in Chapter 12, we translate theory into code. That is, we are going to examine two important RPC-based client/server systems and show how to implement an RPC-based client and server using DCE.

We will use the term ***RPC package*** to refer to a system that supports both the development and operation of RPC applications.

RPCs are an old idea, but standards have been slow to emerge.

Contrary to popular belief, RPCs are not a new concept. All modern RPC packages trace their lineage back to the 1970s and research organizations such as Xerox PARC and Carnegie Mellon University. You would certainly think that such an old technology would have matured to one agreed-upon standard by now. However, too many companies have vested interests in competing products. We will take a look at the technology that seems to be ahead in the implementation war. Later, in Chapter 14, we will focus on distributed programming implementations based on object-oriented programming.

177

Implementation Overview: RPCs

We see the ONC, DCE, and Microsoft Windows NT RPCs as the three most important procedural RPCs. As we shall see, the Microsoft Windows NT RPC is almost identical to the DCE RPC.

ONC/RPC

ONC/RPCs are found on almost every UNIX system.

Sun's ONC/RPC dates back to the mid-1980s and was the first important RPC package on the market. The libraries necessary to run ONC/RPC applications are part of the base software of most modern UNIX systems and are available on nearly all other operating systems. If you have UNIX, you probably do not have to pay anything extra in order to run ONC/RPC applications. However, if you want to develop ONC/RPC applications, then you will probably have to purchase development software from SunSoft or from another vendor.

NFS is the most famous ONC application.

The ONC libraries are everywhere because NFS is everywhere. After all, NFS is merely a sophisticated application built using ONC/RPC to communicate between clients and distributed file servers.

The RPC market (that is, the market for development tools and RPC-based distributed applications) is still fairly immature. However, the DCE RPC package offered by OSF and Microsoft will probably become more important to application developers than ONC/RPC.

DCE is backed by numerous vendors and has more functionality.

There are several reasons for this prediction. First, there are many more companies invested in the success of DCE than in the success of ONC. DCE also provides more complete functionality than ONC to address the distributed client/server issues we introduced in Chapter 2. For example, DCE offers more options for RPC reliability (Chapter 11) and binding (Chapter 13). DCE provides a superior global naming system (Chapter 4). Finally, DCE provides a more extensive set of security services than ONC (Chapter 5).

OSF/DCE RPC

The last section mentioned some reasons for DCE's potential future role, and we will continue to use DCE as a "reference" RPC-based client/server framework. First, we review some DCE background information.

OSF is an industry consortium that provides DCE source code and specifications.

The Open Software Foundation (OSF), a consortium of several large American, Asian, and European computer companies, introduced the DCE RPC package in the early 1990s. This RPC package is based heavily on the Network Computing Architecture pioneered by Apollo Computer and Digital in the late 1980s.

The DCE RPC package is an open standard for remote procedure calls. "Open" is one of those great buzzwords of the computer industry that means just about anything that the inventor wants it to mean. In the case of DCE RPC, "open" means that any company may chose either to license source code from OSF or do their own implementation of the DCE RPC package. So, in a sense, we might say that OSF is merely offering one implementation of the DCE RPC specification. Many large vendors (for example, IBM, Digital, and Hewlett-Packard) market the OSF/DCE RPC package for their own machines. Transarc markets a version of the OSF/DCE RPC for Sun workstations, and Gradient Technologies has a Microsoft Windows version.

The DCE RPC package is the heart of all DCE products, whether base DCE software (such as DFS) or layered software (such as Encina).

In order to run a DCE RPC application, both the client and the server must be on a DCE cell. However, the client and server do not necessarily have to be on the *same* cell. A DCE cell must run at least one CDS (see Chapter 4), one Security Service server (see Chapter 5), and several Time Service servers (Chapter 17).

Microsoft Windows NT RPC

Using DCE, Windows NT can interoperate with other systems, but Windows NT does not supply the framework services.

Since the DCE RPC package is open, Microsoft decided to implement their own version that runs on Windows NT. That is, Microsoft engineers have followed the DCE RPC specification and made an implementation of this package that runs on Windows NT. Microsoft engineers added a few extra features to their IDL that are not available in some other DCE RPC packages.

Thanks to Microsoft, RPC-based application source code is now portable between implementations of UNIX and Windows NT. Furthermore, clients running on UNIX can successfully request services from servers running on Windows/NT, and vice-versa. This is not to imply that all UNIX applications run without modification on Windows NT; however, the RPC part of it should work without modification.

There is a very important caveat about the Windows NT RPC package. Windows NT applications written with the RPC package require that DCE Services (CDS, Security, Time) be running on a cell. However, as of this writing, Windows NT does not come with a CDS. Therefore, in order to run RPC-based applications on Windows NT, there either has to be a UNIX machine running CDS somewhere on the LAN, or you will have to obtain a CDS that runs on Windows NT from some third-party vendor. (Digital and Gradient, among others, have such a product.)

Compatibility and Portability

DCE portability and interoperability have been well tested.

The DCE RPC package has been ported to many different operating systems. The vendors and OSF have gone to a lot of effort to test portability and interoperability. Application developers can create applications from any platform supporting a DCE RPC development kit. The clients and servers that you create can run on any machine that has a DCE run-time license. For example, you can have a client running on an HP-UX machine and a server running on an AIX machine. Similarly, since Windows NT uses the exact same protocol and calls for its RPC package, you can develop clients that run on an HP-UX machine and a server that runs on a Windows NT machine.

The Windows NT RPC package was not ported from the same source as most other implementations of the DCE RPC package. Therefore, the Windows NT RPC package is not "bug-for-bug" compatible with the OSF/DCE RPC package. So, it is possible that a few minor incompatibilities will spring up. Microsoft has also chosen to develop a few optional components of the DCE specification.

Implementation: The DCE RPC

This section creates an example DCE application.

To help you get a better handle on what the development process involves, we're going to walk you through the creation of a simple distributed DCE RPC application. Basically, we are going to take the nondistributed application shown in Chapter 11 and turn it into a distributed application.

Software developers must perform the following steps in order to build a DCE RPC-based application:

1. Write an interface file using the special IDL language.
2. Write client routines and server routines.

3. Write a server initialization file.

4. Using compilers and linkers, integrate the appropriate files. The net result is a client program and a server program.

After following these steps, you will end up with a server program and a client program. In order to execute both parts, quite a bit of system administration set-up is necessary. See Chapter 13 for details.

Step 1: Write One IDL File for Each Server Routine

The IDL file gives the UUID along with the function prototype.

Our sample application from the last chapter consists of one server routine, so we will need one IDL file to describe it. Here is a suitable DCE IDL file describing the interface to the **FindPrimes** routine:

```
[
    uuid(225159c1-28f7-11ce-add1-0000c049d04c),
    version(1.0)
]

interface PRIME
{   long int FindNumberOfPrimes
      (   [in] long int    lower,
          [in] long int    upper
      );
}
```

We will explain this code in a moment. For now, just note that we placed this IDL source code at filename `primes.idl`.

Compiling the IDL File

Compile the IDL source to create two stubs and a header file.

You invoke the DCE IDL compiler to compile the IDL source code. The command we used to compile on a UNIX system was as follows:

```
$ idl prime.idl
```

The preceding command creates the following three files:

• A header file named `prime.h`

• A stub file named `prime_cstub.o` (this is an object file)

• A stub file named `prime_sstub.o` (this is an object file)

IDL looks a lot like C.

The IDL file looks enough like C to give the average C programmer hope that IDL is easy to learn. However, there are enough differences between C and IDL to also give C programmers a quick scare. When it comes down to it, an IDL consists of two parts:

- A way to name the interface
- A fancy function prototype

We now take a look at each of these two parts.

Naming the Interface

The IDL source code contains two pieces of information that uniquely identify the interface. The first is a UUID. In our example, the UUID was

```
225159c1-28f7-11ce-add1-0000c049d04c
```

Paste in the UUID, which is generated by a utility.

In brief, a UUID is a very large number that is guaranteed to be unique. You generate a UUID by running a utility, typically **uuidgen**. Then you cut the UUID returned by **uuidgen** and paste it into your code. (See Chapter 4 for more information on UUIDs.)

The interface also needs a human-readable name. In our example, we decided to call the interface **Prime**. Notice that an interface name is not the same thing as a routine name.

Function Prototype

Is the parameter in, out, or both?

Most of a DCE IDL file looks very much like a function prototype in ANSI C. The only noticeable difference is the IDL keyword **[in]**. A parameter tagged with **[in]** contains a value that is being passed from client to server. Although not in our example, you can also tag parameters with the keyword **[out]**. An **[out]** parameter contains a value to be passed from server to client. Notice that the DCE IDL, just like C, can use **typedef** to declare new types.

Step 2: Write Client and Server Routines

As we described in the last chapter, the client and server routines of a distributed application look just like ordinary routines in a nondistributed application. This is an example of what we mean by "transparency." Of course, there is no shared data. (If there were, the data would not have to be put into procedure arguments.)

Client Routine

Include the header file generated by the IDL compiler in the client source code.

The client in our sample application consists of two routines: **main** and **UserInterface**. Here is the complete client code:

```
#include <stdio.h>
#include "prime.h"

extern void UserInterface(void);

void main(void)
{
  UserInterface();
}


/* This routine is the user interface for the program. */
void UserInterface(void)
{
 unsigned long int lower, upper, NumberOfPrimes;

  printf("Enter the lower integer: ");
  scanf("%d", &lower);
  printf("Enter the upper integer: ");
  scanf("%d", &upper);
  NumberOfPrimes = FindNumberOfPrimes(lower, upper);
  printf("There are %d prime numbers between %d and %d.\n",
  NumberOfPrimes, lower, upper);
}
```

Compile the client separately from the server.

Let's assume that the client was stored in filename `client.c`. To compile from a UNIX machine, you would specify a command such as the following:

```
$ cc -c client.c
```

The preceding command produces an object file named `client.o`.

Server Routine

The server code also needs the IDL include file.

The server routine consists only of the **FindPrimes** routine. Here is the complete server code:

```c
#include <stdio.h>
#include <math.h>
#include "prime.h"

/* This routine returns the number of prime numbers between
   lower and upper inclusive. */
long int FindPrimes(long int lower, long int upper)
{
#define PRIME 1
#define COMPOSITE 2
  int    NumberIs;
  long int current, terminator, NumberOfPrimes=0, i;

    for (current = lower; current <= upper; current++)  {
       terminator = (long int)sqrt((double)current);
       NumberIs=PRIME;
       for (i=2; i<= terminator; i++)  {
           if ( (current % i) == 0 )  {
             NumberIs=COMPOSITE;
             break;  /* Composite */
           }
        }
        if (NumberIs == PRIME)
          NumberOfPrimes++;
    }
 return(NumberOfPrimes);
}
```

Compile the server separately.

We placed the server code inside filename server.c. To compile the server code, we issued the following command:

```
$ cc -c server.c
```

The preceding command created an object file named server.o.

There are only a couple of differences between the distributed and nondistributed versions of our client and server.

One difference is that the distributed versions of both the client and the server include the header file (**prime.h**) created by the IDL compiler. That is, both the client and the server code contained the following preprocessor statement:

```
#include "prime.h"
```

Another difference, not shown in this example, is when arrays are procedure parameters. Recall from the last chapter that pointers cannot be parameters to remote procedures. The nondistributed version of a hypothetical **UseArray** would specify a **DataArray** parameter in the function prototype as follows:

```
float
UseArray(float *DataArray, /* pointer to float */
         int ElementCount)
```

However, the distributed version of **UseArray** specifies the **DataArray** as follows:

```
float
UseArray(float DataArray[MaxElements], /* array of floats */
                int ElementCount)
```

Step 3: Write a Server Initialization Routine

You need to initialize the server and make choices regarding binding and security.

We need to provide a server initialization routine for each server routine. We will take a much closer look at the code in the server initialization routine in Chapter 13, when we talk about binding. For now, we will simply say that the server initialization routine helps the client find the server's location. Much of the work we show here deals with setting up the client/server binding, which is the subject of the next chapter.

A possible server initialization routine for our application is as follows:

```
/* Server initialization routine for FindPrimes. */
#include <stdio.h>
#include "prime.h"

main()
{
 unsigned32 status;
 rpc_binding_vector_t *binding_vector;
 unsigned_char_t *entry_name;
 char *getenv();

 /* Register PRIME interface with the CDS. */
   rpc_server_register_if(PRIME_v1_0_s_ifspec, NULL,
                          NULL, &status);

 /* Use all available transport protocols. */
   rpc_server_use_all_protseqs(
               rpc_c_protseq_max_reqs_default, &status);

 /* Get binding information from RPC run-time routine. */
   rpc_server_inq_bindings(&binding_vector, &status);

 /* Advertise this service in the CDS. */
   entry_name = (unsigned_char_t *)getenv(
                                    "PRIME_SERVER_ENTRY");
   puts(entry_name);
   rpc_ns_binding_export(rpc_c_ns_syntax_default, entry_name,
                         PRIME_v1_0_s_ifspec, binding_vector,
                         NULL, &status);

 /* Register endpoints (places to listen for RPCs).
    An endpoint is generally the process ID of the server
    process itself. */
   rpc_ep_register(PRIME_v1_0_s_ifspec, binding_vector,
                   NULL, NULL, &status);

 /* Deallocate binding information. */
   rpc_binding_vector_free(&binding_vector, &status);

 /* Listen for RPCs. */
   puts("I'm waiting."); /* feedback for sys. admin. */
   rpc_server_listen(rpc_c_listen_max_calls_default,
                     &status);
}
```

Compile the initialization **main** *routine.*
We placed the server initialization code inside a file named `server_init.c`. To compile the code, we issued the following command:

```
$ cc -c server_init.c
```

The server initialization routine is named **main**. Naming the routine **main** gives the server program a starting point.

Step 4: Link the Various Parts Together

At this point, you have written all the code you need to write. It is now time to link the various sources in order to create both a client program and a server program.

Creating the Client

Link all the client routines to create a client.
To create the client program, you must link all of the following objects:

- The client stub object created in Step 1.
- The client object created in Step 2.
- The DCE run-time libraries. There are typically two libraries. One is the pure DCE run-time library, and the other is the DCE multi-architecture threads library.

The way in which you link these objects into an executable depends on the linker you are using. On our system (a Digital workstation running the POSIX-compliant Digital UNIX), the following command created an executable client:

```
$ cc -o myclient client_stub.o client.o -ldce -lcma
```

The `-l` option tells the linker to look at a particular library. The two libraries mentioned in our example are the DCE run-time library (`dce`) and a library supporting threads (`cma`).

Creating the Server

Link all the server routines to create a server.

To create the server, you must link all of the following objects:

- The server stub object created in Step 1.
- The server object created in Step 2.
- The server initialization object created in Step 3.
- The DCE run-time libraries.

We used the following command line to build the server for our system:

```
$ cc -o myserver server_stub.o server.o server_init.o \
-ldce -lcma -lm
```

The command you use to build the system on your server may be somewhat different from the command we used.

Step 5: Test, Debug, and Perfect

You can start testing with the client and server on the same node. New problems can occur when they are on separate nodes.

Debugging a distributed application is more difficult than debugging a nondistributed application. Distributed applications can fail in all sorts of interesting ways that single-system applications never thought of. Furthermore, most debuggers cannot set breakpoints on both the client and the server.

To help the developer test applications, DCE provides a way to build a nondistributed version of a distributed application. Yes, you read that right; the developer can build a version of the application where the "remote" procedure calls are to procedures on the same node. The programmer can use this version to debug the client code and the server code. Of course, there is no guarantee that all the bugs will be found this way. Once the developer actually places the systems on different machines, hidden assumptions about timing, shared variables, state of internal static variables, the host operating system, and many other small details may turn up. For example, consider a remote procedure with static variables. On a single system, only one client will call the server procedure. Once the client invokes the same procedure on a server, however, it is possible for other clients to invoke the same server, upsetting assumptions about the state of the static variables.

DCE RPC: Cost/Benefits for Programmers

The biggest advantage to writing applications with the DCE RPC is that just about every major operating system supports it. Since so many networks are heterogeneous, the programmer gets all sorts of interoperability benefits. The DCE RPC package also solves naming and location, security, reliability, and many other problems.

While RPCs are "transparent," developers, users, and administrators need expanded skills.

The primary cost of developing with the DCE RPC (or any other RPC package) is learning how to use it. The programmer must learn a new language (the DCE RPC IDL) and must learn how to write server initialization routines. The programmer must also become familiar with all sorts of new DCE RPC skills, such as the binding techniques described in the next chapter. Programmers must become accustomed to the new and exotic ways in which distributed applications can fail. Programmers should anticipate a period of discomfort before distributed programming starts to feel natural. However, programmers who are already fairly experienced with UNIX or Windows sockets may become productive somewhat faster.

Companies that develop DCE RPC applications should beware of a hidden cost, namely, documentation. A DCE RPC application requires extra documentation telling customers how to install clients and servers, how to get them running, and how to maintain them.

DCE RPC: Costs/Benefits for System Administrators

Administering DCE RPC applications is a major effort. System administrators require lots of training to run a DCE site. To setup and maintain a DCE RPC application, the system administrator must become comfortable with all sorts of DCE concepts, including DCE services for security, naming, and time.

Summary

ONC/RPC support comes with nearly every modern UNIX system. For this reason, ONC/RPC continues to occupy a prominent position in the UNIX client/server market.

DCE/RPC support is not yet as freely available as ONC/RPC. However, since Microsoft and many leading UNIX vendors have chosen to support DCE/RPC, we expect DCE/RPC to gradually gain momentum.

CHAPTER 13   # Binding Clients to Servers

So far, we have worked with the romantic notion that for every client there's that one special server. We have also assumed that the same client and server remain united through a lifetime of tender RPCs.

Client and server bindings are not permanent.

In actuality, clients and servers can lead far less wholesome relationships. For example, a client can start out with one server and end up with a completely different server. For that matter, a server can be engaged in simultaneous relationships with dozens of clients.

It's a good opportunity to talk about threads.

This chapter examines the whole seedy business in an effort to find out how clients find the server(s) of their dreams. It will turn out that many clients dream of threaded servers, so this chapter also explains threads and how they are used by both clients and servers to improve performance and achieve asynchronous operation.

Binding

How does a client associate with a server?

"Binding" has several different, unrelated meanings in computer science. In client/server computing, **binding** means the mechanism by which a client associates itself with a server. The associated server can be a process on the server node or even a thread within a process.

The binding handle tells where the server is and also contains protocol information.

Before a client can successfully make an RPC to the server, the client must get a **binding handle** to the server. The term "handle" also has a lot of different meanings. Loosely defined, a handle is the data structure with which you grab an object; a handle is not the object itself. For instance, you grab a frying pan by its handle, not by the pan itself. Once you get the pan's handle, you can manipulate the pan. Similarly, a binding handle provides enough information for the client to access the server, but a binding handle is not the server itself.

Respond to the service advertisement, find out where the service is, and reuse that information for subsequent service requests.

The way a client obtains a binding handle in RPC-based programs is, strangely enough, analogous to the way that consumers find cars. For instance, suppose a car manufacturer named Citrus creates a new car model called The Lemondrop. Now, the Lemondrop may be the greatest car since James Bond's Aston Martin, but consumers won't know diddly about the car until Citrus advertises it on TV. Consumers who need a new car will watch the commercial with interest. At the end of the TV commercial, a man with a powerfully resonant voice announces where the nearest Citrus dealers are located. So, the consumers go to the dealership mentioned in the commercial. The dialog at the showroom goes something like this:

> Receptionist: "What kind of Citrus are you interested in?"
>
> Consumer: "A Lemondrop."
>
> Receptionist: "Head over to that door. Mr. Smith, our Lemondrop sales representative, will be right with you."

Let's say that the consumer does not buy the car on the first visit, but prefers to come back for a second and then a third visit. In subsequent visits, the consumer does not have to go through all the rigmarole to find the sales representative. After the first visit, the consumer already knows where the showroom is and already knows where within the showroom to find the sales representative.

You are undoubtedly wondering what this all has to do with client/server binding. Well, just as in car marketing, a client won't know about a server unless the server advertises[1]. In car marketing, a car company places an ad where consumers will be sure to see it. In RPC programming, servers advertise in a place that clients can see; namely, a database controlled by a location server. The server advertisement tells clients where (which node) to find that service.

Once the client knows the server node, the client must then find the location of the service on that server node. Instead of talking to a receptionist, the client typically talks to some small location server on the server node itself. Once the small location server tells the client where to find that particular service, the client now has a complete binding handle to the server. The first visit to the showroom is now complete. If the client needs to make subsequent calls to that same server, then the client need not go through all the location servers since the client already has the binding handle.

There are many variations for locating the service.

We have just described a generic mechanism of finding binding handles. However, there are some variations possible. For example, in the mechanism we described, the client has to endure two lookups in order to find the server. (The first lookup finds the node, the second lookup finds the server's location on that node.) By contrast, on some systems, the client can get a binding handle with only one lookup.

Implementation: Binding in DCE

DCE handles contain the node address and the communication protocol, which are provided by the CDS.

A DCE binding handle contains the following three pieces of information:

- The protocol by which the client and server will communicate. In DCE, for instance, TCP/IP and OSI can be supported.
- The node on which the server resides.
- The endpoint at which the server resides on the node. An endpoint is essentially a port at which the server is listening for requests.

Of these three pieces of information, the first two reside in the CDS and the last one resides in the *endpoint map* of the server node.

[1.] Yes, this really is the correct technical term.

WWW and DCE Use Similar Binding Handles

WWW is not an RPC-based system. Nevertheless, the three pieces of information in a DCE binding handle are quite similar to the three pieces of information in a URL on the World Wide Web. A URL contains a protocol, a server, and a port number. WWW supports a much wider range of protocols than DCE. See Chapter 8 for details on WWW.

A CDS database holds information about every server.

When a server initializes itself, it advertises its interface name (UUID), host address, interfaces, and the supported transport protocols to the CDS, creating a Directory Service entry. A client requests a service by the UUID of the service interface, as originally defined in the IDL. If we were to peer into the CDS, we would see that it manages a database something like the one shown in Table 6. This database lets the CDS look up an interface specified by a UUID.

Interface Name	UUID	Address of Host Node	Supported Protocols
Crunch	b9a76f80-412a-11ce-bee1-0000c049d04c	120.130.18.8	ip
Prime	225159c1-28f7-11ce-add1-0000c049d04c	120.130.18.20	ip & ncacn_ip_tcp
Traveler	ce0cfe41-412a-11ce-8448-0000c049d04c	120.130.18.20	ip
Crunch	b9a76f80-412a-11ce-bee1-0000c049d04c	120.130.18.20	ip

Table 6 Directory Service Entries in a CDS Database

One server can run on several nodes.

According to the preceding table, four servers are advertising in the cell. One server node (at address `120.130.18.20`) is running the **Prime**, **Traveler**, and (two) **Crunch** servers. So, if a client requests the **Prime** interface, the CDS will examine its database and discover that the **Prime** interface is located at host node `120.130.18.20`. Furthermore, **Prime** supports two protocols, ip (connectionless datagrams over `IP` using the `UDP` User Datagram Protocol) and `ncacn_ip_tcp` (connection-oriented virtual circuits using `TCP` over `IP`).

Advanced CDS Entries

CDS supports entries that are a good deal more sophisticated than those shown in Table 6. For instance, a group of servers with a common interface, such as a group of similar print servers, can advertise in a CDS group entry. If all the printers on a LAN advertise in the same group entry, a savvy client that needs printer services can go through the listings and pick the most suitable entry. For example, a client might pick a print server that supports PostScript or might pick a print server that physically is on the same floor as the client.

An endpoint map holds information about servers.

Meanwhile, each server node in a DCE cell maintains an endpoint map. The server places the interface and the endpoint (process ID) in an internal endpoint map. So, the endpoint map at host 120.130.18.20 might look something like Table 6.

Interface Name	Endpoint
Prime	245
Traveler	94

Table 7 An Endpoint Map on Host Node 120.130.18.20

A DCE client takes the following steps to find the `Prime` interface:

1. The client asks the CDS to find a `Prime` interface.

2. The CDS looks in its database and finds **Prime** at host node 120.130.18.20. The CDS also notes that **Prime** supports the `ip` protocol sequence.

3. CDS asks a process (for example, the **dced** on a UNIX node) on host node 120.130.18.20 to look in its endpoint map for **Prime**.

4. The process finds **Prime** at endpoint 245; the process returns this endpoint number to the CDS.

5. CDS returns a binding handle to the client. The returned binding handle specifies the server host node (`120.130.18.20`), the supported protocols (`ip` and `ncacn_ip_tcp`), and the endpoint (`245`).

DCE: Finding Servers on Other Cells

DCE can bind to a server in another cell using the GDA. DCE clients can bind to a server on another cell. This is true even if that other cell is on another site or even on another continent. To help locate servers in other cells, each CDS contains an element called the ***Global Directory Agent (GDA)***.

To help understand the role of the Global Directory Agent, consider Figure 37. In this figure, a client on a cell named **Red** is looking for a particular server on a cell named **Rover**.

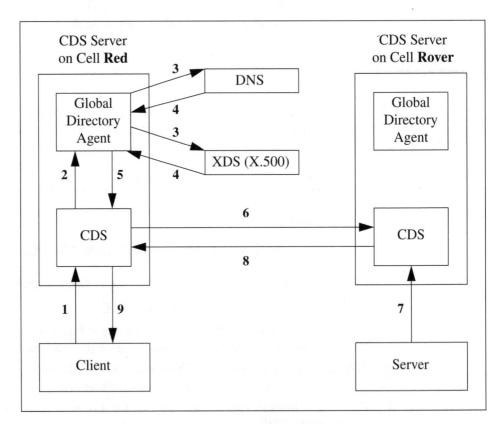

Figure 37 Local and Global Location Services

According to Figure 37, the client on **Red** follows these steps to find a server on **Rover**:

1. The client contacts the CDS to say that the client needs a binding handle for a particular server.

2. When the CDS on **Red** sees that the client is looking for a server outside the cell, the CDS on **Red** passes the foreign address to the Global Directory Agent on **Red**.

3. The Global Directory Agent on **Red** contacts XDS (X.500) or DNS depending on what kind of naming the client has used.

4. Once XDS or DNS finds the address of **Rover**'s site, it passes that address back to the Global Directory Agent on **Red**.

5. The Global Directory Agent passes the site name to the CDS on Red.

6. The CDS on Red contacts the CDS on Rover, asking for the binding handle.

7. The CDS on **Rover** contacts the server node and ultimately obtains a binding handle to the server.

8. The CDS on **Rover** passes the binding handle back to the CDS on **Red**.

9. The CDS on **Red** passes the binding handle back to the client.

DCE Binding for Application Programmers

This section explains what application programmers have to do when writing servers or clients to ensure that binding will take place.

Writing the Server Initialization Routine

Server initialization registers and advertises the service and tells what protocols are supported.

An application programmer advertises a DCE server by writing a server initialization routine. The code for a sample server initialization routine (server_init.c) for the **FindPrimes** example appears in Chapter 12. The server initialization routine provides information about the server to the CDS. The server program needs a **main** routine, so the server initialization routine is typically named **main**.

The CDS needs to know what transport protocols the server understands. The server_init.c example calls **rpc_server_use_all_protseqs** to tell the CDS that **FindPrimes** understands all supported protocols. The server initialization routine also needs to supply the name of the interface to the CDS.

In addition to CDS information, the server initialization routine also has to register its endpoint(s) for the endpoint map on the server host itself. The `server_init.c` example does that with a call to **rpc_ep_register**.

Finally, wait for the client request.

Finally, after the CDS and the endpoint map are taken care of, the server initialization routine has to issue an **rpc_server_listen** call to mark the beginning of waiting for an RPC request from a client.

Writing the Client

The client can select from three binding strategies.

The application programmer writing a client must pick one of the following three binding strategies:

- Automatic
- Implicit
- Explicit

Automatic involves the least work for the programmer and explicit involves the most. We will take a quick look at all three strategies.

Let DCE do it automatically. The programmer never has to consider the handle.

In *automatic binding*, the application programmer expects DCE to find the binding handle whenever the client makes an RPC. When we described the graceful, worry-free, transparent RPC programming model back in Chapter 11, we were assuming an automatic binding strategy. In automatic binding, the client programmer makes RPCs exactly the same as LPCs and lets DCE do all the hard work. Furthermore, the client will use the same server for subsequent calls to the interface. Writing a client that depends on automatic binding is simple. The example DCE client code (`client.c`) shown in Chapter 12 uses automatic binding.

Alternatively, you can get your own server handles.

In *implicit binding* and *explicit binding*, the application programmer takes full responsibility for finding a binding handle. To find a binding handle, the client programmer must write a short routine (perhaps 40 or 50 lines of code). This routine gathers binding handles based on the criteria the programmer requests. The most obvious criterion would be to find all servers having a certain name. For example, the routine might obtain binding handles for all servers on the local cell named **FindPrimes**. Additional criteria might include the kind of transport protocol the client prefers the server to speak.

A client using explicit binding passes a binding handle as the first argument to every RPC. For example, if the client calling **FindPrimes** was using explicit binding, then the RPC might look something like the following, where, for simplicity, we omit code to check for null pointers correct operation:

```
rpc_binding_handle_t a_binding_handle;
...
/* GetBindingHandleByName is written by the application
   programmer; DCE does not provide this routine. */
   a_binding_handle = GetBindingHandleByName("FindPrimes");
   ReturnedNumberOfPrimes= FindPrimes(a_binding_handle,
                                      lower, upper);
```

You can specify a handle with every call.

Explicit binding gives application programmers a lot of control. For example, suppose that **FindPrimes** is running on several different server nodes and that your application needs to call **FindPrimes** several times. With explicit binding, you could connect to a different server node on each call to **FindPrimes**.

Or, you can specify the handle once and it is used implicitly thereafter.

Implicit binding is similar to explicit binding in that both require the application programmer to get the binding handle. However, implicit binding does not give you the control of explicit binding. In implicit binding, once the application obtains the binding handle, the application tells DCE that the obtained binding handle will be used for all subsequent calls to that server. In implicit binding, the client does not pass a binding handle as the first argument to an RPC. Rather, the binding handle is implied.

DCE Binding for System Administrators

You have to start up the server before you can start up the client. Once you start up the server, the server waits for requests from clients.[1] The server continues running unless you explicitly kill it or unless it encounters a fatal error.

Starting the Server

We have written the server initialization routine (server_init.c) to allow the system administrator some flexibility in naming the interface. The relevant lines for a system administrator in server_init.c are as follows, again omitting the error checking that experienced programmers will be sure to include:

[1.] "They also serve who only stand and wait."—Milton

```
/* Advertise this service in the CDS. */
entry_name = (unsigned_char_t *)getenv(
                                  "PRIME_SERVER_ENTRY");
puts(entry_name);
rpc_ns_binding_export(rpc_c_ns_syntax_default,
                      entry_name,
                      PRIME_v1_0_s_ifspec, binding_vector,
                      NULL, &status);
```

The administrator can specify the environment and start the server.

These lines indicate that the system administrator has to assign a value to an environment variable named *PRIME_SERVER_ENTRY*. The value we assign to this environment variable should contain the following three pieces of information:

- The cell on which the server will run; the phrase /.: specifies the local cell
- The interface name (for example, **Prime**)
- The name of the server node on which the interface is running (for example, **JABBAR**)

There are numerous ways to set the value of an environment variable; the ways depend on the operating system and on the shell you are using. On UNIX, in a KornShell, type the following:

```
$ PRIME_SERVER_ENTRY=/.:/STATS_JABBAR
$ export PRIME_SERVER_ENTRY
```

You can now start the server program. From a KornShell on a UNIX system, you can start the **server** by typing the following:

```
$ server &
3837
I'm Waiting
```

Code in the `server_init.c` routine causes the server to register itself with the CDS.

Starting the Client

The way you start up a client depends on the binding strategy you have chosen. We have chosen automatic binding (the easiest) in our example. In automatic binding, you need to tell the client the name of the server entry in the CDS. You do this by setting the value of the environment variable **RPC_DEFAULT_ENTRY** to the name of the server entry; for example:

```
$ RPC_DEFAULT_ENTRY=/.:/PRIME_JABBAR
$ export RPC_DEFAULT_ENTRY
```

Now comes the magic moment when you start up the client and keep your fingers crossed. To invoke the client program on a UNIX system, you simply type the following:

```
$ client

Enter the lower integer: 4
Enter the upper integer: 10
There are 2 prime numbers between 4 and 10.
```

Unlike the server, the client will not run indefinitely. After the initial run of the client terminates, you can run the client again with a new data file and a new server binding.

Server Replication

Back in Chapter 10, we saw how databases could be replicated. Here now, we examine server replication.

You can have multiple, replicated servers for an interface.

Consider a network on which six clients want to access the **FindPrimes** server at around the same time. If there is only one copy of **FindPrimes** running on the network, then that one server will be strained and performance may be rather sluggish. But, suppose we put **FindPrimes** on two different server nodes as shown in Figure 38. By so doing, we have spread the computational load to two different machines. Clients should therefore see improved response time from servers.

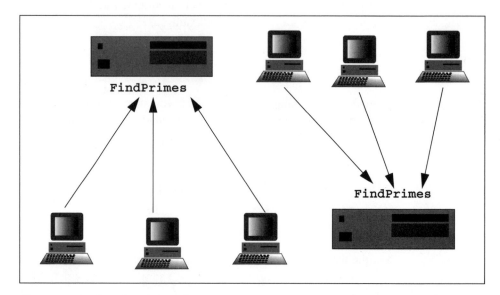

Figure 38   Replicating a Server

Clients must somehow select one of the identical servers.

At first glance, the scenario shown in Figure 38 looks pretty easy to implement. But as detectives in B-Movies say, "Yeah, but maybe just a little *too* easy." The diagram suggests a few questions:

- How did the clients know that there were two different versions of **Find-Primes**?
- How did each client choose its server?
- How did the server loads end up being so balanced?
- Is a client wed to the same server forever?

Notice in this example that, other than differences in performance and location, there is no reason a client would prefer one server over another. There is no state information or data that make a particular server unique.

DCE: Multilevel CDSs and Clearinghouses

CDS itself is a replicated DCE server.

You may never have considered a client/server framework to be a DBMS, and yet a DCE CDS is essentially a special-purpose DBMS. A CDS manages a database of interface names, such as the one shown back in Table 6. The database for a large DCE cell may grow to contain a very high number of interfaces. When you have a situation where one large database serves a lot of clients, you should start to think about replicating that database. DCE provides a multilevel replication strategy.

At the lowest level, DCE caches some important binding handles on the client node itself. If the client needs a binding handle and it is not in the local cache, DCE looks for the binding handle inside a clearinghouse as shown in Figure 39.

Clearinghouses replicate portions of the master CDS server.

A ***clearinghouse*** is a partial replica of the database managed by the master CDS. Typically, a clearinghouse contains only those interfaces that local nodes need. For example, the accounting department and engineering might each maintain separate clearinghouses. The accounting department clearinghouse might maintain a database of interfaces typically used by accountants, while the engineering department clearinghouse would maintain a database of popular engineering interfaces. If an interface cannot be found in a clearinghouse, then the client might possibly look in another clearinghouse. If the interface just cannot be found in a clearinghouse, then the client will have to look in the master CDS database.

Successful location can require interrogating several servers.

Each cell has one master CDS database, and each clearinghouse is a subset of this master CDS database. If the interface is not in the master CDS database, then the client might be out of luck. Of course, it is also possible that the server is on another cell.

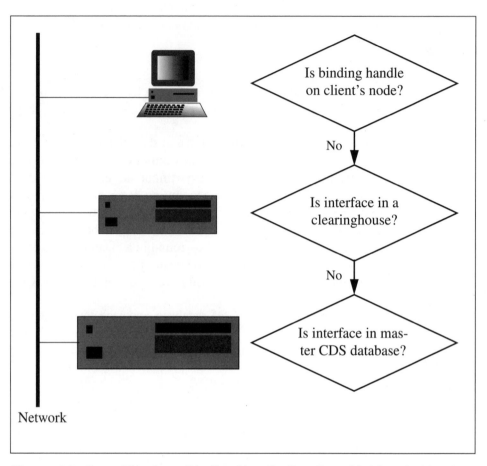

Figure 39 Searching for a Binding Handle Can Be a Multileveled Lookup

Threads

*A server
should be able
to process
client requests
concurrently.*

Sometimes, multiple clients request service from the same server. Therefore, a good system should provide a way for the server to process multiple, independent client requests concurrently. Broadly speaking, there are two ways to handle this situation.

One tactic would be to have the server replicate itself as a separate process every time a new client asks for its services. Each process has its own separate memory space and is scheduled independently by the OS. For example, in UNIX, a process can call the `fork()` system call to replicate itself, creating a totally independent server process to handle the new client request. The new client will then bind to a dedicated server process on the server host. There are several difficulties with the independent process approach:

Processes are not the most efficient way to provide concurrent service.

- Creating a new process is time-consuming to the host operating system because the entire process configuration must be re-created. The process configuration includes memory maps, variable data, and so on. Nevertheless, some operating systems do a good job of minimizing this overhead.
- Independent processes consume significant amounts of memory.
- Process-to-process *context switching* is also time-consuming. In context switching, the operating system switches from one server process to another.
- It is difficult for processes to access and control shared data.

Threads run within a process.

In short, independent server processes are "heavyweight" in terms of initialization time, switching time, and resource utilization and sharing. By contrast, *threaded processes* can execute more efficiently than unthreaded processes. A thread is an independent unit of execution within a process, but all the threads in a process share the same memory address space.

pthreads are the "open standard" and can support multi-processor machines.

Thread support is typically built into operating systems rather than into RPC packages. However, an RPC package may contain some interface to the underlying operating system thread routines. Thread support is built into Microsoft Windows NT, the Novell NetWare operating system, and most implementations of UNIX. Thread support is not built into DOS. POSIX 1003.4a specifies a thread interface, called *pthreads*, that is used by most UNIX implementations. **pthreads** is also an optional component of DCE. Windows NT threads, however, are not compliant with **pthreads**. OS threads support includes functions to create threads, for threads to exit, and to synchronize the threads within a process. Many operating systems permit threads to run concurrently on separate processors in multi-CPU systems.

Threaded Servers

An alternative to making more server processes is to keep only one server on the server system, but to enable that one server to handle multiple clients concurrently. A server built to exploit threaded processes is called a *threaded* server. A threaded server can handle requests from multiple clients without replicating itself. Independent threads of execution within a process, one for each client or potential client, share the same memory and code. Each client, then, will bind to both the single server process and to a dedicated thread within that process.

*DCE allows
you to specify
how many
threads a server
will support.*
The operating system allows each thread its own relatively small stack data space for arguments, results, and intermediate computations. The operating system can create threads quickly and can switch from one thread to another with minimal overhead. Threads are "lightweight" compared to processes.

In DCE RPC programming, the programmer writing the server initialization routine specifies the maximum number of threads that a server can efficiently handle. This specification is made as an argument to the `rpc_server_listen` routine. The server can simultaneously handle one client for each server thread. Any additional client request will be queued until a thread becomes available.

*The server code
needs to be
thread safe.*
Threaded servers must be ***thread safe***. To be thread safe, the programmer must put mutual-exclusion (***mutex***) locks on all sections of code that modify any shared variable. The mutex lock ensures that only one thread at a time can execute the locked section of code. A programmer can put mutex locks on chunks of code as small as a single line or as large as an entire routine.

To keep track of each thread, the operating system stores each client's state in a separate portion of the stack. Each client's thread is allowed to access other system resources, such as dynamic memory.

Threaded Clients

*Clients can use
threads to run
asynchronously.*
Some RPCs take a long time to complete. It would be nice if a client could get some useful work done while waiting for the RPC to complete. To accomplish this feat, clients can use threads. Threads allows clients to gain the performance and design advantages of asynchronous operation while retaining the advantages of RPCs.

Figure 40 shows the RPC flow of control for an application containing a threaded client. In this application, the programmer creates the following two separate threads:

• The main thread, which creates the second thread.
• The second thread (the RPC thread), which makes the RPC call.

After the main thread starts up the RPC thread, the main thread is free to get some useful work done. The main thread performs computations until it needs to wait for the RPC results before proceeding. The RPC thread can then signal RPC completion so that the main thread can continue. Operating system thread synchronization mechanisms, such as semaphores, can be used to implement the waiting and signaling. Alternatively, the main thread can wait for the RPC thread to exit.

Figure 40 shows a possible time sequence for the five events (marked as 1, 2, 3, 4, and 5). However, the events may occur in other orders. For example, Event 5 might occur before Event 4.

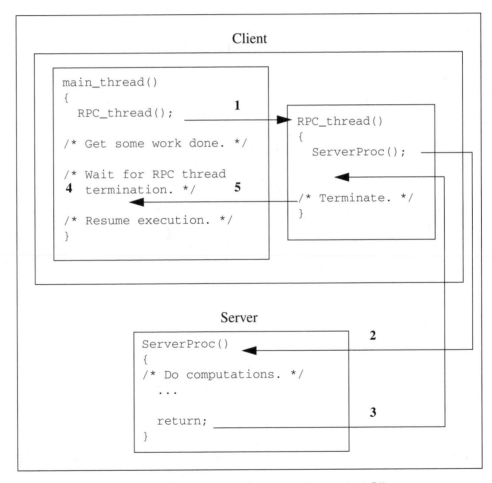

Figure 40 Flow of Control with RPCs and a Threaded Client

Summary

A naming and location service helps clients specify servers. Ultimately, a client must obtain a binding handle to a server that identifies the server's host machine, the server's process, and possibly the thread within the server process. Bindings can be short- or long-lived, depending upon a number of factors. Servers are often replicated to improve performance and availability.

Threads improve server performance and can also improve the performance of some clients.

CHAPTER 14

Distributed Object-Oriented Computing

Distributed object-oriented programming is the next big step.

Object-oriented programming (OOP) is the new frontier for distributed computing. Just as RPCs enable us to create distributed clients and servers using the procedural programming model, ***distributed OOP*** promises to create a world of distributed interoperable objects.

There are several competing architectures.

Distributed OOP technology is not as mature as RPC technology; there are no widely used distributed OOP frameworks to compare with ONC and DCE. However, two interrelated technologies are emerging as front runners in the distributed OOP sweepstakes:

- The ***Common Object Request Broker (CORBA)***
- The ***Component Object Model (COM)*** and its integration with Microsoft ***Object Linking and Embedding (OLE)***

As we shall see, distributed OOP bears a strong architectural similarity to RPC programming. In addition, some elements of COM/OLE are comparable toOpen Database Connectivity (ODBC). (See Chapter 9 for details on ODBC.)

The Benefits and the Vision

OOP is widely used in single-system computing, with C++ and SmallTalk being the two most popular development languages. There are any number of toolkits, object libraries, and other aids for object-oriented development.

OOP on single systems is widely practiced; programmers realize some important benefits.

OOP advocates claim the following benefits:

- Each object defines not only the data to be manipulated but also the set of **methods** (functions) allowed to manipulate that data.
- The actual method implementations are hidden from outside access.
- There is a well-defined set of interfaces to an object. The data can be accessed only through the interfaces.
- Interface inheritance allows more specialized object methods and implementations to be created from more general ones.
- Objects promote tangible benefits such as faster development, code reuse, higher reliability, and simpler maintenance.
- Object interfaces, or **wrappers**, can be put around existing legacy applications so that the legacy code can be easily incorporated into new applications.

Applications can distribute objects across nodes.

Moving beyond single-system OOP, the obvious next step is to implement distributed OOP. Many vendors are already supplying client/server object-oriented interfaces and development toolkits for operation on top of network transports, and, in some cases, on top of RPC frameworks such as DCE and ONC.

OOP and client/server offer compelling synergy.

Distributed objects, then, would seem to combine all the benefits of OOP and distributed computing. Some would say that the ultimate computing *Vision* is of a world in which many robust objects are spread across a network. In the Vision, each object runs on a node specialized to execute that kind of object. The application would simply ask to instantiate an object, and some middleware would magically locate the needed object on the network and instantiate it for the application. In fact, the application would not even have to know where the instantiated object comes from. Whenever an object was needed, it would be provided.

Figure 41 illustrates application programming under the Vision.

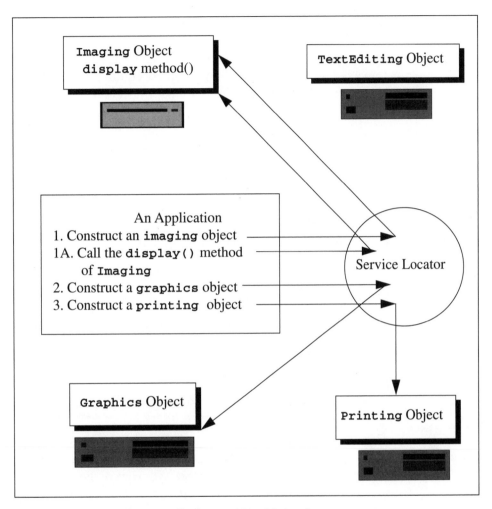

Figure 41 The Ultimate Programming Vision?

Figure 41 does not show where application objects actually run. They can run on the client or on server nodes spread across the network.

Application programming may start to resemble hardware manufacturing.

In grander versions of the Vision, the objects would be spread around nodes on a wide area network, perhaps across the Internet. Application programming would become a matter of browsing through a catalog of existing parts (objects) and requesting them by name, or perhaps even requesting them by capability. For example, a client might request the closest printing object that is capable of handling color PostScript images. The service locator would match the application's request with an actual object.

Different vendors could provide different objects and make them available to customers. The companies creating objects could carefully license their use and charge for access. (Note the need for authentication and authorization.)

Is It Ready Yet?

From time to time, we have made comments about technologies "maturing" or being "still immature." What we mean is that open implementations are not widely available. It may well be that the technical problems are understood, the standards are converging, and so on. Yet, it would be premature, for instance, for a large organization to start developing their strategic applications on that technology, even though pilot projects might be in order. By this measure, then, distributed object-oriented computing is still premature. However, we expect that distributed object-oriented computing will mature rapidly over the next few years.

The objects will be anything but mundane.

Throughout the book, we have focused on server objects providing mundane computer services, such as database access. You might find it more interesting to imagine entertainment servers that serve movies or video objects. The client could be a television containing a low-end CPU. When the user, sitting at home, requests a movie, the application running in the television could make a request for a particular movie object. The movie could be found and then served directly to the television set. Such applications are already a reality, though not widely deployed.

The OOP scene is filled with implementations and strategies, most of which overlap and interrelate in some way. For instance, IBM's ***System Object Model (SOM)*** implements and extends CORBA. We will focus on two implementations: CORBA and COM/OLE.

Implementation: CORBA

The ***Common Object Request Broker Architecture (CORBA)*** is a specification for distributing objects across multiple nodes on a network. CORBA's creator, the Object Management Group (OMG), puts out specifications only, not code.

Nearly everyone supports CORBA.

Many companies, large and small (Sun, IBM, HP, Digital, Iona, Tivoli, and more), have come out with software that is CORBA-compliant or have expressed their support.

CORBA specifies

- An architecture of cooperating client and server components
- A set of functionality
- An interface language for defining objects
- Language bindings to allow C and C++ programmers to access CORBA objects

CORBA, as of Version 2.0, also addresses interoperability. As CORBA 2.0 implementations become available, the distributed object Vision becomes more and more plausible. Furthermore, CORBA-compliant objects will be both portable and interoperable between different systems, much as DCE, ONC, and TCP/IP applications are today.

There are some familiar architectural components, including an IDL and stubs.

As we discuss CORBA, we will encounter some familiar terms, such as stubs, the Interface Definition Language, and bindings. The biggest change as we go from RPCs to distributed objects is that the interfaces become more general. In particular, CORBA interfaces support inheritance.

Here are the major CORBA components:

- The ***CORBA Interface Definition Language (CIDL)***. The CIDL is similar to the DCE IDL, but CIDL is both simpler to use and richer in features than the DCE IDL. The CIDL specifies objects, their methods, exceptions, and object hierarchy (inheritance). The CORBA IDL also provides ways for object references to be passed as arguments to methods. In addition, servers can even add interfaces dynamically.
- The ***CIDL compiler***. This component takes CIDL files as input and generates header files, client stubs, and server skeletons as output. The stubs and skele-

tons play roles similar to the DCE RPC stubs, and, among other things, manage data marshalling and unmarshalling.

There are new components and also new features, including dynamic invocation.

- The ***Object Request Broker*** (***ORB***). The ORB allows objects to make transparent requests to other objects and to receive the responses. The ORB provides interoperability between objects on different systems. The ORB also manages binding, communications, and other details.

- The ***Basic Object Adapter*** (***BOA***). The BOA is a component of the ORB that supports server object activation.

- A ***Dynamic Invocation Interface*** (***DII***). The DII allows clients to discover and invoke new interfaces. In DCE and ONC, procedural interfaces are static and must be known to the developer. With DII, a client can find new interfaces at run time and invoke the methods corresponding to these interfaces.

- A ***Dynamic Server Interface*** (***DSI***). A DSI permits servers to create new interfaces for clients. CIDL also expresses the DII and DSI interfaces.

- An ***Interface Repository***. As the name implies, this component contains interface definitions. The definitions are either static (defined through the IDL) or dynamic (defined to support the DSI and DII).

- An ***Implementation Repository***. This component is a database containing names of object implementations (servers) and their locations. The BOA uses the Implementation Repository to activate objects.

CORBA Code Example

The following is an example CORBA IDL (CIDL) for a **statistics** interface:

```
interface statistics {
    const long MaxArray = 1000;
    exception MathFault {short FaultType};
    float FindMedian (in DataArray[MaxArray],
                      in long ElementCount);
    void Sort (in DataArray[MaxArray],
               out Array SortArray,
               in  long  ElementCount);
    float AvgMinMax (in DataArray[MaxArray],
                     out float ArrayMax,
                     out float ArrayMin,
                     in long  ElementCount)
           raises (MathFault);
};
```

Interfaces allow for exceptions and multiple methods, as well as inheritance.

The preceding IDL code specifies the following:

- The name of the interface (**statistics**).
- A data type declaration (**MaxArray**) that can be used elsewhere in the IDL file.
- A programmer-defined exception (**MathFault**). An exception is an error in the server that the server wants to convey to the client. Servers can also return error indications.
- Three methods (**FindMedian**, **Sort**, and **AvgMinMax**). A client can call any of these three methods. Each method has several input and output parameters designated with an attribute of **in** or **out**. An attribute of **inout** is also possible. The **AvgMinMax** method can raise the **MathFault** exception in case the operation encounters a fault, such as arithmetic overflow, while computing the average.

How Similar Is CORBA IDL to DCE IDL?

The preceding CORBA IDL file is reasonably similar to a DCE IDL file. However, we should note a few significant differences. Unlike DCE IDL, CORBA IDL does not use UUIDs to identify objects. Furthermore, CORBA IDL can define multiple methods per interface; a DCE IDL file can define only one method per interface. In addition, CORBA IDL supports exceptions; DCE IDL does not.

The CIDL compiler generates a client stub and server skeleton just as the DCE IDL compiler generates a client stub and server stub. The CORBA server skeleton plays the same role as the DCE server stub. The CORBA IDL compiler must also produce a header file for use in client and server source code.

How do you access the methods from your programming language?

Language bindings allow a program in C, C++, and Smalltalk (the most likely choice in the long run), or some other language to invoke an object method in a way that seems natural in that language. The C language binding makes it possible for a C programmer to invoke CORBA interface methods using familiar C syntax. For example, the following C client code requests the object methods to sort an array and to find its average:

```
#include "statistics.h"

statistics so1, so2;
Environment Env1, Env2;
float vector [100], f, Avg, Max, Min;

    /*.... Invoke the FindMedian method...             */
    f = statistics_FindMedian (so1, &Env1, vector, 200);
    /* Determine if the object invocation was successful
       by checking for an exception in the environment. */
    if (Env1._major != NO_EXCEPTION) {/* Determine fault */}
    /* Get the average, min, and max                    */
       Avg = statistics_AvgMinMax (so2, &Env2, vector,
                                   &Max, &Min, 200);
    /* Determine if there was a math fault              */
    if ex_MathFault.FaultType != 0)
       { /* A fault occurred. Report it.                */}
    /* More code ..........                             */
```

The preceding code begins by including statistics.h, which is the header file
generated by the IDL compiler. This header file defines all the types and the function prototypes that represent the methods or operations. DCE programmers will
be relieved to see that there is no server initialization routine. The code checks for
generic exception errors by testing Env1._major, and it checks for user-defined
exceptions by testing ex_MathFault.FaultType. The CORBA C binding specifies
these naming conventions.

The interface name is a prefix to the method name.

By convention, the name of each method uses the interface name as a prefix.
Thus, the client code calls **statistics_FindMedian** rather than just plain
FindMedian.

Notice that each time the client code calls a method, the client code must specify
two additional arguments not present in the IDL definition. For example, the IDL
definition for **FindMedian** method specifies two arguments; however, the client
code actually passes four arguments to **FindMedian**. The first argument to each
method is an object reference. The second argument to each method is an environment variable. The environment variable is a structure; one of the fields of this
structure (*FaultType*) holds information about user-defined exceptions.

CORBA: Clients, Servers, Stubs, and ORBs

*An ORB
provides an
interface to
network
transport .*

Interaction between application (client) objects and server objects (often called ***implementation objects***) occurs through their stubs and skeletons. (The server skeleton is really a stub.) The two stubs communicate though the Object Request Broker (ORB), which ultimately communicates through a network transport.

An object can act as both client and server.

Just as with DCE or ONC, remote CORBA clients and servers generally occupy totally distinct address spaces. Therefore, all relevant data must be communicated as part of the client's request. Figure 42 shows the simple CORBA client/server interaction. By comparing this picture with the RPC Programming Model of Chapter 11, we see that the ORB plays a role analogous to that of the RPC run time.

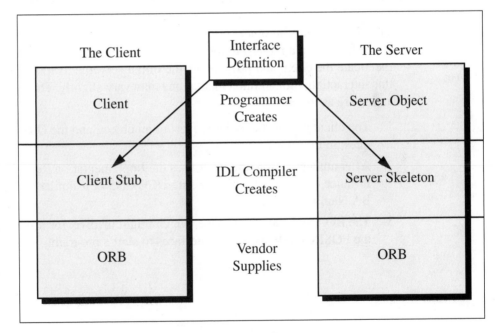

Figure 42 Distributed Objects and ORBs

Figure 42 raises the following questions:

- How do the ORBs communicate over the network?

- Is there any security? Can DCE or ONC provide security or other features? Will DCE and ONC security be consistent with OMG's CORBA security model?

- How are all of the distributed computing problems, outlined in Chapter 2, addressed? Are these solutions compatible with other distributed computing frameworks? For instance, will DCE naming suffice to name CORBA objects?

- What is the messaging format so that object references and data can be communicated between clients and servers over the network transport?

These are all good questions, and thereby hangs a tale. We will explore the interoperability part of this tale in Chapter 17.

CORBA: Client/Service Binding and Object Activation

The BOA starts the server and creates the binding.

The client obtains an object reference, typically from a location service, and uses that reference in a request to the Basic Object Adapter (BOA). The BOA can authenticate the client and provide for the initial server activation. Figure 43 shows this interaction, though implementations may vary slightly. The steps in this interaction are as follows:

1. The client makes the initial request to an object, and the ORB sends the request to the BOA.

2. After authentication, the BOA uses the Implementation Repository to find an instance of the server object (using DCE CDS or a similar service as a CORBA Naming Service).

3. The BOA activates the service, which might involve, for instance, invoking the POSIX `fork` and `exec` interfaces to start a program.

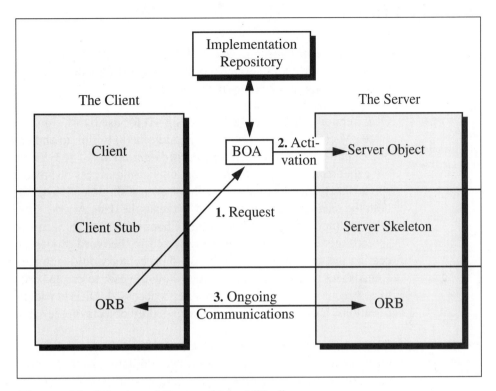

Figure 43 Client and Server Object Binding

Subsequent interactions use the handle.

Once the client object is activated, the client does not need the BOA for further help. The communication mechanism, the object reference format, and all the other details depend on the answers to the questions at the end of the preceding section.

CORBA object references, which include partial or complete binding handles, can be either static and dynamic. Object references have an additional attractive feature not available in DCE: object references can be passed to other objects. Therefore, one object (A) can create an object reference to a remote object (B). Object A can then pass that object reference to some other (possibly remote) object (C). Object C can then access B.

Implementation: COM, OLE, and Object Broker

The *Component Object Model* (*COM*) is Microsoft's object model. COM, among other things, provides services to the Microsoft *Object Linking and Embedding* (*OLE*), leading to the acronym COM/OLE.

OLE is popular for PC applications on a single system.

OLE Version 2 is a set of services designed for use by PC applications (Microsoft Excel, Microsoft Word, Lotus 1-2-3, and others) to link to and embed one type of object into another to create *compound documents*. The OLE document objects are called *containers*. A typical container could access a spreadsheet or part of a spreadsheet, such as a table, graph, or even a single cell. The container accesses both the data and the method used to create the data. A word processor might use OLE to import a spreadsheet table. Changes to the table, caused by changes to spreadsheet data, would then be reflected in the word processor document. Accessing the table from within the word processor would automatically invoke the spreadsheet. Additional capabilities allow the user to create scripts of commands to be executed whenever the container is accessed. OLE is widely used by PC applications, but, by itself, OLE can access only objects on the same system.

COM extends the power of OLE to client/ server systems.

OLE is layered on COM. With COM providing distributed object services, COM/OLE can overcome OLE's single-system limitation so that applications can transparently access remote objects. The remote objects are not necessarily CORBA-compliant.

The OLE interfaces are very different from CORBA's. The first problem is to map them so that a client program can use OLE interfaces to access COM objects. The second problem is to support distributed objects.

Digital's ObjectBroker integrates COM/OLE, CORBA, and DCE.

Digital has proposed one solution to these problems. Here are the component parts of Digital's distributed COM/OLE architecture. There are, of course, other solutions with similar objectives and architectures.

- Digital *ObjectBroker*, which supports CORBA using DCE for interoperability.
- A *portal* on the PC intercepts COM calls, translates them to CORBA messages, and sends the message to ObjectBroker (on the PC) for communication to an object server.
- DCE, which provides for communication between ObjectBroker and distributed objects.

It is transparent to the PC application.

The objective of this architecture is to allow OLE applications to access data objects from UNIX, OpenVMS, and other servers running ObjectBroker. Ultimately, one can assume that the data objects could be on any CORBA 2.0 system. The access is transparent to the PC application user (it appears to be a local OLE access), has all of the advantages of accessing a distributed file or database, and brings the additional advantages of distributed OLE document objects to the PC. Distributed data can be dynamically linked or embedded into PC personal productivity applications. Additionally, COM/OLE with ObjectBroker should provide for interoperability and sharing between existing Component Object Model (the other COM) objects and CORBA objects.

COM/OLE combined with Object Broker can be regarded as an object-oriented information interface designed for PC integration into the enterprise and data center. Figure 44 shows the architecture.

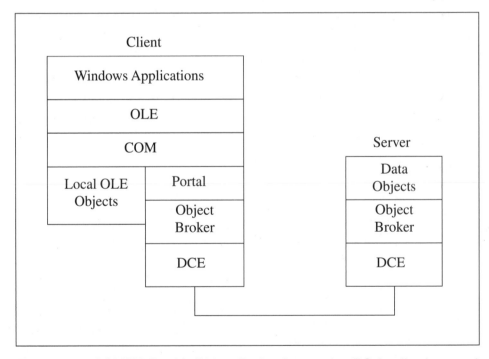

Figure 44   COM/OLE, with Object Broker Integrating PC Applications and CORBA Objects

Object Wars

Several object models, implementations, and interoperability solutions are currently available. Vendor alliances are vigorously competing to promote their special interests. While this situation may be confusing to users and developers, competition should result in stronger solutions if there is convergence to one or two widely deployed standards.

Which object models?

COM/OLE provides the PC developer with both the OLE and CORBA interfaces. Developers are likely to continue to use the OLE interfaces, which are already popular for PC applications. It is also plausible to expect that OLE will become available on UNIX and other non-Microsoft systems, creating an interesting contest between OLE and CORBA for object model dominance.

OpenDoc, DSOM, and CORBA (again).

Meanwhile, as might be expected, OLE is not without capable competition. OpenDoc, originated by Apple and sponsored by IBM and Novell, also deals with compound documents. Distribution is achieved using IBM's Distributed System Object Model (DSOM), which implements CORBA.

Exactly which object models and interoperability architectures will prevail is not clear at this time. It is possible that multiple solutions will survive. Certainly, users will ultimately benefit in the long run as client applications based on OpenDoc and OLE are able to access distributed objects on a wide variety of systems.

Summary

Open, distributed object-oriented computing is still in its formative stage, but standard, interoperable implementations should emerge in the very near future. OMG's CORBA seems to be a part of nearly every strategy and of most products. Chapter 17 discusses CORBA 2.0 interoperability.

Many aspects of distributed OOP closely parallel what we have seen with the RPCs and ODBC. Stubs, interface definition languages, binding, and integration into PC applications are all very much in evidence.

The advantages of distributed OOP and the ability to integrate distributed objects into client applications ensure that COM/OLE and OpenDoc will find wide acceptance in client/server environments.

CHAPTER 15

Distributed Graphics

1975

In the 1970s, vast herds of minicomputers and mainframes roamed the earth. These beasts typically had one powerful CPU driving several dozen "dumb" terminals, such as the DEC VT100 and IBM 3270. Although these CPUs were very expensive, adding extra users was relatively cheap. All you had to do to add a new user was to buy a relatively inexpensive dumb terminal and hook it up to the minicomputer or mainframe. However, dumb terminals had one very important limitation: Dumb terminals could not display sophisticated graphics.

1982

In the 1980s, PCs, Macintosh computers, and UNIX workstations began to displace the minicomputer and mainframe herds. Instead of sharing a CPU, individual users now got their own CPU. Users also started to get terminals that could display sophisticated graphics. Not only did graphics make programs more entertaining, but the graphical user interfaces also made programs much easier to use. The new terminals had lots more features than their VT100-class predecessors. In fact, these terminals developed so many smarts that they sometimes became the single most expensive component of the computer system.

1986

By the mid-1980s, the question became, "How can we decouple terminals from the other components?" In other words, how can we give individual users a powerful graphics terminal without having to give them a powerful CPU and disk drive?

1990

By the early 1990s, *distributed graphics* had become reality. Figure 45 shows a typical modern distributed graphics system in which a powerful CPU runs programs and remote, smart, graphics terminals display the program's output.

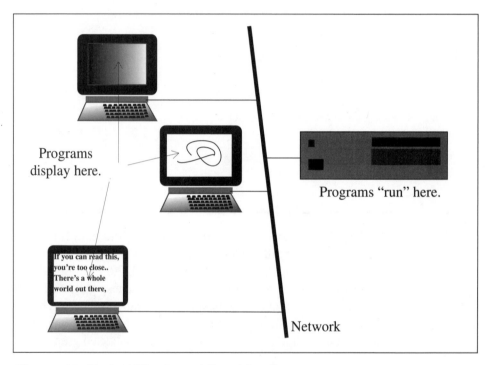

Figure 45 Typical Distributed Graphics System

Synchronous vs. Asynchronous Distributed Graphics

Distributed graphics programs can run either synchronously or asynchronously. A graphics program running *synchronously* cannot issue a new graphics command until the preceding command has been completed. A graphics program running *asynchronously* issues graphics commands without waiting for confirmation that the preceding command has been completed.

Synchronous programs pause frequently.

Suppose a graphics application contains code to draw a circle and then to draw a line. Further suppose that the graphics system is distributed so that the terminal is connected to the CPU through the network. If the graphics program is running synchronously, then this is what happens:

1. The application asks the terminal to draw a circle. The graphics application stops running until Step 4.
2. The terminal draws the circle.
3. The terminal sends confirmation to the CPU that the circle has been drawn.
4. Upon receiving this confirmation, the CPU resumes execution of the graphics program. The graphics program asks the terminal to draw a line. The graphics application stops running until Step 7.
5. The terminal draws the line.
6. The terminal sends confirmation to the CPU that the line has been drawn.
7. The graphics application resumes execution.

Asynchronous programs do not pause.

If this same program is running asynchronously, then the following happens:

1. The program asks the terminal to draw a circle and a line.
2. The terminals draws a circle and a line.

Programs running asynchronously never stop to wait for confirmation from the terminal. For this reason, asynchronous execution tends to be significantly faster than synchronous execution.

Asynchronous is more efficient.

Synchronous execution ends up creating a lot more network traffic than asynchronous execution. That is because each graphics command generates two messages on a synchronous program (from CPU to terminal and from terminal back to CPU), while each graphics command generates only one message on an asynchronous program (from CPU to terminal).

Asynchronous has limitations.

Asynchronous execution does have a few adverse side effects. For one thing, it is almost impossible to display animation asynchronously. In addition, asynchronous graphics programs are harder to debug than synchronous ones.

Costs/Benefits of Distributed Graphics

This section describes the challenges and opportunities in distributing graphics. The bottom line is that distributed graphics are already widely and successfully deployed, but users and programmers need to be aware of the trade-offs.

Costs/Benefits for Programmers

Sorry, but you have to use the API.

Many PC software packages come with an API for graphics routines. Just call this graphics routine, the documentation promises, and a line will be rendered between the specified endpoints. These APIs are relatively easy to use, which possibly explains why many professional programmers avoid them. DOS programmers often create graphics by skipping the API and going straight to the bits in the PC's display memory. (Turn on a bit in display memory and a pixel will be illuminated; turn on enough bits in display memory and a line will appear.) Going straight to memory can make a program run faster.

A graphics programmer cannot easily twiddle bits in the display memory of a remote terminal. Therefore, graphics programmers really do have to go through the API to render distributed graphics. To some "creative" programmers, using the real API is a brutal restraint on freedom. However, trying to see this restraint in the best possible way, we feel obligated to point out that using the API can help produce readable, maintainable code. In reality, this battle (converting from direct access to hardware to using an API) has already been fought and won on many other fronts (disks, I/O of all sorts, memory management, and so on).

Distributed graphics APIs are more complex.

The API for distributed graphics is necessarily somewhat more complicated than the API for local graphics. For example, a line-drawing routine on a nondistributed graphics system requires arguments specifying the line's endpoints. A similar line-drawing routine on a distributed graphics system requires the same endpoint arguments, plus the name of the graphics terminal on which the line is to be rendered.

Network traffic presents problem for animation.

The speed of all distributed applications is limited in part by the speed of the network. However, slowdowns in distributed graphics applications can be particular nuisances. For example, suppose a distributed graphics application runs into a network traffic jam while displaying an image. If that happens, the user might see only half of an image and then have to wait a few seconds to see the other half. Slowdowns are particularly annoying in animation.

*Events
cannot
always be
gathered in
real time.*

Distributed input devices can create significant challenges for programmers. Suppose an input device, such as a keyboard or mouse, is not connected to the machine on which the graphics application is running. In this case, input events have to be relayed from the input device to the application. Now, for some kinds of applications, such as word processors, it is not a problem if the input message is delayed by network traffic. For other applications, particularly those in which the user requires frequent and precise feedback, network traffic jams are a big problem.

*Speed up
performance
by avoiding
unnecessary
network
access.*

Distributed graphics programmers should try to reduce network messages whenever possible. In large part, this means trying to run programs in asynchronous mode. Other ways to reduce network access are more subtle. For example, consider two different ways in which a graphics program could render a rectangle:

- Call a rectangle drawing routine once.
- Call a line drawing routine four times (one time for each line of the rectangle).

On a local graphics application, it does not matter which of the preceding calls the programmer chooses. On a distributed graphics application, calling the line-drawing routine four times creates four times the network traffic as calling the rectangle-drawing routine only once.

In summary, it is somewhat harder to write a distributed graphics program than to write a nondistributed graphics program. There is simply more to worry about.

Costs/Benefits for Users

The use of distributed graphics produces two issues for users, one performance-related and the other psychological.

The primary issue for users is one of speed. Distributed graphics applications tend to run a little slower than their nondistributed counterparts.

The psychological issue for users is that they sometimes feel slighted using special graphics terminals that "don't come with a computer attached." "Computers with CPUs" tend to be given to the organization's heavyweights.

Costs/Benefits for System Administrators

Setting up a distributed graphics system generally involves very little extra work for system administrators. In fact, by centralizing CPUs and distributing graphics, a system administrator's overall workload is usually diminished.

Saving Money by Distributing Graphics

Back in the expansive 1980s, Omnibus Inc. employed 50 design engineers. Each engineer got his or her own UNIX workstation, complete with fancy terminal, CPU, and disk drive. Engineers were ecstatic, but system administrators were getting exasperated trying to back up all 50 disk drives. In addition, each workstation had its own copy of the UNIX operating system, so it took weeks to install operating system patch releases. System administration costs were exorbinant.

In the 1990s, Omnibus replaced their aging UNIX workstation fleet with four powerful UNIX compute server machines and 50 remote graphics terminals. Software installs now have to be done on only four disk drives instead of 50. Backups are also far simpler.

When you think about it, Omnibus has followed a back-to-the-future strategy; they find themselves with a modern version of a 1970s-style time-sharing system. The big difference is that engineers of the 1990s end up with smart and powerful graphics terminals.

Implementation: X Window System

The X Window System (known more simply as X) is the most important distributed graphics system available today.

*X was
spawned from
desperation.*

Before the development of X, UNIX workstation vendors all featured their own proprietary graphics APIs and their own proprietary graphics hardware. Consequently, it was very expensive to take a graphics application written for one kind of workstation and port it to another vendor's workstation. Since porting was so expensive, some software companies in the early 1980s only offered their application on one particular platform and thus forfeited the rest of the UNIX workstation market. Application developers clamored for standards.

*X programs
used to run
slowly.*

M.I.T., in partnership with several UNIX workstation vendors, developed X in the mid-1980s. Initial adoption was fairly slow, mainly because the hardware of the times was far too slow to run X applications efficiently. In these early days of X, an X application might run several orders of magnitude slower than its non-X counterpart. By the early 1990s, however, workstation hardware had caught up to the needs of X, and X buried its proprietary competition. Today, almost every commercial graphics application running under UNIX uses X. In addition, X now runs on PCs and Apple Macintosh computers. Note that X is not embedded in an operating system; rather it is a set of programs and libraries that run independently of the operating system.

What Is It?

X is a client/server system. Most newcomers find the X definition of "server" and "client" rather strange. In X parlance, a "client" is a graphics application program. An X "server" is a program that controls a visual output device (a screen) and one or more input devices (for instance, a mouse, a keyboard, or a track ball).

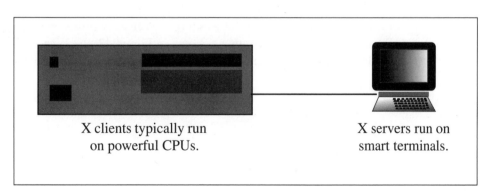

X clients typically run
on powerful CPUs.

X servers run on
smart terminals.

Figure 46   Client and Server Definitions Seem Backwards in X

X clients and servers just seem backwards.

An X "client" typically runs on a powerful machine; the "server" often runs on a comparatively weak machine. A popular cliche says that X reverses the usual meanings of client and server; however, when all is said and done, the X definitions are indeed accurate. After all, X clients really do make requests like, "Draw me a line," and X servers really do service requests. X servers actually render the line on the screen. Similarly, when a client requests a particular input service ("Alert me the next time the user clicks the mouse over here."), it is the X server that satisfies that request.

X protocol defines a low-level interface between client and server.

The client and server programs communicate with each other through the ***X protocol***. This protocol establishes a mechanism for the client to make requests to the server and for the server to relay events back to the client. For example, if a client wants the server to render a line on the screen, the client passes a particular number to the server. The protocol details are important to those porting an X server to a new terminal, but are seldom important to application programmers.

By default, X programs run asynchronously. However, a programmer or user can use a command-line option (`-synch`) to force an X program to run synchronously.

An X server grabs user input and displays program output.

Many different kinds of terminals can act as an X server. (The most common place to run an X server is on an ***X terminal***, which is detailed later in this chapter.) Being an X server really just means being able to respond appropriately to the X protocol. For example, when the client sends a line-drawing request through the protocol, it is up to the X server to respond by rendering a line on the screen. The X server has to understand what it takes for this particular screen to be able to draw a line. Some screens have fairly sophisticated graphics cards that can calculate the line "in hardware." Other screens don't have that level of hardware support and have to rely on the X server itself to twiddle the appropriate bits in display memory. At any rate, as shown in Figure 47, the X server acts as an intermediary between X clients and the screen and between X clients and input devices.

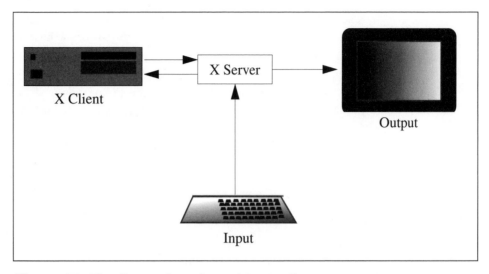

Figure 47   The Server Acts As an Intermediary

X protocol is operating-system independent...

All X clients and X servers understand the same X protocol. The protocol contains no information about instruction sets or operating systems. Thus, any client can talk to any server even if the client and server are running on different kinds of machines. For example, a client running on an HP-UX machine can request display from a server running on a Tektronix X terminal. In fact, one X client could request simultaneous displays on dozens of different kinds of machines running X servers.

X applications are not.

We don't want our enthusiasm to mislead you; the client is itself an application program, and, like all application programs, has machine and operating system dependencies. Thus, you could not execute an HP-UX client on an AIX machine. However, since X source code is highly portable, a programmer can typically port an X client from HP-UX to AIX simply by recompiling.

Hardware and Software Requirements of X

To run X, you need an X server, and ...

To run X, the node to which the terminal is attached must be running an X server.

- If you are buying an X terminal, then an X server automatically comes with the machine. The server is generally installed on a PROM in the X terminal.

- If you are buying a UNIX workstation, then you can be almost positive that an X server is available for your terminal. Usually, the company you purchase the workstation from will supply an X server as part of the base software package.
- If you are buying a new PC or an Apple Macintosh, you will probably be able to acquire an X server for it. Note that X servers are rarely bundled with the base software package that comes on the PC or Apple Macintosh. Therefore, you should expect to pay something extra to purchase an X server.

By the way, an X client node does not have to be running an X server. In fact, some X client nodes do not even have a terminal.

X clients, and ...   X clients run best on powerful nodes that support multiprocessing. Even the simplest Motif applications are memory hogs, so make sure that the X client node has plenty of memory.

a fast network,   An X client node and X server node must be able to communicate through a net-
and ...   work. Network traffic between X clients and X servers tends to be steadier (less bursty) than network traffic between most other kinds of clients and servers. X clients and servers are normally connected through a high-speed local area network. However, you can also connect X clients and X servers via a modem through a regular phone line. (Performance over a regular phone line may be frustratingly slow.) Furthermore, you can also connect X clients and X servers through a wide area network such as the Internet. However, our practical experience suggests that X over the Internet can be painfully slow.

TCP/IP.   For you to run X applications, the transport and network layers need to be occupied by either TCP/IP or DECNET. TCP/IP is the more common choice.

X terminals   The predominant graphics terminal used in distributed graphics systems is called
are smart   an *X terminal*. Quite a few companies make X terminals, so competition is easing
distributed   the price somewhat. Some manufacturers, such as Hewlett-Packard, are all-pur-
graphics   pose computer vendors. Others, such as NCD, specialize in X terminals.
terminals.

The most expensive part of an X terminal is the monitor. Part of the expense is size; most buyers opt for relatively large X terminal monitors. Unlike most computer components, monitors do not tend to go down in price the longer you wait. The other components of an X terminal (a keyboard, memory, an Ethernet controller, a small CPU) will undoubtedly show price/performance improvements as the years go by. However, these other components typically account for a relatively small percentage of the cost.

X terminals
may be the
cheapest
graphics
desktop
solution.
X terminals can provide a desktop graphics terminal for less money than a full-fledged UNIX workstation or even a PC, although the price gap is closing at the low-end of the PC and workstation market. The cost difference is due to the fact that X terminals do not contain many of the high-priced components (lots of memory, a disk drive, a state-of-the-art CPU, and so on) found in UNIX workstations.

X: An Application Programmer's View

X, like most sophisticated software systems, is layered. Figure 48 illustrates the three most important X API layers:

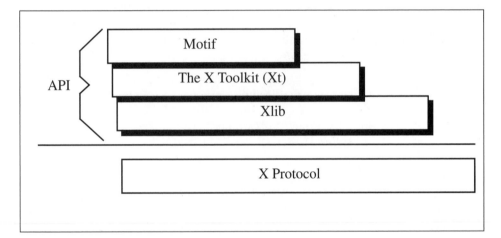

Figure 48   X Programming Layers

We now take a look at each of the three levels.

Xlib

Xlib is the
lowest level
in the API
hierarchy.
The lowest programmable level of X, **Xlib**, is a library of graphics primitives routines. The routines include ways to draw geometric figures, render text, and specify colors and fill patterns. Xlib can be compared to assembly language in that both give the programmer a great sense of control over what happens in the program but at a cost of having to write an awful lot of code.

The start of most Xlib applications is a call to the **XOpenDisplay** routine; for example:

```
Display *DisplayHandle;
char *name_of_display;
. . .
DisplayHandle = XOpenDisplay(name_of_display);
```

Xlib provides a binding handle routine.

The **XOpenDisplay** routine gets the client a binding handle to a server. The Xlib programmer can either specify the name of the server in the code itself or let the user specify it at run time. Either way, the returned *DisplayHandle* variable will be the first argument to all subsequent rendering routines in the application.

One X client can connect to multiple X servers.

An application can call **XOpenDisplay** multiple times in order to establish a connection to multiple servers. For example, the following code fragment calls **XOpenDisplay** twice, once to establish a connection on a node called **magic** and another time to establish a connection on a node called **bird**:

```
Display *DisplayHandle1, *DisplayHandle2;
char *name_of_display1="magic:0";
char *name_of_display2="bird:0";
. . .
DisplayHandle1 = XOpenDisplay(name_of_display1);
DisplayHandle2 = XOpenDisplay(name_of_display2);
. . .
XDrawLine(DisplayHandle1, ...); // render a line on magic
XDrawLine(DisplayHandle2, ...); // render a line on bird
```

(We will explain that mysterious :0 that comes after **magic** and **bird** later in this chapter.)

The user can specify the server at run-time.

The preceding example hardcoded the name of the servers inside the code. In fact, most applications do not specify the name of the server. Instead, most applications get the name of the server at run time. That is, most applications expect the user, not the programmer, to specify the name of the server. The user specifies the name of the server with an environment variable *(DISPLAY)* or with a command-line option (-display). For example, to start up a client named **DateMaker** and tell it to connect to the server on **bird**, you would issue the following command:

```
$ DateMaker -display bird:0
```

The X Toolkit (Xt)

Xt provides a mid-level API.

An application programmer uses Xt to manipulate GUI objects, typically the GUI objects (*widgets*) of Motif. The Xt routines primarily exist as base software for the more sophisticated software that appears above it in the hierarchy.

The X Toolkit provides routines analogous to `XOpenDisplay` that allow an X Toolkit application (or a Motif application) to make a client/server connection.

Motif

Motif is the most important layer.

After vendors embraced X as the distributed graphics base technology, it quickly became apparent that the X community also needed a standard way of building graphical user interfaces (GUIs). A GUI lets a user supply input by pointing and clicking a mouse (or other pointing device) rather than by typing command strings. Sun was first with an X-based GUI product called OpenLook. However, the Open Software Foundation countered with Motif. After a protracted, ugly war between the competing vendors, Sun ultimately conceded defeat. The war was over and Motif had won. In 1994, the Open Software Foundation turned over stewardship of Motif to the X Consortium.

Widgets are the building blocks of Motif applications.

From an application programmer's point of view, Motif is primarily a set of GUI building blocks called *widgets*. To create a GUI with Motif, the application programmer places the appropriate widgets in the appropriate places on the screen. For example, the Motif PushButton widget displays a rectangle with some text or a bitmap inside; when the user clicks the mouse anywhere within the rectangle, the widget invokes a routine of the application programmer's choice. To create a menu, a Motif application programmer can organize several PushButton widgets into a column.

Motif divides widgets into two primary categories:

- *Primitive widgets*, which are the widgets that users actually see. Table 8 shows some of the primitive widgets.
- *Manager widgets*, which programmers use to organize sets of primitive widgets or sets of other manager widgets. Table 9 shows a few manager widgets.

Widget	Purpose
Label	Displays uneditable text or an uneditable bitmap.
PushButton	Displays uneditable text or an uneditable bitmap; when a user selects a PushButton widget, the widget activates a programmer-defined routine.
Text	Lets a user enter and edit multiple lines of text.
TextField	Lets a user enter and edit a single line of text.

Table 8 Some Motif Primitive Widgets

Widget	Purpose
Form	Organizes widgets into a grid.
RowColumn	Organizes widgets into a row or a column; often used to build menus.

Table 9 Some Motif Manager Widgets

Each widget knows how to process a documented set of events. For example, a Text widget highlights a word if the user places the cursor on it and clicks the mouse twice.

You can grow your own widget.

If programmers cannot find a widget to meet an application's needs, then they can create their own widgets. Creating a widget from scratch is notoriously tricky, though Motif Version 2.0 provides a few useful routines to help simplify the task.

Motif programming by hand is hard.

These days, nearly all X applications are written with Motif widgets. Since coding Motif applications is rather complicated, a small industry has sprung up to provide products that simplify the coding of Motif applications. Instead of writing Motif code by hand, programmers can use one of these products (such as ICS Builder Xcessory) to electronically sketch a picture of the GUI and then let the tool generate the appropriate Motif code.

X Naming and Location

X naming and location are built on top of DNS.

X uses an extended version of DNS for the naming and location of servers. It is not sufficient for an X client merely to know on which node a server is running. After all, some X servers may be driving multiple displays and multiple screens per display. For example, Figure 49 shows a sample display name. This is the name that would be passed as an argument to the *DISPLAY* variable or used with the `-display` command-line option.

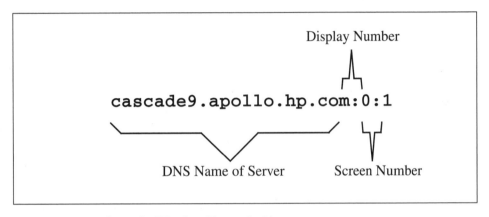

Figure 49 A Sample Display Name in X

In the preceding figure, **apollo.hp.com** is the name of a site on the Internet and **cascade9** is the name of a particular UNIX workstation at that site.

The **0** that follows the first colon symbolizes the display number. If **cascade9** were a multi-user machine, then the display number would identify a particular user's display. (The display number is almost always 0.)

The **1** that follows the second colon identifies the screen number. Screen number 0 signifies the primary screen, and screen number 1 specifies a second screen. If a screen number is omitted from a display name, the screen number defaults to 0.

X Security Services

X security is weak.

X provides only minimal security services. The central principle of X security is that the user sitting at an X server should be the one who decides who is allowed to use that X server. The user invokes a utility called **xhost** to implement security decisions.

For example, suppose Ellis wants to allow anyone to display X applications on his X terminal. In that case, Ellis would issue the following command:

```
$ xhost +
```

On the other hand, if Ellis were not the trusting type, he could issue the following commands to deny access to everyone except Scott and Bernice:

```
$ xhost -          # Deny access to everyone,

$ xhost +scott     # but give access to Scott,

$ xhost +bernice   # and give access to Bernice.
```

Beware of X hackers. You may be wondering why Ellis would want to protect his server in the first place. On the surface, it may appear that the worst that could happen would be for a malicious user to display electronic graffiti on Ellis's screen. However, remember that an X server is also a conduit for input. Therefore, a malicious user could connect an invisible client to Ellis's server and record Ellis's keystrokes without Ellis knowing it. Before long, the client will have collected Ellis's password.

X does not provide any protection for X clients. None is needed; the host authentication security protects against unauthorized use. A user on an X server must log in to the client host.

X: A User's View

Accessing an X server is no more complex than a remote login with, say, **telnet**. X users can run many more applications than would be available on a nondistributed graphics system. Users can run any X client on the network as long as they can log in to the client machine and have execute privileges for the application.

X: A System Administrator's View

X is a big win for most system administrators. That is because distributing graphics to X terminals allows sites to reduce the number of CPUs and disk drives, thus reducing the complexity of backups and installs.

X Terminals: On the Road Again

Socrates and Sons, a training company, teaches onsite courses all over the world. Before each course starts, Socrates and Sons ships a dozen steamer trunks of computer equipment to the course site. The instructor arrives before the course starts in order to set up the equipment.

Socrates and Sons decided to go with the client/server approach to distributed graphics. Inside the largest steamer trunk is a powerful UNIX workstation with a large disk drive. X clients run on this machine. The other trunks hold X terminals and twisted pair Ethernet wiring. After the UNIX workstation is set up, the instructor begins connecting X terminals. Connecting the X terminals is as easy as plugging cables into a connector.

Socrates and Sons found that the entire setup could be done in only 90 minutes. In addition, they can hook into the customer's network via the Internet and access demonstration programs back at the home office.

The system administrator must ensure that the X server is started on every terminal on which X clients will be displayed.

X often confuses new users.

There are two hidden system administration costs to X. The first is that users are often confused by the X environment and therefore pester system administrators with questions like, "Which node is **DateMaker** on?" The crafty system administrator can eliminate some of the hassle by writing scripts that encapsulate the necessary X startup information.

X startup files are notoriously complicated.
The second hidden cost concerns X startup files, such as the .Xdefaults file on UNIX implementations. If a user makes a mistake, and it is easy to make a mistake editing .Xdefaults, all sorts of weird problems can pop up. Naturally, the system administrator will be expected to bail the user out of such jams. The best solution is prevention; the system administrator should create appropriate X startup files and copy them into new users' home directories.

Summary

This chapter focused on the X Windows System as the enabling technology for client/server graphics. However, X is not the only distributed graphics system. The World Wide Web (described in Chapter 8) is also a powerful distributed client/server graphics system. We conclude our discussion of distributed graphics with a brief comparison of WWW and X.

WWW is also an important distributed graphics system.
HTTP, the central protocol of the WWW, solves a different category of distributed graphics problems than the X protocol solves. The X protocol is very good for highly interactive applications such as word processors or drawing programs. The X protocol is also very good at graphics applications where the output has to be rendered "on the fly." HTTP, on the other hand, is very good at delivering large files of previously computed data, such as graphics files in GIF format.

Some client/server experts have suggested that the WWW be extended to support X servers. In this thought-provoking arrangement, a WWW server would essentially act as an X client. For example, a WWW server could send a request to render a circle to a remote X server.

CHAPTER 16   Managing a Client/Server Environment

Chapters 1 through 15 described an idyllic world of immortal client/server applications running flawlessly over everlasting networks. However, in the real world, clients and servers often contract mysterious illnesses and die ignoble deaths. Plus, the networks on which client/server applications run often fail at the worst possible moments.

Systems can fail anywhere at any time. Even normal operation requires management.

In the simpler days before client/server computing, a system administrator could often solve a problem by walking over to the machine room and rebooting a mainframe. Today, however, a server running in London might be managed by a system administrator in San Francisco. A quick walk over to the machine room for a reboot is not always feasible.

Even when all systems are behaving well, there are numerous mundane management tasks to be performed. Servers need to be started, software installed, and so on.

Managing distributed systems is an active area of research and product development. Numerous products, approaches, and even frameworks deal with distributed management in one form or another. Nonetheless, full, integrated client/server management remains an elusive goal.

System management is an active field with numerous products and architectures.

This chapter answers the following questions:

- What do you need to manage in a client/server system?
- Should management be centralized, decentralized, or some combination of the two?
- How do you monitor distributed systems for problems?
- Should there be management frameworks that provide system services for management applications? Should these frameworks be included within the client/server framework? Should management frameworks be any different from general purpose client/server frameworks?

After we answer these questions we will describe some representative management products.

What Do You Need to Manage?

You need to manage a wide array of logical and physical components.

As a system administrator, you need to manage nearly everything, including the following:

- The network
- The host operating system and the resources it controls
- The client/server framework software
- Clients and servers
- Login accounts
- Software distribution and licensing

Managing the Network

You need to manage the network that client/server systems run on. ***Network management*** is usually distinguished from ***systems management***, which is management of nearly everything else on a computer system.

Networks are dynamic beasts; you must frequently add or remove cables, hubs, routers, network interface cards, and nodes. Even with the best hardware, network service can still be unreliable. So, keeping the network up and running can be a time-consuming job, particularly if parts of the network are at a different site.

Managing Operating System Resources

Clients and servers require the underlying features of the host operating system. To maintain adequate performance, you must monitor and control operating system resources such as memory use, CPU use, disk space, and swap space.

Managing the Client/Server Framework Software

You must install, configure, and maintain the client/server framework software. Managing a client/server framework often requires a lot of training and expertise, not to mention software tools. For example, you have to become comfortable with installation, configuration, and management of various subsystems. You also need the management software to be able to carry out these tasks across a large network.

Managing Clients and Servers

System administrators typically manage servers; users typically manage clients.

As a system administrator, you are typically responsible for starting servers and keeping them running. You need to monitor server performance. Furthermore, you need to handle unusual events such as security violations, resource exhaustion, and various kinds of failures. You must also define authorization lists for servers. That is, you must specify the list of who has permission to do what.

Generally speaking, users are responsible for learning how to start and maintain client software (though you might have to push them in that direction).

Managing Login Accounts

The heart of all security in client/server systems is a registry of login accounts, complete with encrypted passwords. You must manage login registries for users and groups. At a minimum, this means working with users to define the information required for a login account. If security at your site is high or if the number of users is large, then managing login accounts can become a major time sink.

Managing Software Distribution and Licensing

Various technological and legal issues make software distribution tricky.

In any but the smallest environment, the management of software distribution is a major problem. Software distribution tasks include:

- Installing software and keeping it updated.
- Ensuring that only licensed software is used. At sites with a good distributed file system it is very tempting to cheat software licensing agreements by making a single-use license available to all users at a LAN.
- Ensuring that the correct binary versions go to the correct machines. For example, a Windows client has to be made available to Windows users and a Macintosh client has to be made available to Macintosh users.

As another example, if a site installs new DBMS servers, you must install the latest ODBC drivers on every client node.

Centralized and Decentralized Management

Client/server management can be centralized, decentralized, or some combination of the two. In a ***centralized management*** scheme, responsibility for the management of all of an enterprise's resources is delegated to a single organization. Centralized management is performed from one location. In a ***decentralized management*** scheme, management responsibility is dispersed throughout the enterprise. That is, various users and system administrators each take responsibility for some aspect of management.

Management is a confederation of centralized and local control.

Many enterprises use a mixture of centralized and decentralized management, often with several management layers. For example, a typical large enterprise centralizes the management of login accounts and backups. However, clients are controlled by individual users, and servers are managed by the groups that use them.

The Internet cannot be managed centrally.

In some situations, the centralized management of client/server systems is impractical. For instance, centralized management of the Internet would currently be impossible. Separate and independent domains cooperate to provide Internet services. Nevertheless, Internet management still works very well most of the time.However, when things go wrong, no one has responsibility for fixing the problem. For example, if the WWW home page you are searching for does not respond, there is not much you can do about it. The server might be down for maintenance, the router providing access to the server may have failed, or the home page's owner may have gone bankrupt. There is not much that a user can do about these problems.

Monitoring vs. Controlling

Many management applications monitor components.

Monitoring means getting information about a component. ***Controlling*** means changing some aspect of how a component is running. In practice, monitoring is far more common than controlling.

In the client/server world, you have to monitor not only the clients and servers, but also the underlying components (such as networks and operating systems) that allow the clients and servers to run. This section contains two examples of monitoring and one of controlling.

Example 1: Monitoring the Network

A system administrator can monitor the network's health from one or more ***management stations***. The management stations are typically UNIX workstations or PCs running management applications.

Each management station periodically polls all of the known devices on the network (for example, bridges, routers, network controllers) to find out if they are operational. If they are, the management stations get some basic statistics, such as the number of packets transmitted and received and the number of error packets rejected. Devices can also report errors by sending alarms to the management stations on their own. From this information, the network management application can draw network maps to indicate which devices have not been located or appear to have problems.

Example 2: Monitoring the Operating System

Many system management applications monitor and report the processes running on the host machines in the network. The information may also include statistics on CPU, disk, processes, and memory use.

The system management application may detect, for instance, that a server is not running on a remote host.

Server performance is influenced by host's load.
If the performance of a server is poor, a management application could monitor how resources are being used on the server's host machine. Monitoring might reveal that CPU use is heavy because the host is running numerous servers. In this case, the system administrator might shut down some servers and move them to different nodes.

Example 3: Controlling TCP/IP

You need to maintain consistent configuration information.
Managing a sizable TCP/IP installation can be a vexing job mainly because networks often contain a mixed assortment of operating systems. Among other challenges, the various systems need to keep a consistent database (a **hosts** file) that maps node names to IP addresses. In addition, some systems on the network need to run routing software to reach other Internet sites.

You need a management application that can control hosts files. Such a management application must be able to write the host files on each machine to ensure consistency. The management application must also be able to start up server processes that control TCP/IP services.

The Manager/Agent Approach

Management applications are often divided into clients and servers.
Systems and network management are typically implemented as client/server applications. The management application is the client, and all the managed systems are servers that provide management information. All the normal client/server issues apply.

Many client/server management tools use object-oriented programming techniques to tame the great variety of devices to manage. For example, most managed devices need methods to reset, start, and stop them. As another example, a network router can inherit methods from a "network interface" class. Instantiations of the methods can then handle these operations for agents, or "managed objects," such as processes, devices, servers, and entire systems. For this reason, management applications have been early users of distributed OOP, and the SNMP and CMIP standards (next section) have OOP features.

In *manager/agent* design, the *manager* is the client, and the managed *agents* are the servers. An agent represents a managed object.

Managers periodically poll agents to obtain state information.

For example, consider a management application to monitor disk space. If based on the manager/agent design, each agent periodically checks the free space on its disk. A manager periodically polls the agents, and they send back their current disk information. If an agent's free disk space goes below a danger level, the agent does not have to wait to be polled; the agent just goes ahead and sends an alarm (a *trap*) to the manager. The manager gathers information from all the agents and displays the results in some useful fashion to the system administrator.

The following factors distinguish manager/agent applications from more general client/server applications:

- Management protocols, especially for network management, must often be lightweight, functioning even in the absence of any operating system. Client/server applications typically require a huge supporting cast of software, including an operating system. Network management agent software often executes on routers and bridges that are not running a general-purpose operating system. Furthermore, since basic framework services must be managed, there is a chicken-and-egg problem of running agent software in the absence of operational framework services.

- Management applications place heavy emphasis on events. A managed agent may need to generate an asynchronous event to indicate a failure, and the manager must be prepared to respond to the event, perhaps showing the device icon in red on the management station's display. Events play a less significant role in general client/server computing, though they do play a significant role in the X Window System.

- Management requests are frequently confined to getting and setting values rather than carrying out more general procedures or object methods.

- A single manager can handle multiple agents. This reverses the client/server model, in which one server handles multiple clients.

Figure 50 illustrates the architecture of manager/agent implementations. This architecture consists of the following components:

- The base of the architecture contains the familiar network transport layer, typically inhabited by TCP/IP.

- The next layer is occupied by a *management protocol*, which is typically occupied by SNMP or CMIP (explained in the next subsection).

- The next layer is called ***management services***; it contains the API for writing management applications and agent implementations.
- The top layer of the manager contains a ***manager application*** that includes the system administrator's graphical user interface (GUI). The top layer on the agent side contains the ***agent implementation*** itself. The agent maintains management information about the managed object. The managed object could be a physical device or a logical object (such as an operating system resource).

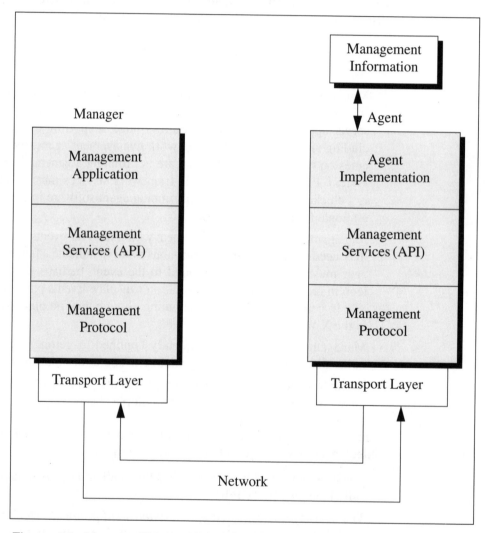

Figure 50 Manager/Agent Architecture

Figure 50 shows only a single agent and a single manager. However, a real-world manager often manages numerous agents. Conversely, on some systems, several managers may access the same agent.

CMISE-Portions of the Manager/Agent Architecture

The *Common Management Information Service Element (CMISE)* is defined as part of the *Open System Interconnection (OSI)* model. CMISE is not an actual implementation or even a specific set of protocols. CMISE defines the following two levels of the manager/agent architecture:

- The management protocol level
- The management services level called the *Common Management Information Service (CMIS)*

Management Protocols

The following are the two most important common management protocols:

- The *Simple Network Management Protocol (SNMP)*
- The *Common Management Information Protocol (CMIP)*

SNMP is everywhere that TCP/IP is.

Nearly all network management and most systems management applications use SNMP, CMIP, or a combination of the two. In fact, SNMP is so closely associated with TCP/IP that it is included in nearly all TCP/IP implementations.

SNMP is the dominant protocol for manager/agent designs. Because of its popularity, it is easy to declare SNMP as the *de facto* standard. In addition, the IETF has given SNMP the *de jure* stamp as well. The SNMP protocol is widely used in network management and is frequently extended to systems management. SNMP is another outstanding example of a solution initially developed by a few dedicated people that became widely used.

CMIP is the top-down standard.

CMIP was created by a standards committee and is not nearly as popular as SNMP for general-purpose network and system management. CMIP is important, however, in certain areas such as the management of telecommunications equipment.

*CMISE
specifies seven
service
primitives.*
All CMISE-compliant management protocols (including SNMP and CMIP) must support seven API *service primitives*. These service primitives implement the request/response and event notification communication protocol shown in Figure 51. Requests are usually confined to getting and setting values. CMIP requests can invoke an action; this request is analogous to a remote procedure call or object method invocation. The response is not necessary for some requests.

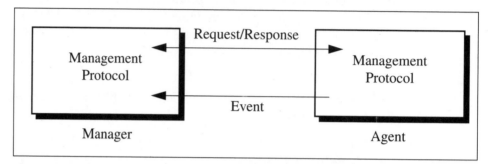

Figure 51 Communication Between Manager and Agent

These service primitives, invoked by the manager, the agent, or both, can request operations on single or multiple management objects. We have placed the primitives into the following four categories:

- Primitives to get and set management information. **M-GET**, **M-SET**, and **M-CANCEL-GET** fall into this category. These primitives retrieve and modify management information.

- One primitive, **M-ACTION**, to request an action on the agent. **M-ACTION** requests that a CMISE agent perform an action, which could be a procedure.

- Primitives to create and remove managed objects. **M-CREATE** creates managed object instances, and **M-DELETE** destroys them.

- One primitive, **M-EVENT-REPORT**, that an agent uses to send an event to a manager.

Management Services

*XMP is a
common API
to the
management
protocols.*
The management services level is not dominated by one or two standard implementations to the same extent as the management protocol level. However, the *Common Management Protocol (XMP)* API appears in several products, including HP OpenView. X/Open has made XMP into a *de jure* standard.

An *MIS provider* converts XMP calls to the appropriate management protocol and manages the information flow between the layers.

Management Information

Agents maintain management information.

To put it somewhat circularly, *management information* is information about anything that must be managed, whether systems or networks. Hosts, user accounts, routing tables, network interfaces, servers, and entire operating systems can all generate management information.

SMI provides information structuring and naming.

The industry-accepted way of specifying management information is through OSI's *Structure of Management Information (SMI)*. SMI is not a specific implementation. Rather, SMI provides for the model, notation, and naming conventions for managed object definitions. SMI requires the following information in order to describe a managed object:

- The managed object structure and attributes.
- Naming rules for the objects and attributes.
- The logical structure for representing management information.
- The object classes and class relationships. Unlike objects in C++ and CORBA, SMI objects do not encapsulate their methods. Instead, the objects are parameters to the XMP or other service calls. One could argue that they are not really objects in the OOP sense; nonetheless, OOP terms are used.

The CMIP implementation of SMI is called the *Guidelines for Management Information (GDMO)*. The SNMP implementation is called the *Management Information Base (MIB)*.

Object Addressing in SMI

Name a managed object with an IP address and an object identifier.

SMI uses its own addressing system to specify particular managed objects. Addresses are used as parameters to XMP and other service APIs.

An SMI address is simply a TCP/IP address concatenated to an *SMI Object Identifier*. The TCP/IP address specifies the node on which an object is running. The SMI Object Identifier specifies an object within the node. All instances of a particular object have the same SMI Object Identifier. Since the TCP/IP address for each node is unique, each object ends up with a unique SMI address.

The SMI Object Identifier for both SNMP and CMIP is a sequence of integers within braces. The object identifier defines a hierarchical naming space or naming tree. The first integer is the branch from the top of the name space, and each integer after that is a branch from the preceding level. For example, all managed objects on the Internet are contained as branches below the following four-integer identifier:

```
{1 3 6 1}
```

The leftmost 1 symbolizes the International Standards Organization (ISO), the next integer (3) symbolizes an organization governed by ISO, the third integer (6) represents a particular organization (the U.S. Department of Defense, which originated the TCP/IP protocols), and the last integer (1) symbolizes the Internet, which was originally a branch of the U.S. Department of Defense. This same address is often written as follows:

```
{ iso(1) org(3) dod(6) internet(1) }
```

Object identifiers are integer sequences, creating an identifier tree.

Sites on the Internet can append additional integers to {1 3 6 1}. For example, specifying 2 in the fifth branch symbolizes management, and specifying 4 in the sixth branch symbolizes private use. Therefore, the following address is usually used for new managed object definitions:

```
{ 1 3 6 1 2 4 }
```

Since this number is used so heavily, SMI defines the following synonym for it:

```
{ organizations }
```

We use { organizations } in the next example.

An Example SNMP Management Information Base

Create the MIB source and compile it.

Part of the task of developing a management application is to create a Management Information Base (MIB). MIB source code is a text file that describes the data that the management application monitors. MIB source code is compiled by a special MIB compiler; the resulting object code must be linked into both the manager and the agent. Many management applications provide customers with the MIB source code so that customers can better understand the application and sometimes even change attributes.

MIBs are analogous to IDLs.

Defining and compiling a MIB can be compared to creating and compiling a DCE or CORBA IDL interface. In all cases, we are defining how the client and server are to interpret the data they send and receive.

Suppose you are a programmer writing a management application that monitors the amount of free disk space. Perhaps you want the agent to send an alarm (a trap) to one or more managers when free disk space goes below a certain threshold. The following is a simplified, hypothetical MIB source code file for our management application:

```
OS-MIB       DEFINITIONS ::= BEGIN

MyCompany    OBJECT IDENTIFIER ::= { organizations 135 }
OpSys        OBJECT IDENTIFIER ::= { MyCompany 2 }
OpSysVersion OBJECT IDENTIFIER ::= { OpSys 1 }
OpSysStatus  OBJECT IDENTIFIER ::= { OpSys 2 }

OpSysName    OBJECT-TYPE
             SYNTAX      OCTET STRING
             ACCESS      read-only
             STATUS      mandatory
             DESCRIPTION "The vendor name"
                         ::= { OpSysVersion 1 }

OpSysVNum    OBJECT-TYPE
             SYNTAX      INTEGER
             ACCESS      read-only
             STATUS      mandatory
             DESCRIPTION "The version number"
                         ::= {OpSysVersion 2 }

DiskUtil     OBJECT-TYPE
             SYNTAX      INTEGER
             ACCESS      read-only
             STATUS      mandatory
             DESCRIPTION "disk utilization, between 0 and 100"
::= { OpSysStatus 1 }

DiskThrsh    OBJECT-TYPE
             SYNTAX      INTEGER
             ACCESS      read-write
             STATUS      mandatory
             DESCRIPTION "The disk utilization alarm
```

```
                                                       threshold"
                                                       ::= { OpSysStatus 2 }

 ... more attribute entries
END
```

The preceding MIB source code defines four object identifiers *MyCompany*, *OpSys*, *OpSysVersion*, and *OpSysStatus*. Notice that each object identifier has a unique SMI Object Identifier. Notice also that the SMI Object Identifiers are hierarchical. For example, the SMI Object Identifier for *OpSys* derives from the SMI Object Identifier for *MyCompany*.

After the four object identifiers, the example MIB source code defines four attributes. (*OpSysName*, *OpSysVNum*, *DiskUtil*, and *DiskThrsh*). Each attribute has four parameters. Table 10 explains the meanings of these parameters.

Keyword	Possible Values
SYNTAX	Programmer specifies a MIB data type. The OCTET-STRING data type corresponds to an array of **chars** in the C programming language.
ACCESS	Programmer specifies **read-only, read-write, write-only,** and **not-accessible**. Our example uses **read-only** and **read-write**. A manager cannot modify a **read-only** attribute but can modify a **read-write** attribute.
STATUS	Programmer specifies **MANDATORY** or **OPTIONAL**. An agent must support a **MANDATORY** attribute, but does not have to support an **OPTIONAL** attribute.
DESCRIPTION	Programmer specifies a comment. Management application does not use this field in any way.

Table 10 Attribute Keywords Used in MIB Example

Standard MIBs can be used nearly everywhere.
The IETF has made several standard SNMP MIBs available to the general public, including the following:

- MIB-I and MIB-II, which monitor TCP/IP statistics and network interfaces on a single node.
- RMON, which monitors an entire network instead of just individual nodes.

Many management applications have built-in support for one or more of the preceding three standard SNMP MIBs, and these MIBs are a common requirement when evaluating management systems.

Limitations of SNMP and CMIP

SNMP and CMIP have quite a few limitations, which we now examine.

Scale and Efficiency

SNMP and CMIP applications do not always scale up very well. One of the main reasons for this is that managers have to poll agents periodically for information. Although polling is efficient on a small network, polling becomes clumsy and slow on a large network because of the number of agents that a manager has to poll. To reduce network traffic caused by constant polling, some agents simply send events to managers. However, a large number of events will still cause problems.

Hierarchical management addresses scaling and performance issues.
The scale problem can be overcome with hierarchical management using a "manager of managers" (see Figure 52). Version 2 of SNMP (SNMPv2) supports hierarchical management by defining managed objects that have both manager and agent roles (a "manager-to-manager MIB"). In a typical situation, the first-level manager-agents gather information, process the data, and create statistics, and then make the results available to the manager of managers at the next level. The first-level manager-agents might also have user interfaces and be responsible for some portion of the management task. This hierarchical design can reduce network traffic in a large organization if there is a first-level manager within each local network. In that way, polling requests to the agents are confined within local networks. The manager of the managers only needs to poll the first-level managers, rather than all of the agents.

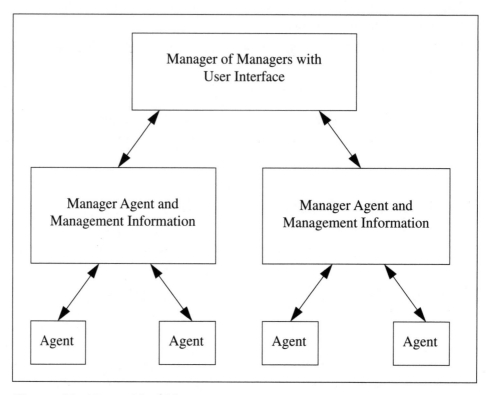

Figure 52   Hierarchical Management

Security

Security is a big problem for management applications that control resources.

SNMP and CMIP have no secure authentication or authorization. Therefore, SNMP and CMIP are best suited for monitoring rather than controlling.

Security is especially critical for agents that control basic system resources. *Secure SNMP*, which is included in SNMPv2, addresses privacy, primarily using DES private key encryption. Data integrity is achieved using a very large 128-bit digest, which is similar to a CRC checksum.

Actions

SNMP does not support actions directly.

In CMISE terminology, when a manager requests the agent to run a procedure, that request is called an ***action***. An action is similar to a remote procedure call (RPC).

For complete CMISE-compliance, a management protocol must support actions. However, SNMP does not support actions; CMIP does. CMIP implements actions through the **M-ACTION** primitive described earlier in this section.

The Future of CMISE

A general-purpose framework can be used for management applications.

SNMP SMI and MIBs were intended to be subsets of the general OSI CMISE architecture. Yet the need for rapid deployment resulted in incompatibilities, making SNMP-to-OSI transition more difficult.

CMISE (along with SNMP and CMIP) only partially implements the client/server model and distributed OOP. More general client/server frameworks, such as DCE and CORBA, have emerged. These general client/server frameworks can be used to develop systems management and network management applications. Furthermore, these general client/server frameworks have their own naming, location, and security models that are not always compatible with those in CMISE. Consequently, the CMISE model might be integrated into more general frameworks in the future.

Management Frameworks Based on SNMP and CMIP

Management frameworks integrate management services, data, and the user interface.

A management framework has different requirements from a more general client/server framework, but there is some commonality. The following three management framework services are essential for developing management applications:

- CMISE-style management information services.
- Data management services for storing and retrieving management information, frequently time-based records. SQL RDMS can be used, although proprietary systems are common.
- A management user interface capability to present management information. Requirements include the ability to draw network maps and to present data in a variety of forms such as strip charts, bar graphs, and gauges.

Some management application frameworks also include support for distributed objects and object interfaces to the management information services.

Figure 53 shows a management framework with several representative management applications.

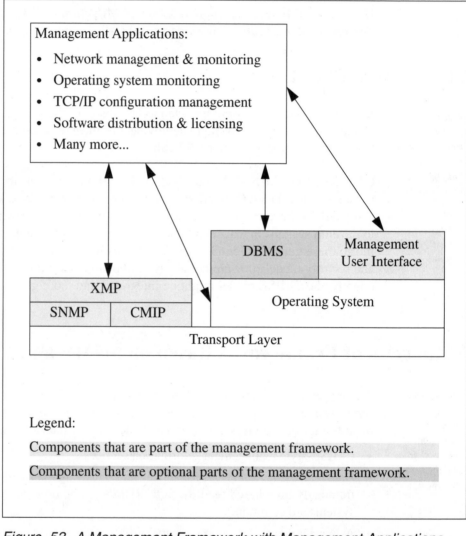

Figure 53   A Management Framework with Management Applications

*Various
products with
different
approaches all
support SNMP.*
We next briefly describe the following three representative commercial products for distributed client/server management:

- Legent Corporation's AgentWorks is an SNMP-based system-monitoring application with provisions for adding new managed objects.
- Hewlett-Packard's OpenView framework supports a wide variety of monitoring and control applications for both system and network management.
- Tivoli Systems' Tivoli Management Environment is a distributed object-oriented framework for system management.

All three products support at least SNMP. However, Tivoli's products have historically relied on distributed objects for management communication.

The three products we have selected represent three different approaches to management. All three products are UNIX-based, but some also run on PCs.

Hewlett-Packard OpenView

*OpenView
attracts value-
added
applications
for both
network and
system
management.*
Hewlett-Packard's OpenView Distributed Management platform supports a framework as shown in Figure 53. In particular, OpenView supports both SNMP and CMIP under XMP and has a Motif-based user interface. OpenView is popular for network management, but it is also being used increasingly for system management.

The OpenView framework APIs are published, and HP actively encourages the development of third-party management applications. As a result, there are OpenView applications for a wide variety of management tasks. IBM's NetView for AIX is similar, and, in fact, uses OpenView components under license from HP.

HP provides a number of management applications that run on top of OpenView, including the following:

- AdminCenter can configure new systems and servers; manage users, groups, and passwords; and monitor software versions, file systems, and peripheral devices.
- OperationsCenter is a focal point for managing events generated by systems and applications throughout an enterprise.
- OmniStorage is for hierarchical storage management.
- OmniBack II provides distributed file system backup and restore.

The industry is moving to standards.

An important feature of OpenView, NetView, and other frameworks is that they are, or are becoming, database independent. The DBMS shown in Figure 52 could now be satisfied by nearly any RDBMS. Formerly, you had to use a proprietary DBMS sold by the same vendor who sold you the management application.

Legent AgentWorks

AgentWorks is an open platform for systems management.

AgentWorks is an SNMP-based framework with applications for monitoring UNIX systems. AgentWorks does not control managed objects. Each product provides both manager and agent software. The user interface is built on Motif.

The following list summarizes four of the central products of AgentWorks:

- SystemManager monitors CPU performance, memory status, file system and disk space utilization, processes, and error log files. The manager can set alarm thresholds and polling rates.
- DomainManager lets you create "polling regions" or domains of hierarchical management, as shown in Figure 52.
- DB Manager monitors database server configuration, performance, disk I/O, and more.
- Agent Factory is a set of tools for developing SNMP agents.

AgentWorks can run stand-alone with its own user interface, or it can be installed to run under Hewlett-Packard's OpenView, IBM's NetView for AIX, and Sun-Soft's SunNet Manager.

Tivoli Management Environment

TME is an object-oriented framework for controlling systems.

Tivoli Systems, Inc. uses distributed objects in its Tivoli Management Environment (TME). TME is a management framework. TME controls UNIX client/server environments. TME and its applications focus on systems management. TME provides data management and a user interface.

Tivoli applications run on top of TME. Some of the more important applications are as follows:

- Tivoli/Works is the core application. You use it to integrate new workstations into the network. It distributes password, group, host, and other configuration files to the new and existing machines. Its capabilities even extend to the management of mail aliases. Tivoli/Works helps to maintain the single-system view.

- Tivoli/Courier distributes and installs application software. You package applications, data, and configuration information into modules. Tivoli/Courier then checks target systems for readiness to receive a module for installation or update by confirming that there is sufficient file system space. Finally, the module is installed, via a "push" operation, on all specified target client systems. The push is done either immediately or scheduled for a later time.

- Tivoli/Print provides a graphical user interface that enables administrators to check print job status, move print jobs to different print queues, reprioritize jobs, and so on.

- Tivoli/Sentry monitors file system usage, printers, and memory. Tivoli/Sentry is comparable to Legent's AgentWorks. You specify services to be monitored, sampling frequencies, and subscribing systems. Tivoli/Sentry provides built-in monitors, but also lets you add new monitors.

- Tivoli/FSM manages distributed file systems. For example, it manages NFS automounters, NFS exports, and file system configuration files.

- Tivoli/Application Extension Facility (AEF) helps you add new functions to customize existing applications.

CORBA will be there in the future.

TME 2.0 supports CORBA 1.1 interfaces. TME will most likely migrate to a CORBA 2.0 management framework for interoperable, distributed objects.

Both the current TME product and its future direction illustrate the point we made earlier; namely, management applications are just one type of client/server application. General distributed computing frameworks, such as CORBA and DCE, can be used for systems management if not for network management.

Summary

Systems management is essential for the success of distributed client/server computing. Virtually all of the distributed resources need to be monitored and controlled. Many existing products are based on SNMP, which was originally confined to network management. In the future, more and more management applications will use the underlying distributed computing framework.

CHAPTER 17

Two Client/Server Frameworks

We have described many parts of DCE and CORBA throughout this book. It is now time to tie all these parts together to show how a complete client/server framework operates.

The Distributed Computing Environment (DCE)

We will now show how DCE integrates its components to form an open, interoperable framework. In addition, we will examine a few features of DCE that we did not cover in earlier chapters. Following that, we briefly describe some DCE value-added products and applications.

Why DCE?

*DCE addresses
the hard
problems and is
available on
nearly all
systems. DCE is
a good
reference
framework.*

Why did we choose DCE as our reference client/server framework? Many other client/server frameworks are more widely used than DCE. (Novell NetWare and ONC/NFS come to mind.) Furthermore, the RPC distributed programming model is not universally accepted. Many say that distributed OOP is the wave of the future. Others contend that the Internet's success obviates the need for anything more than TCP/IP interprocess communication and the DNS. Nonetheless, DCE is in a unique position, and we use it as the "reference" framework for a number of reasons:

- DCE is open, interoperable, scalable, integrated, and available on many host systems.

- DCE is more complete than any other widely available system. DCE addresses the major issues identified in Chapter 2 and thus makes a good reference model for evaluating other frameworks.

- Open and interoperable distributed object systems are not yet available. No single object model or interoperability architecture has yet been firmly established.

DCE Background

*OSF integrated
component
technologies
from many
vendors and
made the
results openly
available.*

DCE is an RPC-based client/server framework that integrates components from several vendors. In 1989, the Open Software Foundation (OSF) began requesting technology from various vendors. Then, OSF selected what it felt were the best components. OSF integrated the technologies and provided the resulting source code, documentation, and collateral material (such as test suites) to the industry. All implementations were designed for portability to POSIX-compliant systems. Over a period of time, DCE has been enhanced, and a number of vendors have shipped it. Interoperability among heterogeneous systems has been tested extensively.

DCE 1.0 shipped in 1992, with several interim releases. DCE 1.1 is the latest version, announced in November, 1994. OSF ships only source code; the vendors port the code to their own or other systems, market it, and provide all support. For example, IBM, Digital, and HP all provide DCE on their own systems. Gradient Technologies offers versions for Microsoft Windows 3.1 (client support only) and Windows NT. Transarc Corporation has a DCE 1.1 product for Sun Solaris. Normally, a vendor uses OSF-provided code, but Microsoft developed its own version of the DCE RPC run time for Windows NT.

It's not just on UNIX any more. DCE is available on most major operating environments from PCs to main frames. DCE can be licensed for nearly any UNIX system; Microsoft's MS-DOS and Windows; Digital's OpenVMS; and IBM's OS/2, AS/400, AIX, and MVS.

DCE is also portable to different network transport stacks, including TCP/IP and OSI.

DCE Architecture

Figure 54 shows the architecture of a DCE environment.

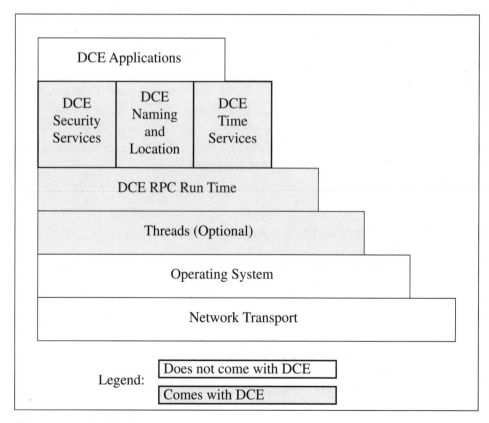

Figure 54 DCE Architecture

Independent software vendors (ISVs) supply DCE applications. DCE applications invoke services from the layers underneath them. All DCE services use RPCs to communicate with each other.

DCE threads are POSIX 1003.4a *pthreads*. A vendor that already supports pthreads in the host operating system would not use DCE threads.

DCE (in the source code from OSF) requires a POSIX-compliant operating system and network transport. The application also uses operating system services directly, and many applications will bypass DCE to use the network transport. A well-designed DCE application, however, should use DCE exclusively for communication and should not directly use TCP/IP, DNS, or any other lower-level service.

GUIs, distributed DBMS, and OOP are not part of DCE.

Comparing Figure 54 with Figure 7 in Chapter 2 (which shows a complete client/ server environment), we see that:

- DCE does not provide a user interface component. Applications use Motif, Microsoft Windows, the OS/2 Presentation Manager, or some other GUI provided by the client system.
- DCE does not provide database management. DCE can be the base for a distributed DBMS (Chapter 9), or a DBMS can coexist with DCE.
- IPC programming interfaces, in the form of sockets or similar APIs, are still available and are used by the distributed user interface, Internet utilities and possibly other user applications.
- DCE can support a distributed OOP model as we discuss later in this chapter.

DCE Cell and System Requirements

Each cell needs the basic servers.

The cell is the basic DCE administrative unit. A cell corresponds to a DNS domain. Each cell, therefore, must contain at least one server each for Security, Time (DTS), and location (CDS and GDS). In addition, there can be replicas for each of these services.

Every participant needs the DCE run time.

Every DCE system, whether client, server, or both, must have clerks to communicate with the servers and the DCE run time library. There is a clerk, acting as a client, for each of the three DCE services (naming and location, security, and time).

Distributed Time Service (DTS)

Previous chapters described DCE's Security, CDS, and DFS. Now we look at the time synchronization service.

Synchronized clocks are needed everywhere.

It is important to synchronize system clocks in a distributed environment. Without synchronization, the clocks could drift, harming system software and applications. The following list describes situations where synchronization is important:

- The Security Service attaches expiration times to tickets. These times must have the same meaning to application clients and servers as well as to the security servers.

- Applications, such as backup and restore utilities, often require synchronization. For another example, in a software development environment, the "modification time" timestamp on source files indicates which files, often on separate systems, should be recompiled during a build.

- Times must always increase so that UUIDs cannot be duplicated. A system that crashes cannot be allowed to restart with its clock reset or set back.

- Applications may use timestamps to schedule events on multiple systems, send events and messages, and log database updates.

DTS keeps system clocks closely synchronized.

The **Distributed Time Service (DTS)** provides a transparent cell-wide time service to synchronize system times, even in a geographically extended cell. In other words, DTS can synchronize clocks even if a cell spans multiple LANs and time zones. While exact synchronization is impossible, DTS can keep all the clocks in a cell within 100 ms (the default) of each other.

For many cells, synchronization to the correct universal time is not vital. In these cells, the only real requirement is that all the nodes have the same time. If the correct universal time is important on your cell, then you must contract with an external time provider such as the U.S. National Institute for Standards and Technology (NIST). Coordinated Universal Time (UTC) is the international time standard used by DTS.

DTS polls DTS servers and averages the reasonable responses.

The DTS servers talk to each other and try to come to some consensus on the current time. It's rather like three people at a bus stop trying to decide what time it is. One person's watch might say 4:05, another's 4:06, and another's 4:04. A sage bus rider might conclude that the time is probably about 4:05. Even, if one person's watch said 2:57, the other two people might still conclude that the time was about 4:05. In a similar fashion, DTS throws out times that seem wildly different from other times.

DCE Cell Configuration

Every cell is configured with framework and application servers.

A cell is the basic unit of DCE administration. A DCE cell may span multiple local networks or even encompass a wide area network. The basic requirements for a cell are as follows:

- Every participating system (client, server, or both) must have the DCE run time and clerks for CDS, Security Services, and DTS.
- Every cell must have at least one CDS server. A GDS server is required if the cell is to interact with other DCE cells.
- Every cell must have at least one Security Services server, containing services for the registry, authentication, and privilege services.
- Every LAN within the cell should have at least three DTS servers. The cell also requires a DTS server connected to a UTC time provider.

Optional components include:

- DFS servers.
- Application servers for various DCE-based applications (developed by the user or acquired from third-party independent software vendors) as required. Database servers are one example of DCE-based servers.
- Value-added products for system management and related tasks.

Figure 55 shows the servers in a typical DCE cell. DCE servers can be on ordinary workstations or on dedicated machines. The network cell probably also includes numerous workstations, PCs, and other client machines.

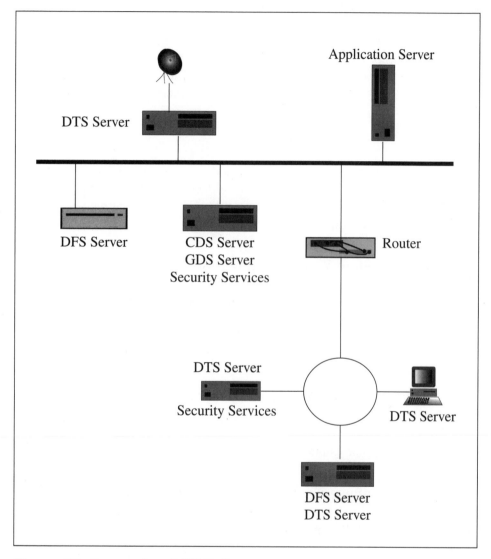

Figure 55   Servers in a DCE Cell

DCE Added Value

DCE provides only a central core of necessary services. As the framework becomes more widely used, it will attract a wide variety of value-added products addressing a wide variety of needs. These products are of several types. We list a few important or representative products here.

Framework Extensions

Framework extensions are additional services built on top of DCE that offer further services for application developers. For example, Transarc Corporation's Encina provides OLTP services to DCE application developers. (The next section details Encina.)

System Service Applications

Products in this class provide general distributed services for system managers and application developers. For example, DAZEL (from the DAZEL Corporation) assists users in distributing information such as spreadsheets and documents to multiple destinations (printers, mail boxes, and applications).

Software Development Tools

There are many DCE-based development tools.

Open Environment Corporation's Encompass/DCE is one of several products that help programmers develop DCE-based client/server applications.

Management Tools

DCE management tools are in demand.

The following tools are available to manage various DCE resources:

- DAZEL's Distributed Access Control Manager is an authorization service for centralized management of DCE ACLs throughout an enterprise.
- Open Horizon's Connection/DCE provides administrators with the ability to audit database access using DCE's Security Service.
- HaL Software System's DCE Cell Manager is a graphical tool for the management of security, directory, and configuration information.

Online Transaction Processing

*RPC extensions
are required for
many
applications.*

Online Transaction Processing (OLTP) systems, long used in commercial data processing, need extensive changes to operate in an open, client/server environment such as DCE. The core requirement is to provide the RPC communication mechanism with transactional integrity so that either the remote procedure is known to have executed completely or not at all. Failures in the middle of the remote procedure have to be detected and any state changes (file updates, for instance) have to be undone. We encountered this requirement back in Chapter 10 during the discussion of database replication.

*Encina provides
a complete set of
services along
with a structured
file system.*

Transarc Corporation's Encina extends OLTP to DCE. Encina is available on many DCE systems, ranging from PCs and workstations to large servers. Encina has several components:

- The Encina Toolkit Executive, layered directly on DCE, runs on each participating node. This component extends DCE RPCs to provide transactional integrity. The Toolkit Executive also includes the Transactional-C programming environment, extending the C language with macros and libraries to allow for declaration or transactions, subtransactions (transactions can be nested), and exception handlers.

- The Toolkit Server Core, layered on the Executive, provides for managing recoverable data, particularly in RDBMSs.

- The Transaction Monitor, layered on the Server Core, is a broker for incoming client transaction requests (transactional RPCs). Security authentication and authorization are performed here, as is server load balancing.

- The Structured File System provides for record-oriented keyed files with random and sequential access, secondary indices, update logs, concurrency control, and recovery. UNIX and Windows files are unstructured byte sequences, which are not adequate for commercial applications, so the Structured File System provides the required capabilities.

- Peer-to-Peer Communication Services provide a communications gateway to the LU 6.2/SNA protocols used by IBM mainframes.

DCE Applications

DCE is a general framework for extending system services to the distributed environment. Not surprisingly, DCE has attracted a wide and diverse collection of application developers. Many end-users have committed to using DCE as the architecture for future development and deployment. Others are deploying pilot projects for the same purpose.

Here are but three examples. All have the common theme of integrating diverse systems, usually distributed among many remote sites.

- Financial. A number of banks plan to equip all their branch and central offices with DCE and its applications. RPC communications are made secure using the DCE Security Services. Encina is often used to manage the financial transactions.

- Telecommunications. Several telecommunications firms use DCE as an enterprise-wide base for management, billing, and other applications.

- Database management. DCE provides services required by distributed database management systems, as mentioned in Chapter 9. Several vendors have announced support for DCE.

Recent DCE Developments

New releases include incremental features requested by users.

DCE 1.1 is the latest (November, 1994) OSF release. Among the enhancements are:

- Internationalization. All DCE user-visible messages can be localized to provide messages in other languages.

- DFS/NFS Gateway. NFS clients can access DFS servers. The gateway translates NFS file requests into DFS requests.

- Extended Registry Attributes. This feature is designed to allow single login across non-UNIX systems by providing a mechanism for associating additional (non-UNIX) security information with users and groups.

- Security Delegation allows intermediate servers to assume the client's identity (PAC) so that it can invoke other protected services on behalf of the original client.

- Administration. A single control program unites all basic DCE administrative functions into one tool.

CORBA and Object Services

CORBA will eventually become a distributed object-oriented operating system.

CORBA is not a complete client/server framework. For example, CORBA lacks security services and naming and location services. The Object Management Group (OMG) has activities underway to add the services that will make CORBA into a complete client/server framework called the Object Management Architecture (*OMA*). The OMG refers to these services as *Object Services* in the Common Object Services Specification (*COSS*). The Object Services in COSS include the following:

- *Lifecycle services* support object creation, copying, movement, and deletion. Objects can be created dynamically or statically.
- *Persistence services* support long-lived objects. Files and databases, with suitable methods, are examples of long-lived, or persistent, objects.
- *Security* supports authentication and access control on objects.
- *Naming and location* supports how applications refer to objects and how BOAs locate them.
- *Time services* support time synchronization.
- *Event notification* supports the transmission of event objects between objects.
- *Concurrency control services* support concurrent access to shared objects.

Another way of looking at OMA is that will essentially be a distributed object-oriented operating system.

Interoperability is the next problem.

Figure 56 illustrates the architecture of a CORBA-based OMA framework. For the sake of simplicity, we have shown CORBA running over an RPC framework, using that framework's services. As we will see in the following sections, this use of RPCs is possible, but not necessary.

Figure 56 looks very similar to Figure 54. However, the CORBA ORB replaces the DCE run time.

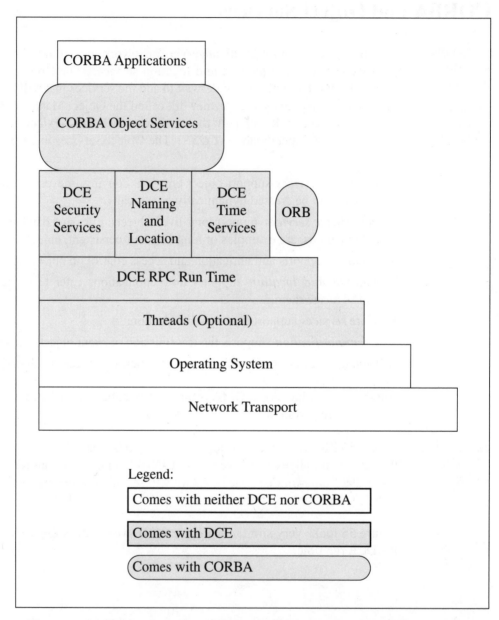

Figure 56 Architecture for a Distributed Object-Oriented Framework on
             DCE

CORBA Interoperability

*CORBA 2.0 is
in progress.*
The Object Management Group (OMG) and its member companies address the problems of interoperability in CORBA 2.0. In an ideal world. all CORBA 2.0 applications would interoperate without hassle. Software vendors could then write objects (using CORBA IDL) with confidence that they would port to any platform and would work with other objects on the same or other frameworks. There are, however, a number of issues to address before all of this can be achieved. Here are a few of the issues:

*How do the
objects
communicate?
How are they
named and
secured?*

- What is the underlying network transport. Is it TCP/IP, or DCE on TCP/IP, or something else?

- How are objects named? If DCE or ONC is used, the naming is fairly well determined. Otherwise, a new naming strategy is needed. It is crucial for interoperability that the same naming formats be used everywhere.

- What are the security mechanisms? Again, it might be preferable to use the services of an existing framework.

*Use an existing
framework, or
create the
services in other
ways?*
The recurring theme is whether it is better to use existing frameworks (such as DCE or ONC) or whether CORBA should supply its own services. For example, consider the first issue. Using just TCP/IP is a low-cost way to supply a network transport. However, using just TCP/IP without DCE means that CORBA will have to reinvent all the RPC-like services (such as reliability, security, naming, and location) that DCE already provides. If CORBA creates its own services, programmers and system administrators will have to master yet another way of doing things.

*You will be able
to choose which
you want.*
These conflicting demands led to **Universal Networked Objects** (**UNO**). In UNO, a **General Inter-ORB Protocol** (**GIOP**) can be mapped onto multiple transport layers. The principal features of the UNO are as follows:

- The GIOP itself, which specifies a Common Data Representation, an Interoperable Object Reference, Interoperable TypeCodes, and message contents, formats, and semantics.

- The **Inter-ORB Protocols** (**IOPs**), which specifies the transport (TCP/IP, Novell NetWare, or whatever) as well as mappings to the GIOP to ensure ORB interoperability.

- The **Internet IOP** (**IIOP**), which uses TCP/IP, is mandatory for all CORBA 2.0 networked ORBs. The IIOP ensures immediate interoperability with other ORBs.

DCE is one specific framework.

- **Environment-Specific IOPs** , which are alternatives to IIOP. The **DCE-CIOP** is the first approved Environment-Specific IOP. These alternate IOPs are seen as being optimized for specific environments. It is reasonable to expect that COM (Chapter 14), which already uses DCE, will evolve to use the DCE-CIOP.

You will be able to bridge between different solutions.

- **Inter-ORB bridges** and **half bridges**, which connect different environments. A bridge must map between different IOPs. This bridge is loosely comparable to a network protocol bridge between, say, TCP/IP and IPX/SPX, or even a link-layer bridge between Ethernet and Token Ring.

Figure 57 illustrates the central components of this proposal.

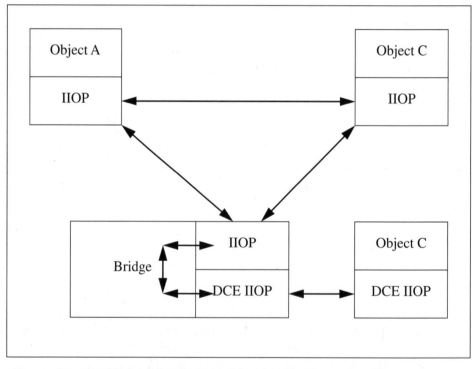

Figure 57 CORBA 2.0 Objects Interoperating Using Full Bridges

Future Developments in Distributed OOP

Pay attention. Interesting developments lie ahead.

It is difficult to predict which way the distributed OOP market will go. Nonetheless, we did say in the preface that we would venture a few risky predictions. So, here are a few for distributed OOP:

- Vendors will implement GIOP-compliant CORBA 2.0 systems, some with the DCE-CIOP and some with IIOP. These vendors will also supply bridges to the other implementations.

- No single implementation will dominate, but Microsoft's version (that is, COM) will certainly capture the non-UNIX desktop and server market. (There, that claim was not so risky.)

- Object services will be implemented competitively by many vendors, with system vendors selling their own versions. This development will create complete distributed OO frameworks.

Changeover will take years, and mixed environments will survive for a long time.

- CORBA 2.0 is only a specification, not an implementation. It will take many years for vendors to deliver implementations with robust portability and interoperability, and it will take additional time for large-scale deployment. Recall that it took over two decades for the relational DBMS to prevail.

- No single framework or model will dominate in the immediate future. Client/server practice will be an eclectic mix of IPCs, RPCs, and distributed objects for a long time.

Summary of Client/Server Computing

We have reached the end of the book, and as the old saying goes, now is the time to "tell 'em what you told 'em." Ours is a sweeping saga of love and betrayal played out against the timeless grandeur that is Rome.

Actually, the beginning of our book obsesses about the client/server concept. Client/server means splitting a program into two or more separately executable programs. The separate programs typically run on different nodes of a network but sometimes run on the same node.

Clients need to find servers and servers need to find clients. To do so, client/server systems rely on a naming and location system. For example, client/server applications on the Internet rely on the naming and location system called DNS.

Client/server security has many facets. For example, servers need to authenticate clients, so that phony clients do not steal services. DCE offers one of the most comprehensive security systems. One of the biggest problems with security systems is that the more security you throw into a client/server application, the harder that application becomes to use and to maintain.

Distributed file systems like Novell NetWare and NFS form a huge piece of the client/server market. A distributed file system enables users to share files that are spread over a network. The World Wide Web is a client/server system that allows users to share (read-only) files spread over the Internet.

A lot of users think client/server means distributed DBMS. Indeed, centralizing a database server makes a lot of sense, especially if you can give each user friendly front-end client software. Microsoft's ODBC specifies a standardized interface between database servers and database clients.

Client/server applications can be coded in a lot of different ways, but we suggest using remote procedure calls (RPCs). RPC packages, like the ones provided by DCE and ONC, take care of most of the nitty-gritty, low-level details of client/server programming. Just as the programming world is gradually transitioning to object-oriented programming, the client/server world is gradually transitioning to distributed objects and to specifications like CORBA and COM.

The X Window System dominates the distributed graphics market. X enables applications to run on one node and to display graphics on another node.

Much of the complexity of client/server computing falls on the shoulders of system administrators. Fortunately, system administrators can get help from a vast array of client/server management products, many of them based on a protocol named SNMP.

We conclude with an appendix describing client/server standards.

APPENDIX A Standards

Throughout this book, we have used the term "standard" with a lowercase "s" to mean a wide variety of APIs, protocols, and specifications. Standards may be developed and provided by official standards organizations, or, at the other extreme, they may simply be embodied in a successful product from a single vendor. Some standards are the work of a few farsighted individuals, and others come from committees delegated by international standards organizations. Vendors may offer the source code to certain standard software, while other standards are only available in binary format.

This appendix lists the standards that are relevant to client/server computing and those we have used in this book. This appendix also takes a brief look at the organizations that create and/or bless standards.

Organizations and Standards Bodies

Here is a partial list of relevant standards bodies and of organizations whose task is to create client/server standards:

- American National Standards Institute (ANSI) is a nonprofit organization of vendors and users. ANSI is also the US member of the International Organization for Standardization (ISO).

- International Consultative Committee on Telegraphy and Telphony (CCITT) has traditionally been concerned with the lower three layers of the OSI architecture, and ISO with layers four through seven.

- Institute of Electrical and Electronics Engineers (IEEE) develops the Portable Operating System Interface for Computing Environments (POSIX).

- International Organization for Standardization (ISO) is involved with many of the standards for networking protocols and system management architectures, including the well-known Open Systems Interconnect (OSI) seven-layer network architecture.

- Internet Engineering Task Force (IETF) deals with everything related to the Internet and TCP/IP. Their specifications are published in the form of "Requests for Comment" (RFCs), which are available on many **ftp** sites. Specific RFCs are listed in the bibliography.

- Object Management Group (OMG) is a membership organization that promotes the theory and practice of distributed object technology.

- Open Software Foundation (OSF) creates implementations that it makes available to vendors in source code form. Portions of OSF implementations conform to numerous relevant standards. In turn, standards bodies endorse other portions of OSF products.

- X Consortium creates standards for the X Window Systems.

- X/Open Company Limited deals with UNIX, network management, and other standardization areas. X/Open is an international group of system vendors.

Standards Pertaining to Client/Server

Name: ASN.1

- **Full Name:** Abstract Syntax Notation One (ASN.1)
- **Sponsoring Organizations:** CCITT, ISO
- **Role:** Data description

Comments: ASN.1 is a formal language for describing the arrangement of data in network packets. It also describes the data syntax for MIB definitions. SNMP, CMIP, and many other protocols use ASN.1.

Chapter(s): 16

Name: C

- **Full Name**: Same
- **Sponsoring Organizations**: ANSI, ISO
- **Role**: Programming language

Comments: C is widely used to implement client/server frameworks and applications. The ANSI standard (X3.159-1989) defines both the language and the standard library.

Name: C++

- **Full Name**: Same
- **Sponsoring Organizations**: ANSI, ISO
- **Role**: Programming language

Comments: C++ is widely used to implement client/server frameworks and applications. As of this writing, C++ is not yet a *de jure* standard; however, a standards committee is working on it.

Name: CMIP

- **Full Name**: Common Management Information Protocol
- **Sponsoring Organizations**: ISO and CCITT
- **Role**: A management protocol using the manager/agent approach

Comments: CMIP defines the procedures and syntax to implement CMIS services for managing OSI-compliant network implementations. CMIP protocol data units (PDUs) specify the exchange between peer common management information service elements (CMISEs).

Chapter(s): 16

Name: CMIS

- **Full Name**: Common Management Information Service
- **Sponsoring Organizations**: ISO and CCITT
- **Role**: An architecture for manager/agent network and system management

Comments: CMIS defines the services required for management of OSI-compliant network implementations.

Chapter(s): 16

Name: COM/OLE

- **Full Name**: Common Object Model/Object Linking and Embedding
- **Sponsoring Organizations**: Digital Equipment Corporation and Microsoft Corporation
- **Role:** PC application integration with CORBA-based distributed data objects

Comments: Implementations are in development at the time of this writing.

Chapter(s): 14

Name: CORBA

- **Full Name**: Common Object Request Broker Architecture
- **Sponsoring Organization**: OMG
- **Role**: Distributed object-oriented computing

Comments: CORBA 1.1 describes the interface language and the functionality. CORBA 2.0, in progress at this writing, addresses interoperability between CORBA implementations.

Chapter(s): 14, 17

Name: COSS

- **Full Name**: Common Object Services Specification
- **Sponsoring Organization**: OMG
- **Role**: Distributed object-oriented computing

Comments: COSS describes object services with CORBA interfaces. COSS and CORBA are the principal components of the Object Management Architecture (OMA).

Chapter(s): 17

Name: DCE

- **Full Name:** Distributed Computing Environment
- **Sponsoring Organization**: OSF
- **Role:** A complete client/server framework based on remote procedure calls (RPCs).

Comments: We have used DCE and its components as examples throughout this book.

Chapter(s): 4, 5, 7, 12, 13, 17

Name: DTP

- **Full Name**: Distributed Transaction Processing
- **Sponsoring Organization:** X/Open
- **Role**: An architecture to support distributed transactions

Comments: DTP defines how applications, transaction managers, resource managers, and communications managers interact.

Chapter(s): 9

Name: HTTP

- **Full Name**: HyperText Transfer Protocol
- **Sponsoring Organization:** CERN
- **Role**: Protocol used by WWW clients and servers.

Comments: Various organizations are working on extending HTTP.

Chapter(s): 8

Name: Microsoft Windows 3.1

- **Full Name**: Same
- **Sponsoring Organization**: Microsoft Corporation
- **Role:** Operating system with user interface

Comments: This is the most common desktop, and hence, client, operating system. It is, essentially, a single-user, single-tasking operating system.

Name: Microsoft Windows NT

- **Full Name**: Same
- **Sponsoring Organization:** Microsoft Corporation
- **Role**: Operating system with user interface and extensive networking and client/server support, including DCE RPCs.

Comments: Windows NT is a complete multitasking operating system with all of the features (and more) of standard UNIX. While it does have a POSIX 1003.1 subsystem, most applications use Microsoft's Win32 API. The two versions are Windows NT Workstation and Windows NT Server.

Name: Microsoft Windows 95

- **Full Name**: Same
- **Sponsoring Organization**: Microsoft Corporation
- **Role**: A complete desktop and client operating system that may supplant Windows 3.1. Windows 95 supports the Win32 API, giving it the features of standard UNIX. It also has an enhanced user interface.

Comments: Windows 95 is not shipping at this writing, but is expected to in the very near future.

Name: Motif

- **Full Name**: OSF/Motif
- **Sponsoring Organization**: X Consortium, which has taken over Motif from OSF
- **Role**: Standard graphical user-interface (GUI) for most UNIX workstations and for many PCs

Comments: The Motif Toolkit is a set of about three dozen widgets and pseudo-widgets that programmers use to implement graphical user interfaces for X-Window Systems. After a long and vicious fight between Motif and Sun Microsystem's Open Look, Sun finally conceded defeat.

Chapter(s): 15

Name: NFS

- **Full Name:** Network File System
- **Sponsoring Organization**: SunSoft
- **Role**: Distributed file system

Comments: NFS is the *de facto* distributed file system, available on nearly every platform. The source code, available from SunSoft, is easy to port to POSIX-compliant systems.

Chapter(s): 7

Name: Novell NetWare

- **Full Name:** Same
- **Sponsoring Organization**: Novell
- **Role**: Distributed file system for PCs

Comments: NetWare is the most popular PC networked file system.

Chapter(s): 7

Name: ODBC

- **Full Name:** Open Database Connectivity
- **Sponsoring Organization**: Microsoft Corporation
- **Role**: PC application access to databases

Comments: ODBC provides services for interoperability, connection and login management, and error processing.

Chapter(s): 9

Name: ONC, NIS

- **Full Name**: Open Network Computing, Network Information System
- **Sponsoring Organization**: SunSoft
- **Role**: ONC is a client/server framework; NIS provides registry services for databases such as users and hosts

Comments: ONC is heavily used on UNIX systems. NFS is the most famous ONC-based application.

Chapter(s): 4, 5, 7

Name: OSI

- **Full Name**: Open Systems Interconnection Communications Architecture
- **Sponsoring Organizations**: ISO and CCITT
- **Role**: Networking protocols and network and system management standards and architectures

Comments: OSI provides the famous seven-layer networking architecture (physical, data link, network, transport, session, presentation, and application).

Name: POSIX 1003.1, 1003.2, 1003.4a

- **Full Name:** Portable Operating System Interface for Computer Environments
- **Sponsoring Organization**: IEEE
- **Role**: Standard operating system APIs

Comments: POSIX 1003.1 specifies the UNIX APIs. Many proprietary operating systems, such as IBM OpenEdition/MVS and Digital OpenVMS, now support POSIX 1003.1. By supporting these APIs, a vendor makes it possible to port application software to a proprietary system without being required to use UNIX. POSIX is also important in allowing framework implementations (such as DCE and NFS) to be ported to a wide variety of systems. POSIX 1003.2 is for shells and utilities, and 1003.4a is the POSIX threads, or *pthreads* which are important for implementing servers.

Name: SNMP

- **Full Name**: Simple Network Management Protocol
- **Sponsoring Organization**: IETF
- **Role**: Network and systems management

Comments: SNMP is a management protocol implementing the manager/agent approach. Version 2, or SNMPv2 addresses security and scalability issues, but is not as common, at this time, as SNMPv1.

Chapter(s): 16

Name: SQL

- **Full Name**: Structured Query Language
- **Sponsoring Organization**: ANSI, X/Open, SQL Access Group
- **Role**: Database query language

Comments: SQL was originally used for single-system databases. Now, SQL commands are frequently passed between client and server in distributed DBMS systems.

Chapter(s): 9

Name: TCP/IP, UDP/IP, IP

- **Full Name**: Transmission Control Protocol, User Datagram Protocol, Internet Protocol
- **Sponsoring Organization**: IETF
- **Role**: Network transport and routing protocols

Comments: This is the essential networking protocol used by nearly every client/server product. There are numerous associated application and service protocols, including **ftp**, **telnet**, and DNS.

Chapter(s): Nearly every chapter has a reference to TCP/IP or some of its related protocols.

Name: X

- **Full Name**: X Window System
- **Sponsoring Organization**: X Consortium
- **Role**: Distributed windowing system

Comments: X is required for Motif. It is available on nearly all UNIX and many PC and Macintosh systems. X terminals provide an inexpensive way to provide a graphics terminal to remote applications.

Chapter(s): 15

Name: XDS

- **Full Name**: X.500 Directory Services
- **Sponsoring Organization**: X/Open
- **Role**: Naming and location

Comments: X.500 provides world-wide naming and location services. Novell NetWare uses X.500; DCE supports both X.500 and DNS.

Chapter(s): 4

Name: XMP

- **Full Name**: X/Open System Management Protocols API
- **Sponsoring Organization**: X/Open
- **Role**: API for network and system management

Comments: XMP appears in several products, including HP OpenView.

Chapter(s): 16

Name: XPG3, XPG4

- **Full Name**: X/Open Portability Guide
- **Sponsoring Organization**: X/Open
- **Role:** UNIX-style APIs, similar to POSIX, but with additional features.

Comments: XPG is a superset of POXIX 1003.1. For instance, XPG adds shared memory, semaphores, and message queues.

Bibliography

These books provide in-depth information or different perspectives on many client/server topics. Where appropriate, we have listed relevant chapters in this book.

[Berlege, 1991] Thomas Berlege. *OSF/Motif: Concepts and Programming.* Addison-Wesley, Reading, MA, 1991. Chapter 15.

[Cheswick and Bellovin, 1994] William R. Cheswick and Steven M. Bellovin. *Firewalls and Internet Security: Repelling the Wily Hacker.* Addison-Wesley, Reading, MA, 1994. This is the authoritative book on Internet security. It details many security threats and what to do about them. There is also a valuable chapter on secure communications that explains Kerberos and various forms of encryption. Chapter 5.

[Comer, 1995] Douglas E. Comer. *Internetworking with TCP/IP: Principles, Protocols, and Architecture*, Volume I. Prentice-Hall, Englewood Cliffs, N.J. Third Edition, 1995.

[Cutler, 1992] Ellie Cutler, et al (Eds.). *The X Window System in a Nutshell.* O'Reilly & Associates, Sebastopol, CA, 1992. Chapter 15.

[DoD, 1985] *DoD Trusted Computer System Evaluation Criteria.* DoD 5200.28-STD, DoD Computer Security Center, 1985. This is the "Orange Book" cited in Chapter 5 that defines single system security levels. It is available via `ftp` from `ftp.cert.org` as `/pub/info/orange-book.z.` Chapter 5.

[Gray and Reuter, 1993] Jim Gray and Andreas Reuter. *Transaction Processing: Concepts and Techniques.* Morgan Kaufmann Publishers, San Mateo, CA,1993. This book covers transaction processing thoroughly, and has brief discussions of Encina and Tuxedo. While we only touched on TPS briefly, this book is recommended for anyone wanting to explore the topic in depth. Chapters 9, 10, 17.

[Kaufman, et al, 1995] Charlie Kaufman, Radia Perlman, and Mike Speciner. *Network Security: Private Communication in a Public World.* Prentice-Hall, Englewood Cliffs, NJ. 1995. The authors provide a thorough treatment of privacy and encryption issues. Chapter 5.

[Kobara, 1991] Shiz Kobara. *Visual Design with OSF/Motif.* Addison-Wesley, Reading, MA, 1991. Chapter 15.

[Krol, 1994] Ed Krol. *The Whole Internet: User's Guide & Catalog.* O'Reilly & Associates, Inc., Sebastopol, CA, 1994. This is a definitive user's guide to the Internet. Chapter 8.

[Liu, Cricket, et al, 1994] Cricket Liu, et. al. *Managing INTERNET Information Services.* O'Reilly & Associates. Sebastopol, CA. 1994. This is a real omnibus on Internet client/server frameworks. It explains how to establish things like WWW servers and how to maintain them. It also explains where you can get the relevant software for free. Chapter 8.

[McLain, 1993] Gary McLain. *OLTP Handbook.* McGraw-Hill, New York, NY, 1993. This is a collection of articles on online transaction processing, including one on Encina. Chapters 9, 10, 17.

[Mullender, 1989] Sape Muellender, Ed. *Distributed Systems.* ACM Press, New York, NY. This book is a collection of articles by experienced distributed systems researchers. There are articles on communication, naming and security, data storage, transactions, replication, and architectures, with a lot of information about specific implementations and research projects.

[Orfali, Robert, et al, 1994], Robert Orfali, Dan Harkey, and Jeri Edwards, *Essential Client/Server Survival Guide.* Van Nostrand Reinhold, New York, NY, 1994. This book is somewhat complementary to our book, covering databases and OLTP in depth.

[OSF, 1993a] Open Software Foundation. *OSF/Motif: Programmer's Reference.* Prentice-Hall, Englewood Cliffs, NJ, 1993. Chapter 15.

[OSF, 1993b] Open Software Foundation. *OSF/Motif: User's Guide*. Prentice-Hall, Englewood Cliffs, NJ, 1993. Chapter 15.

[OSF, 1993c] Open Software Foundation. *OSF/Motif: Style Guide*. Prentice-Hall, Englewood Cliffs, NJ, 1993. Chapter 15.

[Rose and McCloghrie, 1995], Marshall T. Rose and Keith McCloghrie, *How to Manage Your Network Using SNMP: The Networking Management Practicum*. Prentice-Hall, Englewood Cliffs, NJ. 1995. This book not only covers SNMP protocols and MIBs, but it shows how to build management applications, stressing the how's and why's. Chapter 16.

[Rosenberry, Kenney, and Fisher, 1992] Ward Rosenberry, David Kenney, and Gerry Fisher. *Understanding DCE*. O'Reilly & Associates. Sebastopol, CA. 1992. This is a fantastic introduction to DCE. It summarizes all the important features of DCE, including DFS and Security. Chapters 4, 5, 7, 12, 13, 17.

[Rosenberry and Teague, 1993] Ward Rosenberry and Jim Teague. *Distributing Applications Across DCE and Windows NT*. O'Reilly & Associates, Inc. Sebastopol, CA, 1993. Windows NT and DCE RPCs really do work together, and this book shows you how. Chapter 12, 13.

[Salemi, 1993] Joe Salemi, *Guide to Client/Server Databases*. Ziff-Davis Press, Emeryville, CA, 1993. An overview of DBMS and client/server computing, followed by descriptions of DBMSs for PCs, UNIX servers, and mainframes. Chapter 9.

[Santifaller, 1991] Santifaller, Michael. *TCP/IP and NFS: Internetworking in a UNIX Environment*. Addison-Wesley, Reading, MA. 1991. Although the typography and layout of the book are a tad intimidating, this is still an excellent choice for readers who need to learn a lot about TCP/IP and NFS in a short time. This book is power-packed with worthwhile information. Chapters 6, 7.

[Sheldon, 1993] Tom Sheldon. *Novell NetWare 4, the Complete Reference*. Osborne McGraw-Hill, Berkeley, CA, 1993. This is a thorough guide to NetWare, covering everything from physical networks to user commands to NetWare architecture. Chapter 7.

[Shirley, 1993] Shirley, John. *Guide to Writing DCE Applications*. O'Reilly & Associates. Sebastopol, CA. 1993. This is a very well-written, easy-to-understand guide that teaches an experienced programmer how to write DCE clients and servers. It is jam-packed with helpful example code. Chapter 12.

[Stallings, 1993] William Stallings. *SNMP, SNMPv2, and CMIP - The Practical Guide to Network-Management Standards*, Addison-Wesley, Reading, MA, 1993. Chapter 16.

[Stern, 1992] Hal Stern. *Managing NFS and NIS*. O'Reilly & Associates, Inc., Sebastopol, CA, 1992. This book goes beyond its title. In addition to telling you how to set up an NFS environment, it has good discussions of the architecture and implementation. Chapters 4, 5, 6, 7, 12.

[Stevens, 1990] W. Richard Stevens. *UNIX Network Programming*. Prentice-Hall, Englewood Cliffs, N.J., 1990. This is the comprehensive guide to UNIX network programming using sockets and TLI interfaces.

[Stevens, 1992] W. Richard Stevens. *Advanced Programming in the UNIX Environment*. Addison-Wesley, Reading, MA, 1992. This is the comprehensive guide to UNIX programming on a single system. It does not deal with distributed computing (for that, see [Stevens, 1990]).

[Stevens, 1994] W. Richard Stevens. *TCP/IP Illustrated, Volume 1: The Protocols*. Addison-Wesley, Reading, MA, 1994. This book provides extremely detailed descriptions of the TCP/IP protocols and the protocols for standard utilities, including `ftp`, `telnet`, mail transfer, NFS, and many more.

[Tannenbaum, 1981] Andrew S. Tannenbaum. *Computer Networks*. Prentice-Hall, 1981. Englewood Cliffs, NJ. This book explains the seven layers of the OSI Reference Model. It also explains cyclical redundancy codes for error detection, datagrams, virtual circuits, routing, and other topics related to networking.

[Tannenbaum, 1995] Andrew S. Tannenbaum. *Distributed Operating Systems*. Prentice-Hall, 1995. Englewood Cliffs, NJ. In depth and technical, with emphasis on distribution within the operating system.

[Vaskevitch, 1993] David Vakevitch. *Client/Server Strategies*. IDG Books, San Mateo, CA. 1993. This book explains the impacts of client/server computing on business operations.

[Vang 1989] Soren Vang. *SQL and Relational Databases*, Microtrend Books, San Marcos, CA, 1989. This introduces the theory and practice of RDBMSs, Chapter 9.

[Waters, 1995] Karen Watterson. *Client/Server Technology for Managers*. Addison-Wesley, Reading, MA, 1995. This book covers some of the same material as ours, but aims it at a somewhat less technically sophisticated audience.

[Zahn, et al, 1990] Lisa Zahn, et al. *Network Computing Architecture*. Prentice-Hall, 1990. Englewood Cliffs, NJ. The Network Computing Architecture is an obsolete ancestor of DCE. Nevertheless, this book still provides a lot of useful information about RPC operation and design.

Index